The Desegregated Heart

A VIRGINIAN'S STAND
IN TIME OF TRANSITION

BY

Sarah Patton Boyle

.

WILLIAM MORROW & COMPANY

New York, 1962

ACKNOWLEDGMENTS

Many people contributed directly or indirectly to this book. Mention of all of them is impractical, but I cannot omit those below. Some were primarily guides up my steep path, some were friends whose hands reached out at psychological moments, some commented helpfully on the manuscript, and some belong in all three categories. To the following persons I am permanently indebted:

Dr. E. B. Henderson, Dr. Johan Galtung, Nancy Moore, Flora Morrison, Eugene Williams, Otelia Jackson, Stringfellow Barr, Docia Johnson, the Rev. Emmet Green, Vivian Carter Mason, the Rev. J. C. Allmond, Dr. W. Lee Harris, an anonymous local lady, P. B. Young, Sr., Lora Mansfield, Dr. J. Raymond Henderson, the members of Koinonia Community, the Rev. Henry B. Mitchell, Frances Brand, Ruth Haefner (catalyst), Jane Foster (my severest book critic), the Rev. Samuel Wylie (for insight into Corporateness), and the Rev. F. G. Sampson (for a graceful, timely rebuke).

I also wish to thank the editors of *The Christian Century*, *The Saturday Evening Post* and *The Nation* for permission to use numerous excerpts from articles of mine which first appeared on their pages, and *The Post* especially, for also allowing me to quote from their "Keeping Posted" page.

DEDICATION

To T. J. SELLERS who taught me, CHAD WALSH who guided and befriended me, and TED EVANS whose witness shone before me, this book is gratefully dedicated.

Contents

Part 1

THE SOUTHERN NEVER-NEVER LAND

Part 2
Bloodless Destruction

Part 3
Thou Shalt Love

AUTHOR'S NOTE

My primary purpose in this book is to share my discovery that to have joy and peace we must love, and that in the last extremity we can love only by means unfamiliar to most of us. My secondary purpose is to explain what induced me, although I was raised as a typical white Southerner, to take my stand with Negroes against the white South.

The Southern integration struggle is the background of my story, for it was through this struggle that internal changes engulfed me. But the book is not a history of desegregation in my area, and I make no attempt to mention all the important people or events in the contest. Rather, I confine myself to those that in some way bear heavily upon the particular story I have to tell.

The book is not an indictment of the South, of my community, of any organization, or any individual. My experiences are offered as no more than examples of what usually occurs when anyone anywhere in the world undertakes to maintain an unpopular stand on a tense issue, especially if this issue involves the status quo. I happened to be the number one target in my area. I might have been one of the marksmen. Indeed, I was a marksman for a time.

As for the conduct of my particular community in this crisis, my disillusionment in it did not result from its falling short of the average, but from its falling short of my expectations. Its behavior was well above average—probably in the upper ten per cent of Southern communities distinguished for restrained conduct during transition.

It must not be thought that I was the only person here with the courage of convictions or who suffered as a result of witnessing to convictions. Such persons were far too few but there were several, and their inner stories may be more significant than mine. But I do not know their stories. I do know my own. If at times in its unfolding there is an implication that I alone held the banner of brotherhood, the implication is not there because this is what I think, but because this was how I deeply felt at the time. True, I was not supported in efforts which still seem to me important. But it may also be true that others made efforts which seemed to them important and which I did not support. There is no question of my being guiltless in the midst of guilt. One of the surprising truths I discovered is that each of us in his own way commits against others the very same errors and sins.

My loss of faith in all people does not mean that all without exception contributed to that disillusionment. Many individuals did not personally contribute to it. But after the experiences recounted in Part 2, I found it impossible to believe in anyone merely because he or she had not *thus far* contributed to it.

Although I have a husband, two sons, a sister, mother, and many other relatives living in this community, I carefully avoided involving any of them in my story except one son, who being a child at the time would not by anyone be considered "involved" in the usual sense. Naturally, there were varying degrees of approval and disapproval among my relatives as among other persons, and censure from some quarter would result for them from my report that they either did or did not approve my stand at any given point.

To my knowledge none of them suffered personally— except from embarrassment that I am a relative—as a result of my activities, and for this I am deeply grateful. For example, my husband received during the decade less than half a dozen protests (all fairly mild) and neither of my sons received so much as one reproach for their poor choice of mother.

A few important incidents (some good, mostly bad) have been omitted for a variety of reasons. But with the above exceptions, I have tried to set down as accurately and soul-searchingly as I am able exactly what happened, and what I learned as a result.

If what I have written has any value, it is as a simple document of human experience, and for me the core of the book is the solution I found to problems of the human heart.

Part 1

THE SOUTHERN
NEVER-NEVER LAND

CHAPTER 1

Intangible Assets

I WAS BORN INTO A SOCIETY WHICH IN MOST PLACES OUTSIDE the South is smilingly and in quotes referred to as the "Southern aristocracy." Within the South, however, the quotes are almost everywhere absent and the smile, if present, is one of tender, sometimes reverent pride. We believe that our aristocracy is second to none in its inbred knowledge of gracious living, its high purpose in human relations, and its awareness of the true values which lend worth, lovability, and dignity to man. On such an assumption was I reared.

I was taught that my father was a great man. In one larger and one smaller sense I think he was. The larger is summarized in the first sentence of a resolution adopted by the General Convention of the Protestant Episcopal Church, October 1940, following the announcement of his retirement: "Robert Williams Patton, Doctor of Divinity; son of Virginia, citizen of the world; priest of God, servant of man."

Besides this, in his own small world of the Church he certainly was one of the tall figures of his day. The resolution listed an array of achievements in the national Church. More important to this story is the fact that he instilled in me a conviction that the only thing which really matters in anyone's life is a consistent choice of right over wrong.

It seemed natural to me that he was a great man, for I was assured by my mother and grandmother that all our ancestors were great. In slightly lowered tones they said that our family was the best in Virginia. I knew this meant it was the best in the world.

I suspect I wasn't alone among young Southerners in receiving this low-voiced instruction. When junior members of First Families of Virginia got together, there was often a look of conscious kindness on all faces as each dutifully praised the families of the others and carefully ignored his own.

I was told that I was descended from governors, generals, presidents, kings. Instead of fairy stories I was told how my great-great-great-grandfather rode into battle brandishing his sword and shouting, "General Hugh Mercer never surrenders!" Also, how my great-grandfather was called by Daniel Webster "the greatest legal mind of his time" and later became governor of Virginia. (Actually, he was acting governor for I forget how many months.) I was told how one of my grandfathers, a colonel under Stonewall Jackson, "led the Stonewall Brigade" in some famous charge in which his brother—who was the grandfather of George S. (Old Blood-and-Guts) Patton—was killed. I was told how my other grandfather, Franklin Stringfellow, who was General Stuart's aide and his and General Lee's personal scout, had in his possession letters from Stuart, Lee, and Jefferson Davis showing that they thought him the most valuable scout in the South.

This grandfather lived until I was seven. He told me exciting tales of being captured repeatedly and condemned to be shot at sunrise (although he firmly referred to himself as a "scout," never as a spy). He escaped miraculously so often that he was convinced that he was being spared for a Purpose. So he became a minister after The War. (When I was growing up "The War" always meant the Civil War.)

He married a beautiful Dresden-china girl, four feet eleven inches tall, who singlehandedly prevented the escape of a jail full of Yankees, simply by standing guard at the hole they made in the prison wall and refusing to let them crawl out until help came. This she did with pure moral force (plus sex appeal, no doubt), having no weapon of any kind.

She and my grandfather were married under the lovely crystal chandelier in the dining room of the Carlisle House in Alexandria, Virginia, where she had been raised, and where, later, my mother was born. This house became one of the showplaces of Virginia, and having its grandeur and glamorous past reviewed for me by a professional guide, after hearing my mother and grandmother tell stories about their life there, was one of the romantically satisfying experiences of my childhood.

All this emphasis on background inevitably bred in me a loathsome sense of social superiority. But it also gave me a feeling of roots reaching far back—and far forward— into history. I was taught to think of myself as a part of the very backbone of Virginia, which was the backbone of the South, which was the backbone of the nation, which was the backbone of the world. In the years ahead, when Southern editorial pages not infrequently demanded that I leave the South, I was grateful for the indoctrination that my roots were strong and deep.

Being a sensible girl, I received with a grain of salt the information that our family was the best in Virginia. I said to myself, "That's probably an exaggeration. Probably it's only one of the two or three best."

But this—shall we call it "social security"?—was partially redeemed by the fact that real values were entangled in it. Being "the best" carried with it heavy obligations: You owed a great debt to everybody else. If you had "the background to set a standard, you *must* do it," I was taught.

"You must be more courteous, gracious, courageous, honorable, and dependable than others or you forfeit the right to be on top."

The entwinement of snobbery and high principle served to support both. The *noblesse oblige* made it possible to maintain snobbery with a fairly clear conscience, while the ego-satisfaction of snobbery lent a kind of animal good spirits to the grueling task of keeping aloft the standard you were directed to carry.

Incidentally, in the South of my childhood, the phrase "to be on top" didn't have the financial implications it often has today. One's inheritance was entirely of intangible assets. Those "on top" were supposed to have inherited culture, character, principles, possibly—though not necessarily —intelligence, and almost certainly debts.

In fact, most Southerners of my parents' era were raised to feel that it wasn't respectable to be rich. We felt that all patriotic Southerners had lost everything in defense of the South, and sufficient time hadn't elapsed for respectable rebuilding of financial security in a war-impoverished region. If you had money you were assumed to be one of three things: a person who had failed (or whose family had failed) to give everything to the cause of freedom when the South was desperate; or a person who had somehow turned the general desperation of your region to your own profit since The War; or else—Heaven forgive you!—you were a Yankee.

With the memory of large past riches, the Southerner who was "on top" felt only contempt for those who couldn't share his honorable poverty. "The best people" wore poverty with lighthearted pride. Like the hero of Stephen Crane's *The Red Badge of Courage*, who rejoiced in the wound that proved him not a coward, we found gladness in our evidence that we had lost everything for the South.

"The Southern Cause" was of course presented to me stripped of all ignobility. We had "fought The War to preserve our freedom from Yankee oppression, to defend our honor against Yankee insult, and to preserve a noble, gracious and warmhearted way of life unprecedented in history."

My family had an additional source of pride in poverty. As field secretary for the national Church my father received a salary which, while modest, was larger than usual for clergymen of his day; and while we still would have been poor enough for respectability, we would have been moderately comfortable but for two things. First, at my grandfather's death my father had voluntarily assumed debts which he wasn't legally required to assume. And, second, having failed to persuade the Church to vote him sufficient funds to carry out one of the important projects for which he was responsible, he had borrowed on his insurance and mortgaged his property to the hilt in order to do the job right.

He spent his entire life discharging these debts. But when my mother reminded my sister and me that it was because of this that we couldn't do or have the things we longed for, the lilt of pride and satisfaction in her voice made us not mind sacrifices. Her tone said that, since we were the kind of people who always put first things first, we had to do without these lesser material items. So great was the family emphasis on the unquestionable rightness of these choices that, even with many girlhood desires thwarted, I can't recall ever wishing that my father had chosen other than he did.

We were spared, I hope, the worst features of personal pride in this moral achievement by stretching it to include the whole region and assuming that this was the kind of thing that Southerners naturally did. But our regional pride was horrifying.

Of course I was by no means unusual in believing that among all the nations of the world the South shone forth. I recall a popular song which said, "They made it twice as nice as paradise, and they called it Dixieland." We believed that, fervently and deeply. This dogma was the true religion of many of us, whether or not we called ourselves Christians. The South and what we thought of her, her ideals and her people, were more precious to us than anything we learned in church.

We thought our beliefs about her could be reached by pure reason. We would gravely point out that Virginia was settled originally by "the best class of people—younger sons of the nobility, mostly—from England and Scotland." Some of these had drifted south—never north!—with a majority staying in Virginia. This was the reason Virginia was the Mother of Presidents and why most of the nation's greatest statesmen came from the South.

Then, too, an abundance of slaves had granted Southern people leisure to accumulate culture, charm, and human understanding.

The gentle climate may have contributed something. Perhaps it was the grim weather nearly as much as heredity which made Yankees so brash and tense, so chilly-hearted and suspicious of their fellow man.

Yet the facts of breeding mustn't be minimized, we pointed out. If you could breed horses, dogs, and other animals for certain specific characteristics of disposition and body, it was silly to say that these same hereditary laws didn't apply to people. The best people in Virginia tended to meet— and therefore marry—only each other. As a result a wonderful, special breed of people had come into being, as different from other people as greyhounds are different from other dogs.

Thus we smugly reasoned. Yet placed like a jewel in this poor setting of twisted genetic and historical facts, of snobbery and exclusiveness, was something of great value. This was our vision of what our special greyhound breed of man was. For he was not a superman who ruled by power, bending others to his own advantage. He was one whose glory was an inner glory, one who placed culture above prosperity, fairness above profit, generosity above possessions, hospitality above comfort, courtesy above triumph, courage above safety, kindness above personal welfare, honor above success.

We, a defeated nation, stood before the world without power, wealth, success, or real hope of ever regaining any of these, and yet we were able to stand tall and straight within ourselves because we believed we had those things which are good without adornment—those things without which power, wealth, and success are empty victories.

I attributed kind thoughts and high motives to everyone and assumed that they attributed them to me. I expected gentleness, justice, courage, and honor from all. These were the basic nature of man, I believed, and—so believing—was much at home in my world. No one was a stranger to me. I fell naturally into conversation with any person who was near enough to talk to—on street corners, on streetcars, in stores, on trains. I belonged to a great universal fellowship of golden hearts which even included Yankees.

But of all that was wonderful, I was sure Virginians had the largest measure. I did more than love Virginia. I adored her. I felt high pride in her and in the lofty principles for which she had always stood. She was my country. I thought of her as quite apart from all other states.

I recall laughing tenderly over the story of a soldier during World War II, who, when asked if he was an American, replied, "No, I'm a Virginian." His state pride seemed both charming and appropriate. In fact admirable. Virginia stood for the highest aims and ideals in our nation. Therefore, he showed his personal identification with the best.

CHAPTER 2

The Rising Wall

I WAS BORN AND RAISED ON LAND THAT WAS A PART OF THE original plantation which had been a crown grant to my father's family. In my great-grandfather's day it reached many miles in each direction, but that portion which came to my grandfather after division among several children was about 4000 acres. This he cared for with 163 slaves.

He must have been a good master because when they were freed by The War some refused to leave, and most of those who did leave, after a few days of bewildered freedom, returned and asked if they could "work for their keep." Some of these undoubtedly were the most loved companions of my father's childhood. He said so not just with sentimental words, but with his whole body—with warmed eyes, softened voice, and little gestures when he spoke of them.

My maternal grandmother (the one who stopped the escaping Yankee prisoners) used to speak of the house slaves of her childhood and girlhood in a similar way. I still remember the mellow drop in her voice when she told me tales of Mammy Lish. Referring to her own mother and father there was high regard in her voice but not that warm drop.

Mammy Lish comes down to me as a sort of ancestor of

my emotional life, which she certainly was of my grandmother's. It's she, not my real great-grandmother, who is linked in my consciousness with romantic stories of rustling silks and soft candlelight. It was Mammy Lish who warmed my grandmother's canopied featherbed with a pan filled with hot coals from the fireplace in her room, and tucked her in at night.

The tender look and softened voice are sometimes seen and heard even today when white Southerners speak together of Negroes they have known. Until near the end of 1955 I hoped that there were enough of these living waters of love to solve all our problems in the integration struggle. I reckoned without the confused mass of other feelings which are stored in the great hidden reservoirs of our subconscious.

My paternal grandfather (the one who fought under Stonewall Jackson), as well as my great-grandfather, had a large family, and when the estate was again divided at his death, my father received as his share 386 acres of war-impoverished land and a four-room outbuilding once used by my grandfather as a study and place to store his law books. This was moved to a high hill about a third of a mile from the big house. A latticed sleeping porch was stretched across the back, with a kitchen and servant's room at one end, a bath and dressing room at the other—a rather odd looking structure on the outside, but quite functional inside.

The dressing room served the sleeping porch, used by my sister and me and for overflow guests—who were numerous. In summer it was like a dormitory, often giving welcome to seven or eight beds since whole families of relatives visited us for weeks, even months at a stretch.

Large tents were also often raised in the yard when the porch was full. While facilities for extensive entertaining no longer existed in my family—or in most families of the South—the habit of entertaining was still with us. Such as we had we shared with unquestioning hospitality, a blend of genuine human warmth and polite compulsion. All callers as a matter of course were invited to meals and to spend the night. Not to invite them was considered inexcusably rude.

There was hospitality but no feasting. We gave our guests only what was raised on our farm, especially in the garden. Evenings, when the heat of the sun was gone, family and guests, old and young, went into the garden, weeding, working, gathering, and then preparing vegetables for next day and to can for winter.

My father's salary was modest and he carried many debts, but a servant's room was taken for granted in every upper-class Southern home—and you can doubtless see why. There was pressing need for household help, engendered by frequent and long-remaining guests. Moreover, it was close enough to The War for wages still to be infinitesimal.

Nearly everyone above the "poor-white" class could afford a colored girl. You gave her a room, board, your cast-off clothes, and at most three or four dollars a month. Of course, if she needed a doctor, you paid him; and if she had a little property, when taxes fell due you probably paid those. It was a sort of semislavery arrangement, but nobody—that is, no white Southerner—thought it so at the time. We thought ourselves gentle and kind to pay taxes and the doctor.

The servant's room had a slave-quarters atmosphere. It had a cot, straight chair, chest of drawers, washstand, and a bare, unvarnished floor. It wasn't even plastered—just rib-like beams and rafters, with an occasional nail driven in an inch to serve as a clothes hook.

We had no consciousness of being less than kind in this. Negroes' own houses were worse still, so what we provided seemed to us adequate and appropriate. We strained to be kind in every way which occurred to us. That a Negro might yearn for an attractive room even though—or perhaps especially because—she had none in her own home simply never entered our minds. It was assumed that they lived on a lower level than whites, desiring nothing better.

My mother required that our house be kept scrupulously tidy and clean, but we assumed that a Negro's own house, or her room in our house, would be quite filthy. I was instructed not to visit our cooks in their rooms as I "might catch diseases." Also—lest they spread germs—they were forbidden to use the bathroom, required to use an outhouse toilet, a basin and pitcher of water in their room for bathing. And they were forbidden to eat with the sterling flat silver or from the blue willow plates our family had inherited.

Yet all dishes were washed together, no one worried that diseases might be conveyed in the preparation of food, and no restriction was placed on the amount of time I spent with our cooks elsewhere than in their rooms.

There was some grumbling and much soft laughter over the body odors of our cooks, but it occurred to none of us that this could be remedied by letting them bathe in the forbidden bathroom. Negroes smelled bad. This was taken for granted. Their odor seemed as much a part of them as their dark skin. We no more thought of water as a possible remedy for the former than for the latter. We simply accepted Negroes as they were.

My stereotype of the "typical Nigra" grew as a result of a type of indoctrination which was, I think, eighty per cent pure implication, unvocalized and unconscious, on the part of my elders. For example, I can't recall ever being told that the Negro's mental endowments were basically inferior to those of whites, but I was surrounded by a whole pattern of behavior which implied it. I think I was told by my mother that the Negro lacked capacity to appreciate attractive surroundings; but in any case, how could I have escaped such an impression when not only Negro homes in our community were devoid of comfort and adornment, but also the cook's room in our own house?

My father among other things was director of the American Church Institute of the Protestant Episcopal Church, a group of nine Church-supported schools for Negroes in various parts of the South. He was very enlightened for his time, and even went so far as to point out occasionally in my rare contacts with him that the squalor of Southern Negroes resulted from poverty and other social pressures. But what chance had such stray thoughts against impressions gathered from our whole social pattern? Besides, my father's work kept him away from home nine tenths of the time, and my mother was far from accepting his premises. She, too, loved Negroes, but with the same deep tenderness she lavished on her riding horse, her dogs, and other pets. She loved them without the slightest feeling that they were much like herself.

My thoughts became saturated with the assumption that Negroes belonged to a lower order of man than we. Loving them—after my father's fashion at first, and then after my mother's—I quickly learned not to judge them by our standards, but by a segregated, separate standard. I can't remember, for instance, when I first began saying that certain Negroes had "nice homes," meaning nice by "their standards," certainly not by ours. Later, when I wanted to join the human race as an equal, not as a superior member of it, this double standard of values for everything was far more difficult to break down than my outer habits of segregated behavior—and probably also created more resentment among cultivated, keen-sighted Negroes.

Like most upper-class Southern white children of my generation, until I was twelve I was placed largely in the care of colored adults and allowed to play with colored children. I "helped" our current maid-of-all-work who, for some reason, was never referred to as a maid but always as our cook or our servant. I "helped" her in the preparation of food and in all her household chores, but only when I wanted to. It wasn't required as a duty.

My parents instructed me strictly to obey colored adults in our employ, but I was never punished for my sins by a Negro. If I was discourteous, disobeyed, challenged their authority, or otherwise misbehaved in their charge, they must report it to one of my parents. Under no circumstance were they to administer justice themselves.

Colored supervisors characteristically kept Southern white children out of mischief by a combination of moral force and the strategy of keeping them entertained. The typical upper-class white child's relationship with Negroes presented a kind of Utopia of entertainment, protection, and care, without the disciplines and punishments which customarily accompany relations between child and adult. Our fellowship being unstrained by chastisement, there were no dark moments to remember. Memories of Negro nurses for most of us are devoid of unpleasant associations. No wonder our eyes and mouths soften when we recall their faces.

I was with Negroes far more than with whites, and inevitably when I suffered my numerous small injuries, it was in dark arms that I was crooned over. Even now, when I think of the warm companionship of being comforted, it's usually dusky faces which look up from my deep consciousness, and soft, pleasantly thick accents weave a harmony in my inner being with the concept of human sympathy.

There was a vast amount of work to be done, and my mother must have been a rather hard taskmistress, for we never kept a cook long. Thus I had no special or deep attachment to any one of them. Before a strong tie formed, she either left or was fired. She had got "spoiled," Mother would say, and had grown "trifling" or "uppity." (Uppity is a good Southern word meaning impertinent.) I regretted these losses of companions, but none was traumatic.

Just before the United States entered World War I, we had a cook named Coreen. Wages had gone up by then and Mother grumblingly paid her all of eight dollars a month. Coreen had two little illegitimate children whom she had to board out in order to work for us. The board bill was $1.50 a month each.

Coreen used to take me fishing on summer evenings when her work was done. With mutual satisfaction she taught me all she knew of the art. She also helped me dig a much desired "cave"—a hole in the ground covered with old boards. I got a smug sense of security from my plan to stock it with supplies and live in it should the Germans invade. I wasn't much afraid of invasion, looking upon the possibility as adventure and challenge to ingenuity—a challenge which I felt my cave adequately met.

I was more uneasy concerning a whispered-about "Nigra uprising." German spies were rumored to be "stirring the Nigras up." Looking back, I see how well defined already was my typically Southern split image of Negroes. "Bad Nigras" were beastlike, dangerous, repulsive beyond the lowest reaches of white men, even of Germans. But these bad ones didn't include any Negroes I knew. They were all good, and with them alone I shared the secret of my cave.

I had dug it on the steep north side of the hill on which our house stood, a place where the family seldom walked. I thought they never went there, that only Coreen, I, and the hired hands—all Negroes—knew about it. When an uncle who lived with us eventually let slip his knowledge of it, I felt that my secret was exposed and abandoned the project.

When I brooded about the possible insurrection (an even more terrifying word than uprising) I comforted myself with fantasies about being protected by my Negro friends. Never was I in imagination protected by white people. For in my daily life when I fell heir to wounds either of flesh

or spirit I was helped chiefly by Negroes. I derived from
them so many emotional satisfactions that I naturally trusted
them emotionally. But I early learned to mistrust them in
another way.

It was assumed by every member of my family that a
Negro's word was unreliable. This, I now realize, must have
been a heavy pressure toward making it so, for the desire to
speak the truth is largely based on the belief that one's word
is trusted. An even heavier pressure toward falsehood was
their position of dependency, which made duplicity an almost necessary ingredient of success, even of survival. But I
knew nothing of psychological and sociological causes. I took
people as I found them. In Negroes I found an ease and
apparent lack of a sense of wrongdoing when they lied. An
experience in this connection which was traumatic for me,
because so entangled with love, occurred when I was about
four years old.

Our current cook, Rosemary, was full of sunny charm,
playful and tender with me. I loved her and resolved to go
home with her on her "day off"—which began at 2 P.M.
Sunday and ended at 6 A.M. Monday. Ignoring her protests,
I packed my little bag and followed her over the hill.

She resorted to strategy, telling me to return to the house
and get something (I forget what) and she would wait
for me. Obediently I ran back. But woman's intuition made
me pause and look over my shoulder before entering the
house. To my horror I saw Rosemary walking rapidly on her
way.

I dashed after her and caught her. She claimed she was
only going to look at a rabbit she saw run in the bushes, and
I was to return to the house and get that item. She would
wait.

Still doubtful, I demanded, "Do you *promise* to wait?"

"Sure, honey, I promise. I be right there in them bushes,
lookin' for that little rabbit. You run."

I ran back confidently, because my parents had taught me that a promise is never broken. When you promised, that was *it*. But when I returned Rosemary wasn't in the bushes.

Confronted next day with the unspeakable crime of promise-breaking, her lack of guilt feelings was shockingly evident.

"I had to, honey," she said blandly. "You wouldn't of went home ef I hadn't of tol' you that."

I carried my bewilderment to Mother. "People *do* break promises."

"We never do," she countered. "Rosemary is a Negro. They aren't like us. Promises don't mean anything to them."

I don't think I ever again—that is, never until I became integrated at the age of about forty-five—expected the truth of a Negro, or held one fully accountable, as I would a white person, for telling me a lie. Another stone in my inner segregation wall had been cemented firmly in place.

Our farm hands lasted longer than our cooks. We had one hand by the month year-round, engaging others by the day during rush seasons. We kept one of our monthly hands about six years. His name was Tobe.

I regularly helped Tobe do all the interesting things done on farms. We fed stock, harnessed horses, and milked cows practically as a team. I rode beside him on hay wagons and when he hauled wood. I sometimes stayed with him while he ate his lunch, though I wasn't permitted to eat mine with him. He taught me all he knew about the care and handling of horses and other animals. And he taught me many spirituals which I sang constantly in a very untuneful voice.

He was an intelligent man, but he couldn't read or write even his name. He had to sign pay checks with a witnessed mark. I didn't think it either strange or sad that so smart a man was illiterate. In my world a Negro who could read well was unknown. Ignorant-Negro was practically one word. Ignorance was a "racial trait."

All Negroes were Baptists in my community and although I was an Episcopal minister's daughter and granddaughter, Tobe considered me not a Christian because I hadn't been baptized by immersion. He was sincerely concerned about my soul, and tried hard to help me see the light. I still remember some of the lovely faith-filled things he told me about Jesus and His eager forgiveness.

But when I repeated to my parents his exhortations to repent and be baptized, their gentle laughter made it clear that Negroes were dear and quaint but never to be taken seriously about serious matters.

My point is that in their rejection of Tobe's ideas, their emphasis was not that his denomination and mine had different baptismal customs, but that Negroes had ideas which were cute and funny, like those of small children. Yet undoubtedly the majority of white Southern Baptists during this "hard-shell" era would have felt much as Tobe did if they had cared enough about me to be seriously involved in my spiritual welfare.

I was eleven when finally Tobe was fired.

"He's gotten too good for his job," Mother said. "He's more shiftless and uppity every day, and on top of that he had the nerve to ask for a raise. He's not worth what he's getting now."

He was getting $30 a month for ten hours daily and chores on Sunday. But this was considered good pay by current custom. My mother could remember when a hand was paid less than half that much. In any case, I was in no position to judge the justice of her claim. I only knew I was losing the dearest friend I ever had.

For a long time after he left there was hardly any joy in my days. After a little I became ill from sheer loneliness. Both my parents discerned what ailed me and I overheard them discussing it.

My father said, "Maybe we'd better get him back."

"She couldn't be out with him much longer anyhow, darling," my mother objected. "The break would have to come soon."

"That's true," my father agreed. "She's almost too old now."

I sensed in these comments a strange, adult evil descending on me, like the swinging blade in *The Pit and the Pendulum.* A year later it was upon me.

CHAPTER 3

The Southern Code

ON MY TWELFTH BIRTHDAY I WAS TOLD THAT I WAS A "BIG GIRL now" and my relations with Negroes from now on must be formal. The current cook, the farm hand, and all the colored children (hired at 50 cents a day during rush seasons to weed and plant) were ordered to stop calling me Patty and call me "Miss Patty"—for I was never called Sarah.

Worse, I was instructed to insist that they do. I couldn't play with, or even talk to, colored children any more except graciously to greet them or inquire about their welfare. I was to make polite excuses when they asked me to play during their lunch hour or after work.

"Why?" I wanted to know. "Why, why?"

Because, I was told sternly, it was no longer "proper" for me to be "familiar" with Negroes. I was a big girl now. Certain rules of adult conduct must now be observed. It was WRONG to violate these rules.

A dreadful training period followed during which I was watched and rebuked if I forgot any of the many taboos which suddenly came into being. It was similar to the training little girls of long ago endured while being converted from tomboys into "little ladies." But mine was even more unnatural and destructive. It called for repression not only of what was happiest in the years just passed, but also of much that was natural and dear in my human contacts as well.

All that had been best in my life was branded WRONG. It was RIGHT to do what I dimly sensed was contrary to the laws of love and loyalty—to set a wall between myself and friends, to meet overtures with formality—these things were RIGHT.

I remember running into the house heartsick after snubbing the advances of a child of whom I was particularly fond. He had skipped up to me, suggesting that I come along on some small adventure—to search for a duck who had just hatched her brood and left the nest, or to see if the cantaloupes had begun to bloom. Crushing back my desire both for his company and for the fun, I answered stiffly, "No, I can't." Then I added with proper Southern-lady courtesy, "How are you today?" The joy left his face. He lowered his head and walked away.

My mother had watched the exchange through the lattice-work of the porch. When I came in she kissed me and said, "Mother saw and heard everything. That was a good girl!"

A strange combination of depression and pride swept me. I was a GOOD GIRL. But oh, what had I *done!*

Day by day the new habits grooved their way into my behavior, speech, thought. I learned by observation that while you must always be polite and gentle with Negroes, you must talk a little down to them, as to a young child, using a tone of condescension, even an accent reserved for them.

I learned that they provided an endless source of agreeable conversation at social gatherings. You were supposed to store in your memory their quaint sayings, taking special care to remember accurately their dialect, mispronunciations and misuse of big words. These made charming anecdotes through which you could share the fellowship of affection-ate laughter with white friends.

It was quite proper, I learned, to talk for hours with Negroes provided you were adroit in preserving the right balance in your relationship and knew how to keep each of you in your appointed roles. These roles called for your always talking a little down and their talking a little up. Keeping this balance wasn't easy, however, and if you slipped into an equality relationship, even momentarily, you must realize that you had gravely degraded yourself, and undoubtedly forfeited the respect of your Negro companion.

It was proper—indeed, it was *Southern*—to be friendly and chatty with all Negroes, provided you watched the emotional balance and instantly withdrew into a more formal attitude if a note of equality crept in. There were many rules to help one balance on this tightrope, some given verbally, some by implication.

I learned that when visiting a Negro "friend" in her shack, if she offered food it was proper to accept it; also proper (indeed courteous) to sit at her table with her and eat, though you were especially pleased with her "nicety of feeling" if she did not sit down with you, even when invited, but waited on you instead.

However, she wasn't considered uppity if she chose to sit with you at her own table, because in going to see her you voluntarily made her your hostess. Her house was her castle. If she chose to wait on you instead of sitting with you, it was courtesy beyond the call of strict duty. But in your home she was expected to eat in the kitchen—even if the two of you were alone in the house, and even if she were not an employee but a "friend," calling perhaps to bring you a small birthday gift. You never, never, never sat at table with a Negro in your own dining room.

True, if you wanted to be particularly gracious (perhaps because she had indeed brought you a gift, or had come to bring you news of great moment to herself, such as a birth, death, or marriage in her immediate family) it was proper for you to go into the kitchen or on the back porch and eat with her.

In short, there were times when it was courteous for you to bow down to her level; but she must never presume to step up to yours. If she didn't know this, it was your strict obligation to teach her, regardless of how much you might shrink from the task. If you didn't fulfill it you were GUILTY of wronging both her and the South. However, the chances were that her parents had instructed her in these manners as strictly as your parents had you.

Drinking etiquette was different from eating etiquette. If you were a man, you could offer a Negro a drink of whisky if you were having one when he arrived, though he must drink his standing. It would, on the other hand, be uppity of him to offer you one in like circumstances. He must hastily put the bottle out of sight upon your arrival, claiming that he was partaking because of a sore throat or a snakebite. You could then, if you wished, say, "Why don't you offer me one, Jim?" And he would grin from ear to ear at your proffer of fellowship, and saying "Yassuh!" would fetch the bottle forth. You could then, if you wished, sit down with him.

Let me here state, lest I be challenged by another Southerner whose racial etiquette may differ from mine, that I don't mean to imply that these specific distinctions were the same all over the South. Accepted forms vary from state to state, even from community to community, but the above are examples of the kind of distinction between whites and Negroes which exists all over the South. Everywhere one is taught not to treat whites and Negroes in the same way, this rule taking precedence over all other social distinctions.

In my childhood an intelligent, well-mannered Negro of good character was respected a hundred per cent as a human soul, provided the circumstances were strictly nonsocial. But regardless of personal graces and endowments, he did not have the social status of even the most ignorant and disreputable poor-white.* This fact was underscored in countless small ways.

No white man was ever expected to eat in the kitchen, for this would classify him with Negroes. Regardless of his station or the condition of his clothes (perhaps filthy, sweaty), if there was occasion to invite him to eat, he was asked into the dining room. If he smelled of accumulated perspiration, the family was expected to suffer it for courtesy's sake.

If a Negro college president, immaculately attired, and an ignorant poor-white, unwashed and in rags, had arrived at our house near dinnertime, both would have been invited to share our food. But the poor-white would have been brought to table with the family, and the college president have been served separately on the back porch, or—if my father was home—on the front porch or in the living room. We would have felt that sufficient recognition was given to his position by not assigning him to the kitchen. As a further courtesy, my father, mother, or some other adult member of my family, would have sat with him while he ate —probably eating his or her own dinner later, but possibly even joining him with a tray.

Another point at which racial distinction was sharp and biting was in the matter of tipping. I was taught never to tip a white—not even the poorest poor-white—for small services. But a Negro, even a very well-to-do one, must always be tipped. I recall the shock of displeasure I received at the age of about thirteen when a well-dressed

* A "poor-white" is very distinct from a "white who is poor." The phrase implies poverty of mind and spirit rather than of purse. The word "trash" was never added to the phrase among my relatives or friends, though it was implied.

colored man refused my proffered dime for briefly holding my horse while I scampered into the post office for the family mail. This I considered uppity.

Still another distinction was in the matter of courtesy titles. You carefully affixed Mr., Mrs., or Miss to any white person of a lower stratum of society, unless he or she was much younger than yourself. It was considered an invitation to "familiarity" if you didn't, as you would have no recourse save a frank protest (unthinkable!) if a reciprocal dismissal of courtesy title was employed. But under no circumstances did you address a Negro with such a title. If he was a physician, dentist, or Ph.D., it was proper to call him Doctor, if a college teacher, you could call him Professor, or if a minister, you could call him Reverend, but *never* did you *ever* call him Mister.

Once when I was addressing a business letter to a Negro in our community, I asked Mother if I should put *Mr.* on the envelope.

"Oh, no, darling," she said. "You don't use Mister to a Negro even on an envelope. It would embarrass him to death."

And there you have a bit of Southern indoctrination which non-Southerners know nothing about—our belief that "good Nigras" feel as we do about all the details of our system. This explains how kindly, courteous people can be guilty of atrocities like my imaginary illustration of the Negro college president and the poor-white. We really thought—and many white Southerners still think—that the college president himself would prefer it so, his sense of propriety presumably violated as much as ours if we were to invite him into the dining room. Over and over I was told that if I didn't adhere to racial conventions Negroes themselves "would be shocked," "would be horrified," "would be disgusted," "would disapprove," and—occasionally—even that they "would be humiliated."

In the jargon of psychology this would be called "project-ing." We projected our own feelings onto Negroes. Yet originally there probably was some foundation for believing that they shared our feelings. In slavery days, and for a generation following, house servants lived in close, continual contact with their masters and mistresses. The only instruc-tion they received was from their white overlords. There-fore the best and most intelligent among them, being quick to absorb all available knowledge, were naturally the ones to acquire most completely the attitudes of those they served.

Thus many of the best Negroes did completely subscribe to the white Southerner's point of view. And some of these superior, brainwashed Negroes still lived and were known and loved by whites in my mother's generation. They were at ease and vocal with white people and their flattering ap-proval of the ways of Southern ladies and gentlemen carried far.

Also, at the time I was growing up, the college president if asked whether he preferred a tray in the living room to eating with the family, almost certainly would have avowed with haste that he preferred the tray, even if he really felt quite otherwise. He would have been taught from the cradle that to say anything else would give deep offense. It took many years, much courage, careful re-education, and con-tinual hammering from enlightened leaders before even the well-educated Negroes of the South could bring themselves to stop saying what they thought the white man wanted them to say and start saying what they themselves really independently felt.

This corroboration by Negroes fortified my instruction in the rules of the Southern way of life. Without the con-firmation of these Negroes (usually only implied but some-times actually verbally affirmed) I certainly would not have learned the rules so well, and probably would have rejected them much sooner. As it was, I patiently learned and believed them all.

In the wasp-waist era, women grew so accustomed to squeezing corsets that they suffered backache when they left them off. Thus the confining stays of segregation molded my thoughts and behavior. Yet my heart was never quite bound. And this is true, I find, of many white Southerners.

CHAPTER 4

Product of the Code

WHEN MY TRAINING PERIOD WAS OVER, I WAS AS CLOSE TO A typical Southern lady as anyone ever is to a typical anything. My mind had many partitions and my heart many levels. I was a mixture of high idealism and contradictory practice, of rigid snobbery and genuine human warmth. I moved in a segregated pattern which isolated Negroes both in my thinking and in my behavior, yet in my heart we were close and in my imagination we understood each other.

My deep faith in people, especially Southerners and particularly Virginians, included Negroes in a partitioned way. Summarizing, you might say that my religion was humanism, my denomination Southern, and my church Virginia. As I worshiped in this church, all around me I saw beautiful stained-glass windows of people I knew, and handsome carvings of solid human traits.

But when our faith is that people are wonderful, it is essential that we regard ourselves as wonderful—else we are monstrosities amongst our marvelous kind. To maintain such a belief we need a lot of help, but if we are white Southerners we readily find that help in our stereotype of the Negro and our fictitious relationship with him. These props support our Never-Never Land vision of nobility in ourselves, the South, and mankind.

I loved Negroes and, in my segregated way, respected and admired them as individual human personalities. I believed that our relationship was complementary and mutually satisfying, somewhat in the way that a relationship between a man and a woman is satisfying if he enjoys dominating her and she enjoys being dominated. When a Negro didn't "keep his place" I felt outraged, much as some men feel when a woman tries to wear the pants.

My indignation was triggered by a sense of guilt. I had learned that equality relations with Negroes were WRONG, and that it was my fault if a Negro attempted them. Therefore I was immediately on the defensive at the first hint of familiarity.

When no racial conventions were violated, I loved Negroes with the unobstructed outgoingness of a child. With them I felt snugness, richness, tenderness. I wanted to please, share, give. I took joy in belief that I gave them joy, and comfort in the thought that they loved me. Because none I then knew were educated, we had no intellectual companionship, yet I felt closer to them in fellowship, more at home with them, than with the closest white friend.

Their virtues as well as their faults were fixed and exaggerated in my mind. I pictured them as superhumanly artistic and creative, contented in hardship and ill fortune, good-humored and humorous, loyal, faithful and warm. Note that these are all highly lovable qualities compared to the more arid "Anglo-Saxon virtues" of industry, chastity, honesty, and honor, which I believed the Negro race constitutionally lacked.

No moral judgment resulted in me from a discovery that a respected colored acquaintance fell short of any or all of the "Anglo-Saxon virtues." Lack of moral judgment for "typical" faults is reflected even in our Southern administration of law. While Negroes are regularly given maximum sentences for such crimes as assaulting a white woman, they are generally given minimum sentences, often suspended,

for theft, perjury, disturbing the peace, drunkenness, assaults
of all kinds when confined to their own group, and many
other crimes and misdemeanors. Self-respecting modern Negroes resent this as much as they do less kind forms of
discrimination. But I didn't know that then. I thought my
gentle judgments had no other source than love.

My over-all image of the Negro was of a character pic-
turesque, charming, and lovable. The fixed faults I assigned
to him probably contributed as much to my affection as the
fixed virtues. After all, once we've defined any friend's
character, many of us like him to act characteristically. We
smile indulgently when good old firebrand Jim blows his
top on an expected occasion. We may even be a little dis-
appointed if he doesn't. And if kindhearted but gossipy Sally
fails to flatten our ears with a new scandal over the tea
table, we may feel let down. She isn't running true to type
that day. Our sense of character is violated, our amused
affection thwarted.

In the same way, "typical" Negro faults aroused in me
tender, satisfying laughter, not cold-edged ridicule. For the
person laughed at, such a distinction may not be as clear
as for the person laughing; yet it is a valid one.

If a colored woman had an illegitimate child she did not
drop in our estimation. For this was "typical." Or if a
colored man lied or stole from us, our regard was not damaged or our love reduced. These were matters in which we
and he were admittedly different, and we thought it unfair
to apply our standards to him.

It was almost unheard of to call in the police even if the
item stolen was valuable and the thief wouldn't return it.
This was the sort of thing settled between oneself and one's
Negroes. It was unSouthern to bring the law into it. There
was a feeling about it like shooting birds on the ground
—for you knew that no judge or jury would take a Negro's
word against a white's.

I thrilled to the nobility of this custom of taking the loss rather than calling the police in these cases where we knew the victim wouldn't have a chance once legally accused. The fact that a Negro's word was practically no good in court didn't seem to me inequality before the law but merely common sense, since truthfulness wasn't a "Negro trait."

Was there any foundation at all for our belief in racial faults and virtues? This much: The so-called Anglo-Saxon virtues are those which come easily to people who are on top, because their rights and welfare are secure. If all your essential needs are provided for, there is little temptation to steal or lie, and your women aren't much tempted to sell themselves for money or protection.

Moreover, there were and are special pressures affecting the American Negro in regard to these traits. Under slavery, for instance, on some plantations Negroes were not permitted to marry, and on many were not encouraged to do so. A good slave was worth thousands of dollars, and it was thought that the unwed produced more offspring. A people who had long received approval for indiscriminate breeding could hardly be expected to attach much guilt to it only two generations after being freed. Segregationists love to quote hard, statistical percentages of illegitimacy among lower-class Negroes, but this is a blot on our escutcheon, not theirs. Among people of whom a large number still remember grandmothers raised in slavery, it is remarkable that so many endorse high standards of chastity, rather than that many still do not.

Long after slavery, lying was often necessary for survival under a system where colored men were totally dependent on the good will of whites. As for stealing, a man who is giving his whole strength to serve another but is paid less than a living wage need not have a subnormal conscience if he habitually appropriates items of trifling or no value to his "masters," but of enormous use to himself.

Northerners often drop their liberality when they come

South and discover that the Southern stereotype of the Negro's weaknesses didn't rise from our imaginations alone but has at least some foundation in experience. If only it had no foundation at all, the vicious circle of this stereotype would be less hard to break. When I was growing up I knew only severely underprivileged country Negroes, and practically all of them had at some time been caught red-handed in small thefts.

In these circumstances, it was actually an act of love to accept dishonesty as a racial trait, for this freed individuals from what would otherwise have been a serious moral stigma. Had there been more in my environment to guide me, I could have followed the path of love a little further into the realization that under certain conditions dishonesty is a universal human trait. As it was, I took for granted the fact that Negroes stole, were ignorant, lived in shacks, dressed in rags, and year-round ate corn pone and fat-back. It wasn't until after 1950 that I made a clean-cut leap from the racial-trait idea into the larger view of human cause and effect.

I was raised to attribute to Negroes a quaint code of their own. Good Negroes, I knew, never took money, but only battered hats and other discarded items stuffed away in an old trunk or clogging an unfrequented bureau drawer. I knew that I should respect their feeling that this was "not stealin' but takin'." A Negro was seldom called a thief—to his face, anyway—unless he stole money (more than small change), a piece of jewelry, silver, or something else of similar value. Such thefts were rare.

You said to him, "James, you shouldn't have taken that coat from the wardrobe in the spare room. I can still use that. You'll have to bring it back." Then, if he was a good Negro, you probably added, "But there's one in the trunk to the left of the steps in the garret. You can have that."

James, neither admitting nor apologizing for his theft of

the first coat, would sneak it back, then openly fetch out the one you gave him, beaming and thanking you. You both felt friendly and good about the whole transaction—or you did, and you thought he did.

You would rather employ a Negro who knew what was proper to steal than one who was rigidly honest. Such scruples in him seemed stilted and affected. It was like a person's always saying "do not" instead of "don't."

More important (though less conscious) was the fact that a rigid standard on his part deprived you of an opportunity to express your affection through gentle acceptance of his weakness. It felt good to show him kindness when anger and harshness would have been justified. It helped you to think of yourself as a noble-hearted person who knew human relations to be more important than material possessions. This was valuable to you. It undergirded your self-respect, assured you that you were the right kind of person. And this assurance, more even than business success, breeds contentment in human beings. My "paternalistic" relationship to Negroes gave me the release of unobstructed, uncostly love, and provided me with easily found ways of proving myself gentle, high-principled and kind.

I thought my relationship with Negroes altogether beautiful. I would instantly have rejected a suggestion that incidents like the one with James might sap his self-respect as much as it built mine. By giving Negroes acceptance despite their trying "racial faults," I thought we were giving both them and ourselves gifts of worth. We loved them as they were, faults included. "Isn't this," I would have asked, "the foundation of all healthy relationships?"

About that I was of course right. But I missed a serious malignancy in this otherwise healthy body. With rare exceptions we loved "our Negroes" downward but expected them to love us upward—to give us acceptance, not despite our faults, but *as though we had none*. To me our relationship felt wonderful. It brought out the best in me. I assumed it felt wonderful to them and brought out their best, too. It was a traumatic, heart-twisting experience when I learned this wasn't so.

My sense of fellowship with Negroes had an odd tie-in with my snobbery. I thought a special love and understanding existed between my "class" and Negroes, and that they had an uncanny ability to recognize "quality folks." Also, I had been taught a sort of individual snobbery which was superimposed on, and quite apart from, my social snobbery. I thought the best Negroes shared in this. Here is how it worked:

While any white man was socially above any Negro and accordingly must be treated with respect, a Negro of character, sensitivity, and intelligence was humanly above a less decent white. I thought the best Negroes accepted both social and human scales and knew that while our social relationship was unalterably fixed by race, our human relationship was devoid of limitation.

An extreme case of the distinction between social respect and human respect is set forth in Rudyard Kipling's *Gunga Din*, where he describes the British soldier's love and admiration for an Indian water boy whom he treated worse than he probably would his dog. The summarizing sentence goes:

> "Though I've belted you and flayed you,
> By the livin' Gawd that made you,
> You're a better man than I am, Gunga Din."

I had of course never been guilty of physical abuse of a Negro, but this was a type of thinking which I thoroughly understood.

I believed I had a more solid basis of mutual acceptance with Negroes than with whites, our relationship being on a deeper level than the social one which while fixed and

RIGHT was trivial compared to the feelings which rolled like a subterranean river beneath it.

I expected Negroes to recognize me as "quality," that is, as having inherited and been taught certain desirable traits and sensitivities. This gave me a snug feeling with them, as though we shared a pleasant secret, or as though we belonged to an exclusive secret club. We Southern whites and Negroes understood and loved each other, each knowing how to give the other many psychological pleasures and gratifications—this was a premise I took for granted.

Corporateness was an important satisfaction in our club. It wasn't just that I, as an individual, loved Negroes and believed they loved me. I believed that between Negroes and my whole stratum of Southern society there was a continuous flow of understanding, love, tenderness, and well-wishing, and that we all were equally content with the rules which regulated our lives together. With a mixture of discomfort and amusement I recall an incident which illustrates my confidence that Negroes felt just as I did about the South.

I was twenty-one and traveling by train to visit relatives in Florida. The round, chocolate-colored face of the porter with its gleaming white smile made me feel immediately at home, and I tried to talk to him. I used the playful tone, broad Negro accent, and "typical" vocabulary which white "club members" customarily used in addressing colored ones —much as lovers of children often use baby talk when addressing tots. At about my third word his smile absorbed into his face. He replied in crisp, precise English.

Baffled but undaunted, I inquired, "Whah you from?"

"Virgin-i-a," he replied, using the extra syllable which no normal Southerner, white or colored, ever exerts himself to include, preferring to conserve his energies for more important matters.

I reached for my purse and fetched forth a quarter. "Ef

you from Vuhginyah I'm gona give you a li'l some'en extri,"
I beamed.

He failed to beam back—or to take the money.

"Here's fo' you bein' from Vuhginyah," I insisted innocently.

His stiff face revealed a struggle I didn't understand.
Then—probably because I was so young and manifestly unaware of giving offense—his features slowly softened. He
took the quarter. With gentle coldness he said, "Thank you."

I never forgot this incident, but I didn't comprehend it
for nearly twenty-five years.

The maid of my Florida relatives did not disturb my
stereotype. From a caramel-colored face, her lustrous black
eyes burned with an intensity which suggested hot, animal
passions. Lithe and trim, you instantly thought of her as
moving and peering through jungle thickets. Her education
stopped dead in the middle of second grade, and her chief
concerns were sex and conjure. Though my experience in
both was quite limited, I found them intriguing topics, and
we talked often in the kitchen and on the back steps. One
potent spell she revealed to me was directed at keeping a
husband—in her case, a lover—faithful.

You saved the handkerchief or towel he used when you
went to bed together (I didn't know what she meant by this
but was ashamed to ask her) and you took it unwashed
to the forest. You cut a large chunk from a tree "on the sun-
down side" and you nailed it back with the cloth under
it, using two nails at the top and two at the bottom. As soon
as you had thus nailed him up your man would "lose his
nature" with other women and wouldn't be able to "go
with nobody else."

I was doubtful of the effectiveness of this effort, but the
objective impressed me as singularly appealing.

I treasured Carry's formulas as much for the pleasure of
repeating them mirthfully to white friends as for their im-

mediate interest. They were conversation pieces guaranteed to amuse and amaze, and were valued additions to those I had already gathered down the years. I even thought of publishing a collection of conjure recipes, but found that when placed together they lacked sufficient variety, ninety per cent of them being centered on how to acquire and hold your man. This was done by three means.

The first was making yourself irresistible. Methods were standard. There were things you could eat or drink, things you could put under your pillow, in your pocket or shoe, and things you could brew and rub yourself with. I once induced a hotel maid to sell me a set of "love roots." You had only to drop one in your favorite scent and "hit'll draw de men like flies, ain't one be able to stay 'way." I kept these on display for years, pointing them out to the delighted laughter of guests on all occasions.

The second means involved consolidation of conquests. Here you could render your man impotent with other women or merely unattractive to them.

The third was the simple destruction of a specific rival's sex appeal. This was best done by sneaking into her room and putting beans, or any of several other items, under her bed. Unfortunately, this was effective only so long as the item remained there. If she cleaned under her bed once in a while you were nearly helpless.

In leaning heavily on Negroes as a source of conversation when talking with whites, I was following, as I've already noted, an established Southern custom. Stories of the quaint sayings and doings of Negroes were once—and still are in many areas—the number one topic of social chitchat. Sometimes these were deeply moving little vignettes, revealing great pathos or nobility. Sometimes they were simply quotations from some humorous Negro's conscious wit. But most often they concerned colorful misuse or mispronunciation of words.

My mother loved to tell of one of our hired hands warning her that the brush at the edge of woods must be cut as it would soon "be crouchin' on de far end of de yard." He meant encroaching, but his error was so much more expressive than the intended word that our family and some of our white friends from then on spoke of the "crouching woods." This is one way of creating language.

Sometimes, however, these stories had no point but the blunder. These made me increasingly uncomfortable as I matured. It seemed to me horrid to listen with a straight face to what another human being said to you in good faith and then giggle over it—even though tenderly—to a third person. Surely this verged on betrayal. The "funniness" of ignorance only made my heart ache. Somewhere along the line a faint glimmer of understanding had pierced my segregation wall. Was it my pullman porter who had got through? Or was it an art-student maid I once had briefly known?

She was the color of natural brown-sugar-taffy and pretty, with even teeth and arresting dark eyes. She was about my age and short, like myself, but even thinner. Perhaps she didn't get enough to eat, for she was working part time as a maid to send herself to Howard University.

"I like your work," she said one morning as she cleaned my room in a second-class Washington, D. C. boarding house. She pointed to a pile of drawings I had brought home from the Corcoran School of Art. "I study art, too," she added shyly.

As she dusted, we talked a little about our special interests and problems in our art training. And for several months we repeated this pleasant experience whenever I chanced to be there at the time she cleaned. Her name was Evelyn, and I had called her by it from the beginning. But one day as we talked she suddenly called me Patty instead of Miss Patton.

I felt my entire interior congeal. A Negro had failed to call me Miss! *And I was as guilty as she.* How unseemly my attitude must have been to invite such a thing! I experienced a terrible wave of depression, mixed with a kind of horror of myself, as though I had suddenly stumbled on the discovery that I possessed some repellent abnormality. It was my fault—well, certainly partly mine—for I must have somewhere let our relationship become an equality one, thus inviting "this kind of thing."

I said nothing to her at the time but my sleep was tormented by a frighteningly dark and ugly cloud of guilt. I felt trapped. How could one go backward and escape? Yet I couldn't go on. There was only one way out and I dreaded it. It would hurt her, and I felt torn by the thought. *She* must suffer because *I* had permitted familiarity! Oh, my mother had warned me about this. Yet "this sort of thing" must be stopped at once. It would be WRONG not to stop it— WRONG for her, as well as for me and the South.

It wasn't clear to me why it was WRONG, and it didn't occur to me to analyze it. But I knew it was. I felt as a small child feels when caught in some enormous breach of the family's moral code.

I avoided meeting Evelyn for days. Fear of an encounter hung over me, almost like the impending death of a friend —which in one sense of course it would be. Inevitably it happened.

One day, as I was putting the last pin in my hair, there was a quick knock on the door, then the handle turned.

"Good morning . . ." I said, carefully not adding "Evelyn."

"Good morning, Patty," she replied.

Tinglingly, heavily, my heart sank down. I straightened my back and faced her. I dragged my eyes to her face.

"Evelyn," I said in a faint, tight voice, "you mustn't call me that. People might not understand." This was what I had been taught to say in such cases. I didn't know what it meant, but it did make the rebuke a little less personal, as though possibly I didn't agree with these people who didn't understand.

The look I dreaded came into her eyes. "All right," she said quietly, and went on with her work.

We didn't talk much after that. With both of us trying not to meet, it was easy to keep apart.

Perhaps it was later in this same year that I met a girl at art school whom I particularly liked. She had moved her easel next to mine for a certain study, and we talked often as we worked. She had a creamy skin, soft brown ringlets and the most broodingly lovely hazel eyes I had ever seen. There was a ready warmth, a sensitive awareness in all her responses and I couldn't recall ever being so quickly and fully drawn to another personality.

One day she came in with a deeply wounded look in her eyes. She said she was leaving school, and she gave me all her art supplies. I couldn't get past her look to ask why she was leaving.

A few weeks later my father was chief speaker on some occasion at Howard University, the big Negro institution through which my boarding-house maid was working her way. I went to hear him speak, and there in the choir box I saw the girl who had left the Corcoran. So that was why! Though she looked white, she was a Negro, and had been found out. At that time the Corcoran accepted Filipinos, Japanese, and Chinese, but not Negroes.

Conflict seized me. How wrong of her to practice such a deception! Yet how awful that she had to leave school for such a reason! I wanted to go up to the choir box and speak to her after the service and say I missed her and was sorry. But the words when I tried to phrase them stuck in my brain. I felt shy and confused. Surely she had done WRONG in trying to cross over. But somehow it was more wrong—more basically, structurally wrong—that she wasn't permitted to go where she wished, that she was punished for being born of another race.

Not knowing what to say I didn't approach her. But whenever I remembered the incident afterward, which was often, I felt ashamed. She was a friend. Our spirits had touched. I should have let her know that such a contact is an eternal thing.

CHAPTER 5

The Tidal Wave

THE INCIDENTS REVIEWED IN THE LAST CHAPTER SHOULD HAVE made me question the perfection of our Southern way of life. They didn't. It was as though water purifier had been put into a contaminated reservoir but left in sealed bottles. These incidents were little centers—bottles—of genuine truth and experience which remained sealed off by my indoctrination and training, unable to permeate and purify my over-all conception of the Negro people and their situation in the South. During the next twenty years other sealed bottles were dropped in my reservoir.

I was married at twenty-six to Roger Boyle, a young teacher of dramatic art at the University of Virginia. It was in the depth of the Great Depression, when the University was struggling with a drastically slashed budget, and job opportunities of all kinds were rare. Roger was lucky to be engaged even under a special arrangement whereby he did the work of an instructor but received the salary of a student assistant. Our total income from all sources was less than a hundred dollars a month.

I liked the challenge of making ends meet and contentedly collected such data as that rice was cheaper per serving than potatoes, tea per cup than coffee, and that I could entertain a room full of people for one dollar if only I invited them to tea, not dinner or cocktails. Incidentally, I later worked my accumulated economic wisdom into an article— my first—which I promptly sold to a leading women's magazine for a sum which staggered me and induced me to substitute nonfiction writing for portrait painting as my source of personal income.

I searched out and rented for $20 a month a tiny basement apartment of one room, bath, and makeshift kitchenette. I delighted in its location, just back of the University, only two blocks from the building where Roger taught and directed student plays. Better still, it was a short block from one of the several ghettolike pockets of Negroes which the city of Charlottesville harbors. Of course no social stigma accrues from living next to Negroes in the South, provided your relationship is that of their employer, and I knew that their proximity would enable me to have service at minimum wages.

Foregoing a maid entirely was one sacrifice to poverty which I didn't propose to make. Cooking I enjoyed, as it is creative, but routine chores I abhorred. My plan was to have an untrained teenage girl drop by for an hour after school each day, clean my tiny flat and wash the dishes, which I would stack and accumulate for her. In exchange, I could offer the girl the experience of her first job, my cast-off clothes and one dime an hour, or fifty cents a five-day week. On week ends we visited my parents, only twenty miles away.

My offer proved as acceptable as I anticipated, and I tried out several eager applicants before finding one who satisfied me. The mother of the girl I finally engaged even stopped by to beg me please not to throw away any garment, regardless of its condition.

"Don't make no dif'ence if we can jus' wear it once before it fall apart—we wants it," she stated with familiar emphasis.

The pathos eluded me. Poverty in Negroes was a racial trait. I felt only a pleasant glow, knowing that I had nothing to give which couldn't be worn at least a dozen times before it fell apart, and one or two items were hardly worn at all, only out of style.

My requirements were that the girl know her place, do her work quickly, and show appreciation of the opportunity I was offering by making a real effort to learn what nice people expected of their maids. Then she could get a better job later, using me as reference. Unconscious of exploitation, I felt rather magnanimous.

One girl I tried, named Rose, irritated me by making no effort whatever under instruction to improve her poor performance. No ambition! I thought. But she had a poignant little face; so instead of firing her on Friday, I engaged her for another week as my art model.

She was pleased at the prospect of posing for an artist, but to my dismay returned wearing, not her work costume— a skirt and picturesquely ragged blouse held together with a huge safety pin—but a characterless garment with a forlorn lace collar. So evident, however, was her pride in how nice she looked that I hadn't the heart to protest, so I simply created the old blouse from memory.

She was a marvelous subject. Through her sensitive, softly tan face a vibrant melancholy spoke of longings and hopeless visions. I was both moved and aware that her unfulfillment resulted from being a Negro but I thought of it as unalterable tragedy, like the frustrations which intelligent animals must endure because they have no hands. Tenderness surged through me but no consciousness that act or attitude of mine might contribute to her weal or woe.

I never allowed my sitters to look at their unfinished portraits, so Rose knew nothing of my reclothing her in rags until the picture was done. Then she stepped forward smiling, her expressive eyes eager. They fell on the face, moved downward and froze. Her lovely slim fingers which I had carefully portrayed crept to the little lace collar which I had ignored.

With quiet dignity she said, "I'd like to go now, please."

Straining my budget, I handed her an extra quarter with her half-dollar wage. "You were a fine model."

She didn't smile or thank me. With grace she walked slowly away.

The portrait was the best I had done at the time. It appeared in several art shows. But I took little pleasure in it.

The next two incidents which prepared me to recognize the South's unconscious cruelty were not related to Negroes but to Jews. There's little anti-Semitism in Virginia, and until these experiences, I was hardly aware of the handicaps with which Jewish Americans contend.

In the early years of my marriage, before my children were born, I often employed my knowledge of facial anatomy in directing stage make-up for my husband's department. One night as I strove to convert a handsome young student into a doddering old man, he remarked that he had just decided to become a doctor, then added:

"But I don't think the Med School here will take me."

"Why not?" I demanded, knowing he was bright.

"I'm Jewish."

"Does *that* matter?"

"It does. Oh, Jews are accepted here—if they aren't too numerous—but at present there're quite a few in Med School already."

I hope he erred in suspecting that unofficially we employed a quota system at the University, but the point here is not the degree of truth in his accusation but my reaction. I was horrified and brooded long over the fact that in a nation which owes its greatness to the assimilation of many minorities, a clever, attractive young person had been made to feel excluded because he was a Jew.

A year or so later, a blond, Norwegian-looking student

confided that he was a "crossed-over" Jew. That is, he had decided to pass as a Gentile to escape rejections and handicaps which go with the heritage that was his.

Again, I was greatly shaken. Something in me seemed struggling to get free. I had a strong feeling that this problem was mine, that I had a job to do in connection with it.

I bought a book called *The Making of the Modern Jew*, by Milton Steinberg, and carefully read it from first to last, noting the terrible stresses and suffering brought upon a vivid, gifted people through other peoples' persistent exercise of prejudice, misinformation, and faulty generalizations. But there seemed nothing I could do about these many inequities, except of course offer Jewish acquaintances more personal understanding. So, a whole case of bottled new insight was lowered into the reservoir of my daily life.

It isn't surprising that my first conscious knowledge of discrimination came, not directly through glaring examples of it around me, but deviously. We can seldom see evils which blanket us. Overfamiliarity plus personal involvement results in a kind of snow blindness. Perception of our own iniquities almost always comes first through shocked discovery of these same sins in others. We cry, "How awful! *I* wouldn't do that!" Later, we may ask timidly, "In my own way, do I perhaps a little . . . ?" Still later comes mature confrontation by the fact that in ourselves are the very same evils which we condemn in others.

The small amount of anti-Semitism in the South made an appropriate reaction of horror possible for me, just as in other sections of the country persons who are hardly conscious of discrimination against the minority most rejected in their own region often are able to receive a full vision of the Southern Negro's plight.

I recall with what mingled rage and amusement I later confronted a friend who after years of rejecting my growing information and insight about discrimination in the South, suddenly with passion began crusading for justice—to Indians in the Middle West!

She returned my wrath with interest when I pointed out that her conduct was precisely that of her pet aversion—Northerners who try from afar to straighten out the South. Here in Charlottesville there is an active and justly concerned group of workers for the Indian, and they have my heartfelt applause. But I thought my friend should realize that "interfering Yankees" deserve applause, too.

Little, I fear, would be accomplished in regard to most great human problems if "outsiders minded their own business," thus depriving insiders of the benefit of a perspective which distant persons alone are able to give. Moreover, in the larger sense there are no outsiders. We are all members of the human race, all inhabitants of a shrinking globe. As American citizens we are rightly concerned with every region in our nation, and as world citizens we are rightly concerned with injustice everywhere. But it is also true that once we have learned to distinguish the characteristic contours of evil in the distance, we have lost our excuse for total blindness, and we should then look homeward, too.

In my own case, without this uninhibited look at the many evils of discrimination as applied to Jews, I might have continued longer loving Negroes in their place, yet unaware that for them this place spells unfulfillment, frustration, heartbreak. Like so many others, I might not have taken my caring out of its frame and made it functional in the context of today.

In addition to the experiences I have told, I will review only one which transpired prior to 1950 when my real awakening took place. Sometime during the 1940's when socialist Norman Thomas was making one of his recurrent bids for the presidency, I chanced to hear a radio broadcast from Socialist Convention Headquarters. The speaker was a Southern Negro, though I noted uneasily that I wouldn't have known it had he not said so. Neither his choice of words nor accent displayed the familiar characteristics which I considered racial.

He spoke of America and how her performance had fallen short of her glorious Constitutional promises to her people. Suddenly he offered himself as an example and used a phrase which now is overfamiliar but then was fresh to me. It drove in like a spear.

"I have lived in the South for more than forty years but here on this platform is the first time that I have known human dignity."

The words stayed with me. Their impact, I now know, almost broke my sealed bottles of purifying awareness. With all my belief in our love, kindness, and generosity toward the Negro, I knew that this one essential thing we had not offered him: He was our pet, often even our child, but he was not, he was never our equal; he was not, he was never given human dignity.

But despite an occasional splash as a sealed bottle fell into my private reservoir, the years of my early married life moved smoothly, peacefully by. The Southern world of white supremacy was like a serene bay under stars of gallant ideals and a friendly sun of belief in each other. Surrounded in imagination by adoring colored folk who basked out lazy lives in our summer-hearted Southland, despite brief moments of discomfort, I still accepted my indoctrination, hastily bottled all information which belied it, and smugly glowed my way from youth to middle age.

Then without warning which most white Southerners could recognize, a tidal wave rose titan-high in the South's calm bay of the status quo. It reached me in July 1950, when my husband—by then an associate professor in the recently merged Departments of Speech and Drama—brought home news that a young Negro lawyer had opened suit for admission to our law school.

"They expect him to win," Roger said. "Next fall we'll probably have our first Negro student, after a hundred and twenty-five years of operation."

Shocked to the point of physical tingling, I felt rather as I did when the first moon rocket zoomed up: The space age had begun! A human-relations space age was beginning in the South.

I felt lighter. Although I hadn't known it, my chest had been in a plaster cast and now was sawed free. I could breathe!

But sudden guilt pangs accompanied my relief. The tidal wave swept into my private reservoir, banging my sealed bottles together until they broke, releasing my captive insight into the general stream of my thought. The whole Southern scene appeared in a new light.

The South had somehow committed enormous injustice. Here was proof: The University was founded by Thomas Jefferson, who voiced the premise of our nation, that all men—all, not some—are born equal and free with inalienable rights. Yet now a qualified Virginian, a practicing lawyer in our commonwealth, a man already graduated from law school in another state, who had passed our own state bar examinations, such a man had to sue to enter our state-supported school, solely because he was classified as Negro.

For the first time I clearly heard the voice of Justice ring out above the clamoring of my well-learned Southern code. But mutterings from the code could still be heard:

"Watch out! You're soiling an altar cloth. Something pure and honored is in jeopardy!"

I was filled with shame for violating the code. Such feelings as I had just harbored could lead to familiarity with Negroes! These feelings were only childish—

No, by heaven! they weren't! They represented the inner structure of the universe, which long ago I had glimpsed at Howard University as I faced a friend who could not go where I went or do what I did. Oh, no. This time I was not wrong. The South was wrong.

As this heresy broke free from my center, I felt myself growing tall. From my new height I saw how small and cheap, mechanical and far from the basic works of the Creator, are many of the laws, customs, and beliefs of the South. Later my personal stature dwindled—many times in the years ahead it stretched and shrank, like Alice in Wonderland, but from this day I had tall moments to remember.

Suddenly I saw plainly, as though it were a color print, the face of Tobe, the hired hand at whose firing I fell ill. It was as though a dam burst with the waters of longing for all that I had lost along with him. I loved Negroes. They were my people, more mine and in a truer sense than my own blood kin. I loved them and they loved me. We were part of each other. Yet down the years, without my even knowing it, they had struggled against overwhelming injustice in a land which calls itself just!

"If this colored boy comes here," I told myself, "I'm going to make him welcome, and I aim to make no secret of it either."

But the voice of my old code still muttered: "You'll encourage him to forget his place. Then he'll disgust people, and it will be *your fault*."

I shrank to my normal size—smaller! Again I was a twelve-year-old being taught what was PROPER. "But if I'm *careful*," I pleaded, "wouldn't more contact with him be proper than with any Negro not a student?"

"You'll go too far. You can't preserve that delicate balance."

My stomach felt queer. Oh, the cruel consequences of losing that balance! But still, I couldn't, I *couldn't* let our first Negro student come to the University and just ignore the fact. I would have to take a chance.

"I won't be frightened by the possibility of mistakes,"

I resolved. "Mistakes can be corrected. Empires are built on errors."

Then a new thought struck. What would happen to *him*? He might be lynched! He certainly would be hurt in some terrible way. Oh, why did this have to happen now? We weren't ready yet. We needed more time to do it without disaster. What chance had a lone Negro in the midst of 3000 hot-blooded young Southerners who didn't want him here? And if I encouraged him to forget his place—!

Didn't want him here? Was I sure? *I* wanted him. And if I wasn't a typical Southerner, who was? Surely others wanted him, too. We could form a ring around this colored boy, guard him. The best Southerners always had taken care of their Negroes.

I felt as men must have felt when wartime armies were manned by volunteers. My inner land of shining ideals and eternal principles was calling for an army to fight the tyrant nation of propriety and custom. I had to sign for service. It was a time for reckless giving. Personal cost must not be counted. The value of the individual disappears in war. Only the welfare of one's country matters then.

I drew a slow, sweet breath, the ugly fear gone for now. An exciting, pleasant fear of change remained. Unfamiliar problems lay out there in space—new worlds to discover, explore, overcome. Hope was out there, too. Something lovely, lost in childhood, quietly awaited recovery. Long-buried yearnings might now be satisfied. Roots stretching back into my earliest knowledge of tenderness were sending up sap. I felt as displaced persons must feel when news comes that soon they will see long-lost kin. I was enriched by the very thought of a Negro student at the University. Everything of greatest worth in my life seemed centered here.

CHAPTER 6

Everybody Else Is Prejudiced

GREGORY SWANSON WAS THE NAME OF THE TWENTY-SIX-YEAR-
old Negro lawyer from Danville, Virginia, who in 1950 challenged the University of Virginia's right to continue the
practice of segregation. In doing this, he challenged also
the law of our commonwealth which forbade "race mixing"
in tax-supported schools. When he applied for admission to
our school of law, he was—as he knew he would be—refused.

Actually, a state institution had no choice but to refuse
him. Even if the University's board and administrators had
been unanimous in wanting to admit him, it would have
been illegal to do so until the Supreme Court declared our
state law unconstitutional. Since this can be done only if
there is a plaintiff, no state institution anywhere in the South
could legally accept its first Negro student until he sued.

Quickly learning these facts, I realized that as yet I had
no clue concerning the attitudes of University officials
toward Swanson's admission. The same legal procedures must
be followed whether they secretly wanted to have him or
abhorred the idea. Furthermore, it is naturally awkward for
an administrator, or even for a lesser employee of the state,
to deliver himself of an opinion which is contrary to state
laws and policies. Therefore, one could only guess what was

going on inside the minds of the defendants of this suit. I knew my guess might not be much better than that of a rank outsider. If I wanted to make an "educated guess," I must do detective work.

Swanson was by no means the first Negro to apply for admission here. But in the past the University, like other state-supported Southern institutions, had met the dilemma of the state segregation law versus justice to Negro tax-payers by a simple device of giving colored applicants scholarships to Northern schools of their choosing. Negro students had seemingly been satisfied with this arrangement —until the advent of Mr. Swanson.

To the inevitable, affable question, "And now what school have you decided to attend?" Swanson gave a new answer: "Well, sir, I've decided to come *here.*"

I wasn't there to see the faces of those on whom this answer struck, but I've many times seen the expression which falls like a mask on almost any Southern white when a Negro steps out of HIS PLACE. It's a look of wide-eyed amazement mixed with stern-mouthed indignation.

Swanson didn't fool around trying to soften the look. He was a lawyer. He moved into court—with the National Association for the Advancement of Colored People solidly behind him.

J. Lindsay Almond, then commonwealth attorney, later governor, informed the University authorities that there wasn't hope of a ruling other than in Swanson's favor. Black or white, he was legally a son of Virginia, and he had applied for courses not offered at Virginia State College, the state-supported institution for Negroes. On this important point hung the invincibility of his suit.

When news of the suit hit the headlines, it was the number one topic of private conversation, and at larger gatherings it was more carefully avoided than election-year politics. I went on a round of visits to student and faculty wives of my acquaintance, everywhere slipping in the question, "Well, how do you feel about having a Negro student here?" Answers ran like this:

"I think it's about time at Mr. Jefferson's University!"

"I happen to hope he wins, but most of us will feel pretty bad, I reckon."

"Oh, personally, I think segregated education is a handicap to both races, but I'd probably be run out of town if I went around saying that."

Rapturously I began to canvass for private opinion in real earnest. My findings? That roughly 90 per cent of the women in the University community favored admission of Negroes to our graduate schools. Like me, some had been shaken loose from hitherto unquestioned moorings by the incongruity of a suit for equal opportunity at Mr. Jefferson's* school. Others had been conscious of the South's injustices to her colored citizens for a long time. But without a single exception that I can now recall, each firmly believed that she was probably a lonely democratic star surrounded by a void of prejudice.

I applied for enlightenment to our sociology department. Professor Lambert Molyneaux pointed to a South-wide poll of university and college faculty members taken in 1948 by the Southern Conference Educational Fund, Inc. It had inquired whether or not the professors favored integration in Southern graduate and professional schools. Sixty-nine per cent of the returned ballots, even including those from South Carolina, Alabama, Georgia, and Mississippi, declared themselves in favor.

Dr. Molyneaux also informed me that only a few weeks before Swanson opened suit, a sociology student, C. Lee Parker, had polled 300 of the University's students, selected

* It is traditional here to pay tribute to the immortality of our founder by calling him "Mr. Jefferson," as though he lives in flesh as well as in spirit.

at random from various graduate and professional schools. He had asked if they would object to Negroes in their classes. Of the ballots 72 per cent were returned, and on 73 per cent of these "No objection" had been checked. Only about 5 per cent objected strongly. Written-in comments on the no-objection ballots indicated that these young liberals, too, regarded themselves as isolated renegades who could expect little support from fellow students.

A pattern which made sense to me had now clearly emerged. The majority of *educated* Southerners were ready to throw off the yoke of injustice to Negroes whenever it was called to their attention. Most of those who weren't ready would become so, I thought, if given the facts. Plainly needed here was only good leadership. Doubtless it would come forth shortly, the South being noted for great leaders.

The press, however, was not reassuring. Newspaper comment on "the impending situation at the University" gave no hint that Swanson's admission might be welcome to any of us or that any Virginians except Negroes might rejoice in the justice of his winning his suit. Unchallenged by public statement, written or spoken, there rose before the mind's eye a picture of a lone American citizen struggling for inalienable rights against unanimous opposition from the institution which Thomas Jefferson founded.

I felt a rising inner pressure to do something about it. But what? There seemed nothing I could do.

For most of the many whose feelings were similar to mine, this pressure settled into a dull ache. Being a writer, I inevitably burst into words. I wrote Swanson a letter summarizing what I had learned.

"Dear Mr. Swanson," I began, feeling queer and proud. This was the first time I had ever addressed a Negro as Mister. Something old and rigid had given way.

"Dear Mr. Swanson: I feel impelled to speak for the many Southerners who are silently on your side . . . I speak

as a Virginian for the many Virginians who will be happier
if you are admitted to the University, and will be humiliated
if you are not . . . Many more than you probably believe
sincerely want you to come and will be consistently glad
that you are here. Even some of those who are not glad will
be filled with respect for your willingness to bear and to
suffer so that those who follow you will be less burdened
and freer from pain. Salaam. More power to you. And good
luck! Sincerely."

I felt good. I had said what I wanted to say. Perhaps I
should say it publicly. I could send the letter to the *Richmond Times-Dispatch,* the state's largest newspaper. There it
would reassure the maximum number of Virginians. The
possibility of resulting personal attack wasn't very disconcerting to me, because I had been raised to believe that "the
best people make known their convictions on all important
issues, and then stand behind them, come what may." The
worst thing that possibly could happen to anyone was personal failure to stand up for what he believed.

But when I showed the letter to several ardent newly
discovered liberals among my friends, without exception
they were aghast at the idea of its publication. "The paper
would be deluged with letters denying what you say, and
the net result would be the opposite of what you intend,"
one advised. Another expressed an opinion which I later
learned was a rhythmic refrain throughout the South: "Emotion runs too high on this subject: The less said about it
the better."

This seemed sensible advice at the time, and I followed
it. But as I became seasoned in the struggle for human
rights, I passionately repudiated it, concluding—as I still
hold—that belief in the wisdom of that incantation is one
chief obstacle to progress in democracy in the South. It
has snatched leadership from just people in their search for
the solution to our Southern problems, and has tossed this

leadership to the loudly vocal and emotionally disturbed. Requiring good-willed citizens to gag themselves, it leaves public statements to those who are driven by wild horses of fear and hate.

Because of belief by many of the sane and just that "the less said the better" official decisions on this issue have been based on premises held chiefly by the worst elements. Such premises often are founded on pure illusion. In consequence the Southern struggle in some areas has been a comedy of errors—or rather, a tragedy of errors.

I didn't send the letter to a newspaper. But I sent it to Gregory Swanson. Reading his reply a few days later, I was pulled in several directions. My letter had comforted and strengthened him. For this I was glad. But I had *misled* him —Oh, I had! He said he was looking forward to our being great friends and to many other enjoyable relationships at the University. This implied social equality! Something gripped me with digging, cold fingers. Clearly I had already made Swanson FORGET HIS PLACE!

"Maternalism" also reared its determined countenance. Swanson's vocabulary was too large. The educated Negro, as portrayed by minstrel shows and other fun-pokers, always collects long, unwieldy words and employs them, à la Mrs. Malaprop, indiscriminately. True, Swanson used them skilfully and knew what they meant—which I sometimes didn't. Even so, his use of long unusual words underscored the stereotype. From this I must protect him. I spent a tortured night and in the morning took to my typewriter.

I said I hoped I hadn't led him to believe that he would be happy at the University, or to expect "the lowering of social barriers, for I don't think this will occur, even with a few . . . I hope I am wrong but I think your isolation will be such that you will feel like a lone man on one side of a wall with a throng of hostile people on the other. I wrote in an effort to convince you, not that the wall would not be there, but that the hostility would be largely an illusion . . . The multitude who will stand solidly behind the wall are not united in a single attitude toward you . . . The large, kindly but timid majority wishes to see justice done but is fearful of sudden change . . . Take what courage you can from the knowledge that even though we remain on the other side of the wall, many of our hearts are with you, many are working quietly on your behalf, and many are humbled by your courage and inspired by your will to win."

Then I drew a long breath and wrote:

"Watch that high vocabulary. It will make some people wonder uneasily whether you're being snooty or defensive. Simplicity is the most disarming of virtues and is a trademark of true greatness . . . The chief merits of education are indirect and lie in the fact that it broadens our horizon, deepens our understanding and prepares us for better service to our fellow man.

"The mere accumulation of knowledge is sterile, and the use of large unusual words where small, familiar ones would do is a symbol of such sterility. It is, in fact, a form of snobbery, similar to the one which has caused you much suffering. To help your people to a larger life and to combat successfully the pettiness of mine, you must be above such things. I think you are above them, but it is only natural to fall into error occasionally, especially in the desperately confusing position in which you find yourself.

"Do you want to know how to open the door to the power, simplicity and human warmth which you must have in order to be a spearhead for your people? It is done by never thinking of yourself. Exclude yourself from your picture of your life. Do nothing for your own sake; plan nothing for your own profit; make no effort to defend yourself as an individual; ignore in your own heart your personal achievements. Let your joy and satisfaction be in your ideals, your outgoing love, your faith in the rightness of what you do.

"If you recognize this for eternal truth, and not for a string of clichés, then you are more than an individual worthy of respect; you are the right man for this job.

"In any case, the best of luck to you. Cordially."

It was a very long letter, written throughout with a sincere desire to help which must have communicated itself to Swanson, for he didn't take offense at my lecture—though it may have marked the conception of an adverse reaction which later seemed to step full grown from his brow. At this point, I appeared to have won a friend. He wrote me by return mail:

"You must realize that your correspondence is a very rare experience for me, in fact, the first of its kind, for I have never had one of your position to speak so honestly and objectively. Therefore, it is only natural that I should be appreciative of your sympathetic interest and advice. But I suppose I'm more impressed by your spiritual depth than any single characteristic which I have been able to get from your letters. That is the basis for the optimism which I have: you spoke of the fact that you may have misled me. No, I am not misled. I understand you fully, and I believe your advice is the best that could be given. I sincerely believe in the spiritual or intrinsic qualities of all humanity. I shall rely heavily upon that belief when coming to the University, regardless of the treatment which I may receive . . . I expect my pursuits to be most challenging, but in the ultimate I believe that some good will have been accomplished."

I shall close this chapter with that example of successful intergroup communication. It was many months before I experienced another.

CHAPTER 7

Noncommittal Answers

WHEN GREGORY SWANSON WON HIS SUIT I WROTE HIM MY congratulations and offered to help him find a suitable place to live—in the Negro community. I talked further about his vocabulary, my "maternalism" obtruding even more. His reply seemed slightly cooler than his first two letters.

He said that T. J. Sellers, local district manager of a Negro insurance company and Charlottesville editor of a Negro weekly newspaper, *The Tribune,* had agreed to find him lodgings, but added politely that he was sure Mr. Sellers would welcome my help.

On the assumption that only a white person could make satisfactory arrangements about anything, I at once called Mr. Sellers—very conscious of the courtesy prefix and proud of using it, for it was the first time I had applied it vocally to a Negro.

Back over the wire came brusque, clipped English, hauling my memory across years to the enigma of my Pullman porter on the Florida train. Now, as then, beneath smoothly enunciated, stilted courtesies there flowed an undercurrent of unspoken rebuff. It registered just below my consciousness, leaving me vaguely shaken.

He said he had engaged a room for Mr. Swanson at Carver

Inn, the Negro hotel. (I hadn't known there was one.) He would be happy, however, if I could find something closer to the University and more reasonably priced. He appreciated my concern.

Slightly dampened without knowing why, but with maternalism unchecked, I hung up and searched the classified section of the telephone book. By their addresses, I identified as Negro a Baptist and an Episcopal minister. Calling each, I asked if he knew of an appropriate room for a University student—in the Negro section.

Chill undercurrents and precise English again greeted me. No, they knew of no place better than the one *Mr.* Sellers had found.

This Sellers must be very efficient, I concluded. Obviously he had consulted the ministers already. But what about their calling him "mister" to me, to say nothing of their all referring to the prospective student as mister? If I graciously chose to apply courtesy titles, that was one thing, but it verged on impertinence for them to do it to me.

And that wasn't all:

The Baptist minister had let me know politely, but not very politely, that if I really wanted to help, I would stop looking in the Negro community and try to get "Mr. Swanson" in a dormitory with other students.

Using laudable restraint, I had with gentleness pointed out an obvious truth: "Now is the time for gratitude, not more pushing. Trying to move too fast will only lose what's already been gained."

I was shocked to hear my unseen listener's soft, ironic chuckle undulate from the earpiece. Such rudeness was unbefitting a minister.

Later I realized that this laugh was a highly Christian substitute for the impulse to slap me flat. In two sentences I had voiced two stereotyped opinions which are universally infuriating to members of the South's oppressed minority.

These opinions pivoted on the phrase "move too fast" and on the word "gratitude."

Nearly a century after the Emancipation Proclamation, Negroes are still in many ways enslaved by our system, and few of their leaders can hear the expression "move too fast" applied to their aching crawl toward full citizenship without yearning to chastise the offender.

Both from mass media and from well-meaning individuals, the word "gratitude" drips like water torture upon the heads of those who find little to be grateful for. Quarter-portions of overdue rights, guaranteed in full to all citizens by our Constitution, are offered as generous gifts for which effulgent thanks are seemly; brilliant, well-trained Negroes are told to be grateful for unskilled jobs at subsistence wages; all are told to be grateful for a love which is blind not to their faults but to their needs.

But I was in a white prison. I knew nothing of that outside world, the Negro's thoughts, knew only that I was acting in a spirit which they seemed not to recognize. I was sure that University authorities were acting in this spirit too, even though their change in policy had been court ordered. Vaguely but deeply troubled, I moved from telephone to typewriter and wrote a letter to Swanson which contained this paragraph:

"He thinks they ought to put you in a dormitory, but if we can't at this point be filled with gratitude that you're here at all, I doubt if this additional minor victory would make us happy either. I'll bet you agree with me that the surest step toward getting what we want is to be grateful—*visibly* grateful—for what we get."

Even then, my boner quota for the day apparently was not filled. My master boner (revelation of which I shall hold until I can go into it thoroughly) was further on in that fateful letter.

Feeling only pleasure that I had identified myself with the

Negro's problem in my use of "we," I posted the letter just in time to reach Swanson before he left Danville for the University—so I didn't expect a reply by mail. But uneasiness grew when he failed to telephone. Had I wounded him in some way? My heart ached at the thought.

As his silence continued, I decided to take the initiative. I had a good excuse, having resolved to write an article about his advent here. Printed in one of the big national magazines which sometimes bought my work, it would help both Swanson and the cause of "nonsegregation"—as it was then called among whites. An interview with him was essential.

I phoned him at his hotel, Carver Inn, and asked if he would see me about an "important matter." His voice was cold, even sullen, when he said he would.

I hoped his manner resulted from shyness. If from hurt, his wound was serious. The possibility that it was cold fury —or even cold fear—never occurred to me. That a Southern Negro could have such feelings toward a member of the "club" was beyond my power to conceive. Full of anticipation, I drove to the Inn. Something lovely was about to begin, I was sure—a new kind of relationship, rooted in nostalgic memories.

Carver Inn is a large white clapboard house with a pillared porch. It was once an ample private dwelling. With astonishment, I saw that the interior was quietly colorful and well kept. I had expected a Negro hotel to be dingy.

As Swanson moved across the reception room to meet me, my reaching emotions drew back like a snail's antenna. A big, light-skinned man, he confronted me with a blankness on his broad face which, even allowing for the possibility that he was naturally dead-pan, I knew must be intentional. Nobody could be so devoid of expression except by an act of will. Clearly it was a defense. But against what?

His conversation was about as spirited as his face.

I expressed hope that he had understood my last letter.

Yes, perfectly. Period. (No room in his tone or look for me to insert a question concerning what he had understood by it.)

Would he help me with data for the article?

Yes, a biographical sketch would be mailed to me within two days. Period. (No sign of pleasure that I planned such a piece.)

Had his experiences at the University been pleasant so far?

Yes. They had. Period.

"No unpleasantness at all?" I persisted, my hopes and gratitude rising.

"I'm just one of the fellows," he answered slowly. "That's the way I want it. I'm treated just like any other student. I'm just one of them."

My heart contracted with a new ache. Such a natural, simple longing for a boy in college, yet for him so beyond hope of fulfillment. I had wanted a glimpse inside him. Now I had it, and with it a glimpse into the cavernous tragedy which I and all my ancestors had fostered in the South.

I rose to go. He accompanied me, and on the bottom step of the porch he seemed to melt.

"Those first two letters you wrote—" his voice was rich— "they meant so much. If there were more people like you—"

He broke off, but he had said enough. My thoughts soared back to beauties that were tender, loves that were sweet. Oh, I didn't care what it might cost me to clothe his dreams in a little reality. I couldn't make him "just one of the fellows"—not our first Negro student, spotlighted, after 125 segregated years—but perhaps I could gain for him a little more acceptance. I would spare no effort, pay any price.

I knew less than nothing about race relations—much less. But I knew how to go about writing this type of article. My data must come directly from the source, not filtered through the minds of other writers. So I pushed forward into an authentic, firsthand learning experience not shared by the University's other incipient liberals who had sprung into being like tiny mushrooms during Swansons's suit. Their new desire to understand more realistically the Negro and the South was satisfied by browsing in the University library. Among predigested answers to profuse questions, they settled back, well informed but with the soil of their minds still unplowed. On the other hand, the neat grassy meadow which was my inner life was soon, through personal involvement, uprooted and harrowed until nothing familiar was left.

I decided to interview the three Negroes I had talked to on the telephone. Mr. Sellers, editor-insurance man, was out of town, but both ministers agreed to see me. Fizzing with good will and determined to make it known, I rang the Rev. Mr. A.'s doorbell with self-satisfaction and confidence worthy of a month-old puppy.

A tall, golden-brown man, with sharp, thinking eyes and a practice of not looking at you except in darting, soon-spent glances, opened the door.

"Come in."

He led me to a comfortable, airy study. Clean, I noted. "I've come for information I just found out I haven't got," I said, beaming and using my "club" voice of intimate condescension.

The air grew so electric I was almost executed. In a New England accent and Webster-perfect words he replied, "If there is any possible way in which I can assist you, I shall be quite glad."

Hastily dropping as much of my club manner as was conscious, I told him that Swanson's suit had awakened me to a new awareness of injustices and I was hoping to find some way I could atone.

"I commend you for your attitude," he said without fervor. "If more white people would take your position, the situation would improve."

This rocked me slightly. It sounded as though *he* were talking down to *me*—morally, anyway. True, he was a minister, but it would have been more fitting if he had said, "You sure are a wonderful lady. My heart is full of gratitude that somebody like you is taking over at last."

I told him that most educated Southerners felt as I did and would pitch into the fight against "injustices to our colored people" if only they had assurance of not being alone. Less educated persons needed to be informed before they would "change over to our side." (I was proud of that "our side.") But I thought I could help dispense both assurance and information.

I paused, looking at him expectantly. There was no hint of enthusiasm either for my good news concerning the attitude of whites, or for my offer to put my shoulder to his wheel. Unlike Swanson's, his face was quite readable. It was chill, stiff, hostile. Also, it reflected something I could not translate, except that it was unpleasant.

"May I ask a question?" I inquired.

"I'll attempt to answer."

"Just what do Negroes think about segregation?"

Amazed I saw anger leap into his eyes. "That's a question no one can answer. Ask what *I* think, and I can tell you."

"Put it this way," I amended, fumbling hastily for words which might be more pleasing. "How do Negroes *feel* about it?"

He leaned forward as though about to rise. "I can save us both a lot of time by suggesting that you simply ask yourself how you would feel if *you* were a Negro."

I took the hint and left, dampened, sadder, but no wiser.

Well, he was the man who had suggested that I should try to get Swanson into a dormitory. He probably was just a chronic sorehead. I would doubtless fare better with the other minister.

But I didn't.

The Rev. Mr. Z. was a large man, nearly white, with a

strikingly beautiful wife who could have passed for a Spaniard. I remember thinking that although his features little resembled those of Mr. A., his expression was similar— stiff, chill, hostile, and, again, that unidentified look. Was it suspicion? It couldn't be! What on earth could they suspect me of?

My good news about the attitude of educated whites once more fell flat; again my declaration that I intended to help Negroes elicited no enthusiasm; as before, my questions received minimum, noncommittal answers.

To my main question, Mr. Z. gave a reply which varied from Mr. A.'s but only in his choice of words: "A Negro can be expected to think and feel about segregation the same way a white man of a similar temperament and degree of intelligence would think and feel if subjected to comparable ill-use and humiliation."

Today I know that both ministers were trying to get two points across to me which I shall discuss in Chapters 11 and 12. I failed to grasp them at the time, seeing only that my questions were evaded.

Either these men were giving me the run-around, I concluded, or else they assumed I had information which in fact I did not have. How could I know how I would feel if I were a Negro? Hadn't I asked the question precisely because I wanted to know? I had no idea what kind of "ill-use and humiliation" Mr. Z. meant, so how could I conceive how anyone would feel upon meeting such experiences? My imagination had no foothold when people spoke of mistreatment and hardship with that bitterness in their eyes and voices.

When I rose to go, Mr. Z. stretched up to his extensive height, squared big shoulders, and tipping a pale face upward, looked past and over me to the upper corner of the room. A cold, leaden quality was in his voice as he said:

"I often wonder, you know, what kind of thinking makes it

possible for light Negroes like myself and wife to be born and yet be segregated. On the streets and in the fields of the South you see Negroes of all shades from pitch black to lily white, pitch black to lily white.

"Ask yourself sometime how these different shades came about, and then ask yourself, 'What about this so-called segregation?'" He paused and looked at me. "You say people you know love Negroes and want justice and happiness for us. What kind of love and justice is it that makes us all different shades and still all on the wrong side of a ten-foot wall!"

Inside me something clicked softly. My conscious mind ignored it. I remembered what he said but not for six years did I grasp the ghastly thought he was striving to convey: That in life's most intimate relationship there never had been segregation in the South, and that these were white men's own sons and daughters, sisters and brothers, cousins, uncles and aunts against whom they built segregation walls.

Only Mr. Z.'s bitterness got through to me at the time. I wondered if all nearly white Negroes felt so resentful. I have learned that the most caustic dose many Negroes have to swallow is their own "white" blood.

Defeated, but challenged and deeply stirred, I returned home.

CHAPTER 8

We Want a Negro

GREGORY SWANSON'S BIOGRAPHICAL MATERIAL ARRIVED NEXT
day. Full of human interest and potential drama, it even
included a few early impressions of the University. Added
to what I already knew about the white community, it would
make possible a good article without the data I had fruitlessly
sought from the two ministers.

With unaccustomed ease I whipped out a first draft of
a piece called "We Want a Negro at the UVA." It compared
favorably in interest with any rough of an article I had ever
sold. Timely as it was, and fraught with far-reaching implications, I was sure it could be placed in one of the big
national magazines.

It briefly reviewed my qualifications to speak as a typical
Southerner and revealed what I had learned about the University community, telling of our fears, hopes, hurting conscience, and our awareness that Thomas Jefferson would not
approve our practice of exclusion. In covering Swanson's
own history, emphasis was thrown on the patience, stamina,
fortitude, and natural capacity required for a Southern Negro
to fight his way up through poverty and many handicaps
to where Swanson now stood.

It pointed to the amazing courage needed to break a

pattern of segregation which was valued by many and which had stood for 125 years. Swanson, isolated and beyond the help of anyone of his own race, confronted alone several thousand young Southern students whose intentions toward him he could not foresee. I described him as I saw him— quiet, unassuming, determined, brave. I closed with the affirmation that he was opening our hearts and minds and not merely the institution he had sued.

Reading the piece over I was pleased. It glowed with fair-mindedness and good will, and would go far toward creating the best possible climate of opinion for Swanson at the University and for "nonsegregation" in general. A member of the University News Service staff who read it heartily agreed, and another staff member assured me, "This is the kind of thing we would like to see published."

As I waited for Swanson in the News Service office in the famous Rotunda, where he had agreed to meet me and go over the piece, I anticipated his reaction with pleasure. Through glass doors I could see the terraced green lawn sweeping down to the graceful white pillars of Cabell Hall. On either side of The Lawn (never, never at the University called the campus) stretched a chain of ancient, charm-laden dormitory rooms and professors' houses designed by Thomas Jefferson. How good that at last his spirit would triumph, I mused. I was grateful that I could play a part in promoting that triumph.

This joy would be my compensation, I decided. I wouldn't keep the money for the article. I would make it as a small payment on a large debt I owed. The check probably would be for a thousand or more and I would give it to Swanson as a kind of scholarship for opening our doors. What fun it would be to hand it to him. If he recoiled from taking it for himself, he could pass it on to the National Association for the Advancement of Colored People.

At last I saw him walking as though carrying a heavy

weight. Reluctance emanated from his every line and movement. He didn't want to come! *Why?*

I pushed back disappointment. He hadn't read the article
yet, I reminded myself, and doubtless he expected something quite different from what I actually had written. It
didn't occur to me that he simply wished nothing to do with
me, and that he knew well it would be quite impossible for
me from the context of my racial attitudes to write an
article which would be acceptable to him.

After greeting him rather effusively, with a notable lack
of response from him, I handed him the manuscript. "Read it
ruthlessly for errors, please," I beamed. "There may be a lot."

We sat opposite each other at a small table. As he read,
I tried to follow the text upside down, weighing it against
his probable reaction. He couldn't, I was sure, fail to be
touched as well as pleased by the way I had written it
without a single concession to inherited prejudice.

Expressionless, he read it through. Then, without raising
his eyes from the page he said, "And you intend to *publish*
that?"

A slight tremor in his voice moved me and I answered
softly, "Yes. But I'm not afraid, because something more
important than me is at stake here—the foundation of our
faith as Americans and as Christians. I'm hoping that it's
timely enough for *Reader's Digest*."

"You intend to publish *that* in *Reader's Digest?*" His eyes
were still down, his voice tremor stronger.

"Please don't feel grateful, Gregory. I feel privileged to
help."

He looked up then. If I had been standing, I would have
stepped back. His eyes were the incarnation of hostility, fury.
"I suppose I can't stop you. Still, I wish you would refrain
from printing that kind of thing about me—at least while
I'm at the University."

He rose, turned, walked through the door and down the Rotunda steps without glancing at me again.

My distress must have shown, for one of the women on the News Service staff who had read the manuscript came quickly and put her hand on my shoulder. "I don't understand either. I thought he would just love that article."

Walking home, my whole interior felt as if it were in a compressor. What did he mean by "that kind of thing"? *What* kind of thing? How could anything in that article possibly offend him?

In the next few days, I reread the article many times. It continued to seem a clear-cut, straightforward statement from a faculty wife expressing one hundred per cent approval of Swanson, and good will in regard to the whole movement toward equal rights for Negroes.

Reading it over again just before beginning to write this chapter, I marked over a dozen places where either my choice of words or the implication behind them would offend many Negroes, and the whole piece dripped sentimental maternalism. In addition, I realize now that Swanson must have been filled with fear that its publication would more than ever spotlight him and set him apart. But at the time I saw no connection between his attitude toward the article and his remark only a few days earlier which had moved me so deeply: "I just want to be one of the fellows." So segregated were Negroes in my inner mind that I thought of Swanson as already having achieved maximum conspicuousness simply by being at the University. Since most of the students and faculty were Southerners, this assumption actually was quite realistic.

I still think it great misfortune that the article wasn't published. Written as it was entirely in the language of white Southerners, it would have had a stronger, more direct effect on unenlightened persons than anything I was able to write after I was better informed.

Add to this the fact that it would have come at the outset
of the integration struggle, when every news and editorial
spotlight was trained on the University, and when the majority of normal Southern whites were feeling their way to
discover what their reaction to integration should be.

It might have had more influence on the climate of acceptance of Negroes than everything I have written since.
Though I know this is little enough, if I had it to do over,
I would ignore Swanson's displeasure and publish the piece
—with his corrections of misstatements if possible, if not,
then with whatever errors I was unable to track down without his help. It was time to speak. I muffed the best opportunity to do it I have ever had.

Poring over the manuscript in 1950 with my wounds still
bleeding, I could think of only one possible explanation of
Swanson's anger. He must think I was trying to exploit him
for money!

Just then the *Richmond Times-Dispatch* blazoned on its
editorial page a letter from a Charlottesville man. He made a
suggestion which, in those innocent days, sounded fantastic
and fanatical: Why not close any state-supported institution
which the Supreme Court ordered to admit Negroes?

Close the schools for the sole purpose of denying our
Negroes rights which our own white judges declared were
constitutionally theirs! I was rocked like a reed in the wind.
The unspeakable injustice and cruelty of such an intent, the
poor sportsmanship of refusing the winner his winnings after
such a fight, and the sheer rudeness of the suggestion which
contemptuously ignored the Negro's listening ear—all this
disrupted my phantasm of Southern principles and courtesy.
Such iniquity voiced by one Southerner *must* be answered
by another. Never mind warnings that a public defense of our
Negroes would only stir up trouble!

I marched to my typewriter and wrote in reply that many
of us associated with the University, both in faculty and

student body, felt strongly that "we must not submit to a prejudice grounded in conditions which no longer exist, and thus continue to humiliate the living spirit of our founder. . . ." And far from maintaining rigid segregation by closing our doors, we hoped that "our action in opening not only our doors but also our minds to a people whom we have too long oppressed will help other institutions on the verge of similar action to hesitate no more."

I was keenly conscious of having laid my neck on the railroad track as I mailed this missive to the *Times-Dispatch*. To publish such a letter in one of the South's most widely circulated newspapers was to lift a voice as loudly as it could be lifted in Virginia. To my knowledge, this was the first time a white Virginian had spoken above a whisper in support of integration at the University. Even my most liberal friends doubtless would disapprove.

But I had spoken primarily for the benefit of Negroes who had been insulted. I hoped my reply would offer some balm. I also hoped my publication of a statement where I would incur the maximum risk of personal attack with no remuneration would constitute proof to Swanson and others that exploitation was not my aim. I took it for granted that I would receive when the letter was printed, as it shortly was, expressions of appreciation both from Negroes I knew and did not know.

None came.

I understand this silence better now. One factor in it probably was that the segregation pattern grips colored Southerners as well as white. Even when their suspicions are quieted, it seldom occurs to one to reach out either in sympathy or approbation to a white adult. They usually think of us as secure within and without, in need of nothing they can give. Much later I learned that my letter created a sensation among Negro leaders, not one of whom thought of commenting on it to me.

Their silence was confounding. My image of Negroes as full of quick praise and appreciation for kindnesses was dear to me, and my dependence on their approval was great. I concluded that in their eyes I had blundered again.

On the other hand, the expected attack from whites didn't come. No reply challenging my statement appeared, not even one from the writer of the letter I had rebuked. And on the home front, three persons whom I had not suspected of being liberal halted hurried steps on the street and in stores to thank me for it.

"I was hoping somebody connected with the University would answer that letter," one said.

My head swam. I had lifted my voice in defense of Negroes against the affirmed position of the white South, and white Southerners were the only ones who thanked me for it!

But their thanks were privately expressed.

I still believe that if even five per cent of the many who evidently approved my stand had *at that time* joined their voices to mine, the whole course of events in Virginia might have been changed. Politicians carefully scan letters on editorial pages, and were now eagerly seeking the public pulse. What they read were tirades by thinkers like the man whose published letter I had answered. Less consciously the average citizen, prefering to move with the trend, also sought the public pulse. If just persons were to set the trend, the moment to make themselves heard had come. They let it pass.

The press hammered on. While occasionally there was an admission that to accept Negroes in our graduate schools was only fair, "How can we stop them?" was the reiterated theme of editorials and speeches. None even hinted at what I knew to be a fact—that integration would be agreeable to many Southern whites. The assumption was that now Negroes had got their foot in the door, "the lawn of the University would soon be black," that every colored Tom,

Dick, and Harry would stampede for admission, while white students would correspondingly withdraw. Some predicted that as "the black flood" swept in, the University would become an all-Negro school.

I rather expected the black flood myself, but I resented the insulting—both to Negroes and whites—assumption that all whites would withdraw. I was very sick at heart. Perhaps what troubled me most was the persistent implication that the *right* way for Southerners to feel was that integration was unthinkable. This was nothing more nor less than *reindoctrination* of attitudes which a great many Southern people who were either kindly or thoughtful were about to lay aside. And I knew that such an implication is the kind of thing which creates opinion. Convince a man that he ought to feel a certain way and pretty soon he believes that he does.

In short, it was as clear to me at this point as it is today (although my evidence was much less) that in 1950 a very large slice of the white South stood at the crossroads in its attitude toward its colored citizens and was psychologically capable of turning either way.

But if this pounding continued, malleable people would be confirmed in old prejudices and would be influenced to think as the press assumed they already thought. And convinced liberals would become more sure that each was too isolated to make an effective stand. And resentment among Negroes certainly would rise—and their attitude toward us become worse. A vicious circle would form.

Such was my gloomy prophecy in the fall of 1950, two months after the first light pierced my cell in the white prison where I had always lived.

CHAPTER 9

Library Liberals

WHAT HAD CHANGED SWANSON? WHY HAD HIS ATTITUDE toward me in his first two letters been the opposite of what it was now? Determined to reach the root of the mystery, I reread my carbon copies of my letters to him. In the boner letter I found a paragraph which halted me.

It had been framed through fear that I had encouraged him to FORGET HIS PLACE. I had felt I must make it clear that he shouldn't call on me at my home. "Race mixing socially," as it was called, was not acceptable even to liberals, I was sure. Attempting it would only "arouse the opposition," endanger Swanson's welfare, and retard progress in nonsegregation at the University. Thus motivated I had said in this letter:

"I wish there were some way we could know each other personally. I want us to very much. But I don't quite see how it can be done. It would be humiliating to us both to be clandestine about it, and would be unwise to be open about it. For us there can be no middle road between those two, for there's no privacy where I live."

This was the master boner I mentioned earlier, but after repeated readings of the paragraph, I still saw in it only a possible source of hurt feelings. Might Swanson have con-

cluded that I was ashamed of his friendship? Oh, surely
he would have recognized the good sense of not stirring up
indignation unnecessarily, surely realized that I was thinking
of his protection more than of my own—even though maybe
I was thinking of mine, too.

The astonishing fact is that it was not until ten years
later when I reread the correspondence that I grasped what
I now am sure was largely responsible for his sudden re-
pudiation of my friendship. Almost any woman, even though
half-witted, could be expected to see in my remarks the
implication they might carry for a man. But a factor in my
upbringing stood like a boulder between me and such
recognition.

There are two distinct schools in handling the Southern
interracial sex problem. One consists in warnings against
"the bestial natures of Negroes." This school makes white
girls super-sex-conscious and continually on their guard
against doing or saying anything to "inflame the primitive
imagination" when dealing with Negro men. The other
school employs an opposite method. Ignoring entirely the
simple scientific fact that Negro men are members of the opposite sex, it encourages white girls to regard them rather as
one does male dumb animals. The latter method was used
with me.

Probably no data is available which offers a clue to
whether the majority of Southern white women learned in
the better-known or lesser-known school. But it happened
that many of my friends belonged to my school, and joined
me in thinking that persons taught the other way were
unpleasantly evil-minded.

Since by its very nature, the sex-suppression school is
conducted only by implications which are never verbalized,
and since, also by its nature, the super-sex-conscious school
is very vocal, the later gets all the publicity. I have yet to
find a Negro who knows even of the existence of the sex-

suppression school. Resultant misunderstandings are virulent. I wonder, even, if they have not been largely responsible for some of the rape cases which blare out now and again from Southern headlines.

Suppose you have on the one hand a woman raised to be unsexed in her thinking about Negroes, with a consequent tendency to behave in relation to them as though sexual desire did not exist. On the other hand, you have a normally virile young man who was raised to believe that all white women conceive of Negroes as in a constant state of lust toward them. Surely she would often, through sheer inappropriate innocence, speak and behave in ways which would appear to him inviting. She might even make him blush at the unabashedness of what he would take for overtures.

Hauled into a Southern court for "attempted rape," such a luckless Negro would be sure (but probably afraid to testify to this effect lest he be lynched by irate relatives or admirers of the girl) that he had been deliberately lured and then betrayed. The girl would be equally certain that she had been insulted without provocation.

But if the above theory were well founded, one might point out, wouldn't there be more cases of interracial "assault" than in fact there are? Yes—were it not beaten into the heads of vigorous colored youths by their elders that to take white women in their arms, be they ever so willing, is virtually certain death.

A favorite story often accompanies these warnings. It involves a description of the reproductive habits of a certain species of lizard, among which the female characteristically kills the male when the mating act is complete. A little later on in my intergroup education, one day as a colored youth dismounted from my bus in a white neighborhood, I heard an older Negro call after him, "Watch out for lizards, son!" I was amused that I knew what was meant.

However, it was not this kind of suspicion (or at least not

suspicion along this line alone) which I had read in the eyes of the two ministers. Such two-way misjudgments extend into many areas other than sex. Operating in a wide range of human concerns they are, I think, largely responsible for the snarl into which race relations have got in the South. That an occasional individual from either group is able to fight his way through the confusion to some kind of understanding and normal friendship with members of the other group is a miracle.

Most of the Negroes who knew of my sudden concern for integration assumed that I intended some form of exploitation. Many admitted as much to me when I finally gained their confidence. It seemed to them a logical explanation of my unusual behavior in the light of what they had been taught about the character of Southern whites. To them the least likely interpretation was that I was dedicating myself to their cause without thought of tangible reward. My first letter to the press (or even my first several) was not for most Negroes convincing proof that I did not have some hidden self-seeking purpose.

I, in turn, was unprepared for their suspicions. During the first years of the '50's I regularly expected a type of response from them which was far indeed from what I usually got. Bruised from their buffeting, my bewilderment was childlike.

But there was no recognition of this from them. Bewilderment in a white does not readily register with a colored Southerner. He tends to credit whites with being sharp of mind and correspondingly dull of conscience. Unjustified respect for our brain-power mothers disdain for our moral impotence. Negroes who imagine that we see the situation with Socratic clarity are understandably contemptuous of our conduct.

My practical training as a writer, besides teaching me to seek facts at their source, had taught me to pursue the reason for the rejection of a piece of my writing. I sometimes submitted a manuscript to above a dozen magazines, until at last it either sold, received editorial criticism, or exhausted my list of market possibilities. I followed this pattern with my letters and manuscript "rejected" by Swanson.

I took them in turn to several newly discovered white liberals among my friends, three of whom were seasoned in interracial work. Could they offer me clues concerning why these innocently conceived efforts had given offense? Indicative of the width of the chasm which separates the thinking of white and colored Southerners is the fact that all these deeply concerned persons were as baffled as I. Only one had a sensible suggestion. This was my family physician. Though like the rest of us, he saw nothing wrong with the manuscript, he spotted at once the guilty paragraph in the letter.

"Why obviously he thought you were making passes at him," he told me with conviction.

The suggestion seemed so preposterous that I didn't even consider it, but continued to circulate the letter and beg for help. If someone had seconded the suggestion, a small crack might have been made in my psychological block. No one did.

But something else became apparent to me as a result of this seeking: Southern white liberals do not necessarily know any more about the Negro whose side they are on than do the segregationists who oppose him. The people I consulted had no colored friends in the sense that they had white friends. Some had acquaintances among educated Negroes whom they called friends, but in no case that I know of was there the kind of intimacy which results in uninhibited exchanges of personal confidence. The relationships were rather like those between club or business acquaintances. Some fervent supporters of "nonsegregation" had not even attempted a conversation with an educated Negro. Their enlightenment was almost entirely of the library variety. In my blindness I had asked aid of the blind.

I telephoned T. J. Sellers, editor of *The Tribune*, the local Negro newspaper, explained my problem, and asked if he would read and criticize the material. Probably filled with curiosity, he said he would. So I attached a request for a brutally frank report, and mailed the items to him.

When his reply arrived a week later, I read it, unbelieving.

About the letter he carefully said only that he thought Swanson did not understand the language I spoke, but the manuscript he reviewed in detail. Point by point he laid my Southernisms bare. It was no mystery to him, he said, why Swanson was not moved to write "rave notices" concerning it. This was why:

In paragraph one I had referred to slavery, a tactless habit of white Southerners, with whom the mere sight of a Negro seemed to conjure up nostalgic recollections of those good old days. I had also pridefully affirmed that nobody on earth "could accuse me of being a Yankee," thus revealing that I felt no shame for the South's far-reaching continued crimes against her Negro citizens. I had clearly implied in several places that although we wanted Swanson at the University, his brothers, sisters, or friends were not included in the invitation.

Then I had tried to whitewash the University by depicting her as open-minded and openhearted as the morning, even suggesting that she was restrained from extending justice to Virginia Negroes only by the law and by considerations of the Negro's own welfare; Swanson and other informed persons well knew that this was not in accordance with fact. Another glaring departure from fact had been my interpretation of the role of the NAACP.

Worse still, near the bottom of page two I had begun to build the impression, continued throughout the manuscript, that Swanson and his family were quiet, easy-going colored people with "not a trace of defiance" against a system which had made intolerable their own lives and the lives of others of their race. Thus I had isolated Swanson from the cause nearest his heart.

Finally, the tone of my whole article suggested the one hundred per cent Southern conviction that "privileges" were not for Negroes, and that it was only through the wonderful generosity of whites that they could expect to obtain those rights which actually are guaranteed to every American by our Constitution. He closed with this statement:

"There is a New Negro in our midst who is insisting that America wake up and recognize the fact that he is a man like other men. He is entirely out of sympathy with the gross paternalism of the 'Master class' turned liberal."

When I finished reading T. J. Sellers' letter, I leaned against the living-room wall, breathing hard. I was indignant at being addressed in such manner by anyone, especially a man, and particularly a Negro. But I had asked him to be "brutally frank," and I had little patience with people who voice such a request and then renege when it is complied with. So I reread the letter slowly, forcing my reluctant mind to follow and weigh his points.

Only two facts emerged: First, that I was thoroughly misunderstood by Negroes; second, that they were thoroughly misunderstood by me. The disrupting impact of both together resulted in literal physical shock. Weak, cold, numb, I stumbled into bed.

For days I thought of nothing but that letter and what it revealed. My sense of loss was indescribable. I felt as a lover might if he were standing under the window of the girl he thought returned his devotion, and was pouring out a beautiful song of adoration, offering her his life, his all, when suddenly she shouted down in a harsh voice, "Stop that noise!" and banged the window shut.

No greater dislocation of my thought and emotion could

have resulted if I had been catapulted to another planet. Nothing I saw in Negroes was familiar. I had landed in a nightmare world, among people who neither liked nor understood me, and whom I could not understand.

After a week I brought myself to answer the letter. "I appreciate your courtesy in taking me at my word and answering my question with complete honesty," I began, then went on to admit that I was somewhat taken aback by the number and magnitude of my sins, and felt that the best thing I could do at that point was to retreat into the background. I would make no defenses, offer no explanations of my intentions, I said: "People who are chronically misunderstood must look for the explanation in themselves, and I'm indebted to you for the clues you have given me."

As I posted the letter I thought that for a long time to come I would have no appetite for the Negro's struggle for freedom. I had been mistaken. It wasn't my dish after all.

CHAPTER 10

I Nearly Die Aborning

I WASN'T TO GET OFF SO EASILY.

Return mail brought from T. J. Sellers a gracious, though indirect apology for his punches and a frank appeal not to pull out from this struggle for a more democratic South. He listed famous white women, including Mary Overington White—one of the founders of the National Association for the Advancement of Colored People—who, though battered, had persisted until their contributions to humanity were large.

I wrote thanking him for his encouragement and said I thought the only hope of cleaning up the mess was for each side to "fasten instantly on evidence of positive good will and understanding from the other, and make an effort to pass over the negative, of which there was inevitably a good deal . . .

"What made me feel hopeless," I went on, "was a marked tendency in Negroes to fasten on the negative and minimize the positive elements in any overtures of friendship from white persons . . . It must be realized that even a small such overture is significant and indicative of sincere human reaching, for we whites have nothing whatever to gain by such an act except human contact."

I wrote the letter with the sincerity of one human soul seeking to make itself understood by another. Sellers replied that he could not agree that a tendency to fasten on the negative was a "marked racial trait" with Negroes, nor agree that whites had nothing to gain from the practice of Christianity except human contact, since on a world-wide basis whites were in the minority.

The timbre of his response was so far from the intent of my letter that I felt as if I had been hit in my middle. But this time I was not stunned. I reached for my typewriter:

"Stop reading my letters with your positive eye half shut and myopic and your negative eye all-seeing in reverse. Shame on you as a newspaper man for not even reading my words aright, let alone my meaning.

"I did *not* say that fastening on the negative is a racial trait with Negroes . . . And I did *not* say that we have nothing to gain from 'the practice of Christianity except human contact.' I said we had nothing but that to gain by an overture of friendship. True, no one can fail to be just, fair or kind without hurting himself more than he hurts his neighbor. But an overture of friendship is more personal. When a white man makes one to a Negro, it can mean only that his heart is wide open, for what can he possibly gain from such an act except an exchange of human love—and even this he must pay for in many losses."

Healthily angry and not a bit apologetic for it, I posted this letter by return mail. His conciliatory reply failed to lure me from silence. Many years intervened before I realized that this was the first time I had ever reacted to a Negro as an equal, minus all the inhibitions and condescensions of my clan. My reaction was one of clean-cut annoyance with another person who underrated my thoughts and feelings.

It took me perhaps half a decade also to learn that one of the blind spots of most Negroes is their failure to realize that small overtures from whites have a large significance.

Few have patience with a white at the halfway mark of conversion. They want total acceptance or none. Acceptance with reservations seems to them more insulting than flat, honest rejection.

I now realize that this feeling inevitably takes possession of one in the bitter struggle for equality. Indeed, I share it. Yet I wonder how we can expect total acceptance to step full grown from the womb of prejudice, with no embryo or infancy or childhood stages. It is only with a sad heart that I can guess how many potential liberals must have been stampeded back into the prison of their conservatism by confrontation with experiences similar to mine.

I was close to stampeding myself. I wanted to return to my Southern womb, with its snug satisfaction and emotional security. I couldn't. I had learned too much. "He that increaseth wisdom, increaseth sorrow," right enough, but wisdom is a one-way street. Gone was my belief that "our Nigras are happy and satisfied, adore and respect us, and regard our many kindnesses with gratitude." I had seen behind the idyllic, painted backdrop. I couldn't believe it was a picture window any more.

I have known no experience more distressing than the discovery that Negroes didn't love me. Unutterable loneliness claimed me. I felt without roots; like a man without a country; perhaps like a child who has just discovered that he is adopted, or like a dog whose family has taken a vacation, leaving him with an empty house and yard and a next-door neighbor who impersonally dispenses correct measurements of food.

Had I always imagined their love, even in my childhood? Had I confused a painted backdrop with reality even then? My heart refused this possibility. They may have put on acts to gain favor with white adults, but surely a child can't easily be misled in the matter of who loves him. Maybe some of their heartaches spilled over in love for their small white charges. Maybe some of the wounds our elders gave them were transmuted, even healed, in love for us. Only real love could have been poignant enough to drive so deep in me and in others I knew. Why, I was forty-four years old and *still* tenderness on a dark face struck a more vibrant answering cord in me than it did on a white face; thought of friendship with a Negro lifted my heart more than thought of it with a white; trust from a Negro bound me more tightly than trust from a white; and, oh God, rejection from a Negro hurt more than from a white.

The fact that since I was twelve it hadn't been PROPER for me to associate with them didn't change the fact that within me they were a symbol of comfort, love, and security. True, they had moved into the background of my life, but that background was the pivot on which my whole life swung. True, I had accepted the fact that I must sit in front and Negroes in back on streetcars and buses, but a feeling of snugness and tender awareness went with seeing them there. Was that feeling really not mutual? Did they really not know how I felt? When I looked smilingly back at them, did they think it a prideful smile?

My sense of loss was corporate as well as personal. It was *our* love that Negroes had rejected, not just mine. I recalled a friend's remark following her trip North: "I got homesick for black faces. Nothing up there but white people. It made me feel like a foreigner." Would she have been homesick for black faces if she had known how their owners felt about her?

A professor's wife had said, "By me, the worst thing about inflation is that I've no money for a colored cook. It isn't the work I mind; it's not having a Negro around. I feel lonely. White people just don't take the place of Negroes—not with me." How would she have felt if she had known what I knew?

Knowing what these others did not know, I was in a certain sense excluded from a corporateness of which I had once been wholeheartedly a part. I held an ugly secret which made hollow our conception of the South. I could no longer vibrate in unison when someone struck once-cherished notes concerning the rich charm of our relationship with "our Negroes." Now only a great silence and emptiness in me answered the striking of that familiar chord. A world had been destroyed inside me.

There was no summer-joy for me in streets where once I had loved to walk. I looked into dark faces as they moved past and thought, "They don't like me. They think I'm mean, hard. They think I want only to use them for something."

Even my physical vision shifted with the change in my inner seeing. I saw in dark eyes expressions which once I had been blind to. Their slow passage over my face held often a harsh, defiant look, as though they dared me to affront them.

My interior contracted into something tight and rigid as my love seeped out through the wound of knowing I was not loved. A hardening stole through me, a shrinking away from Negroes. Resentment rose. Their suspicion was unjust, undeserved! I realized that their faith in the white man's hostility was being materialized in me. The beginning of racial enmity was taking hold.

Heaven help us, I thought. In the whole South the hidden love which Negroes don't believe in will turn to this ugly thing that they do believe in. We often do create things we believe in.

This must not happen! I would *not* have this barren, frozen tundra instead of the June fields I once knew. Oh God, was there no way back to a warm heart?

√ Then I thought, Whose fault is it that they mistrust and dislike us? Everybody wants to love. If they don't love us any more it must be our doing. And that means it's *my* doing, because I'm one of us.

I felt relief from the numbing chill of resentment. Penitence hurts but is a defrosting pain. I was creative again, giving birth, not freezing, drying up. My mind turned, able once more to seek answers.

One day as I drove along a highway I saw standing near a country store, evidently waiting for a bus, a plump, jolly-looking woman with a shining face the color of powdered coffee. Lacking only the red bandanna, her face was a near duplicate of the one familiar to all purchasers of pancake mixes. Liquid sunlight rolled cozily through me. I halted my car.

"Wanna ride t' town?" I asked with my most lilting "club" accent.

"I sure does, honey," came the joyful reply.

Settled on the seat, she was all friendliness, comfortable chuckles, and easy gratitude. "Honey, you's jes' the sweetes' thing to give me this good ride!"

A struggle went on inside me. I didn't want to spoil this homelike atmosphere by obtruding that awful outer-space element which bewildered and hurt me. But I had to know whether she was really what she seemed.

I chose my words carefully. "I'm glad Gregory Swanson has come to the University. Let's hope it's the beginning of the end of this segregation foolishness."

The liquid sunlight froze in a solid block around me. I glanced quickly at my companion. Her face was frighteningly changed. Gone was the shine of friendliness. Her cheeks and mouth were rigid, eyes hard. With the rusty edge of hatred, her voice ground out her words.

"It ain't right how they treats us. When I waits for the bus in the store, I can't sit nowhere, make no dif'ence how late the bus is an' how tired I gits. An' if I buys somethin' to eat I can't eat it in the store with the white folks, even if they's sweaty and dirty and I's clean. Rainin' or sleetin', make no dif'ence, I got to go outside to eat."

Here again was the picture I didn't want to see. Hour after hour, day after day, from the time they were children, this was the kind of love, justice, and equal chance for happiness that "our" Negroes got from us. And we never grasped the content of the pattern which we had been taught by rote, but had the incomparable stupidity to expect them to return our love.

"It's terrible," I said humbly, "but it's going to change now —soon."

"Oh, no-o-o, not soon, not soon, honey chil'. There's sufferin' ahead. I jes' hopes that brave boy at the Univus'ty don't git hurt. Once I seen the body of a man that got lynch'. I don't never wanna see 'nother!"

In a flash of horror I realized that lynching had a present reality for Negroes which it lacked for me. I spoke of it, had even feared for Swanson, but to me it was primarily just a word—a remote atrocity of mad mobs, as distant from my life as revolution. But for Negroes it was a hideous memory, and ever-present possibility even, that might happen senselessly to any one of them any time.

I tried to reassure her, but I was talking about things which were more living for her than for me. When I deposited her at her destination, I knew I had not succeeded.

CHAPTER 11

Hurt Until You Give

KEEPING OUT OF THE NEGROES' STRUGGLE FOR EQUALITY SHOWED good sense, I knew, but it brought me no quietness of spirit. When Swanson's suit began I had taken it for granted that I would battle for justice to "our Negroes." Having learned such people really didn't exist, surely I was released from my involvement. Yet somehow I wasn't. I had no doubts as to who was right, and I was therefore in the struggle on the wrong side by my very neutrality.

Bits of Mr. Sellers' letters haunted me. He had said that citizens like myself were needed. And he had closed one letter with the admonition, "Keep up the good fight." My father's dying words had been St. Paul's contented avowal, "I have fought the good fight; I have finished the course; I have kept the faith."

The good fight. Yes, it was! Even though the Negroes doing the fighting bore no resemblance to those I had loved all my life, they were right, and my beloved South was wrong. They were right, and that made it my fight, too.

A friend was fond of reversing a familiar slogan "Give until it hurts" to "Hurt until you give." I was hurting.

There was no comfort in the thought that the whole thing was none of my business. Not only were my heart strings tangled round it, but also I had been raised to feel that any issue which concerned the welfare of others *was* my business.

My father had often said, "If you see a public need which isn't being met or a public responsibility which too few are assuming, that probably means it's *your* job. A Christian is supposed to do something about needs and responsibilities."

At other times he would say, "Never leave an important job undone on the assumption that someone else will do it. Whenever we decide to 'let George do it,' the job usually goes undone. George isn't as hard-working or reliable as most people think. Besides, who is this George anyhow? *You* are. I want you always to remember that."

I remembered it.

I was plagued by the question of how much justification there was for Negroes mistrusting our good will. In my personal experience I had not, so far, found much basis for their belief that whites were determined to deny them rights. Once the whites were made to understand that their own assumptions were confused and false and that human rights really were involved, they seemed ready enough to grant these rights. This certainly had been true of me, and also of most of the University people I had talked with when I made my little private survey before Swanson came. I resolved to continue my investigation of how much ill will there actually was.

While Swanson's suit was in progress I had talked one day to a University administrative official, agreeing with him that Swanson was sure to win and that it would be a good thing for everybody when he did.

"But there's been a great deal of opposition among alumni," he said. "Letters of protest have poured into the Alumni Office."

"May I see them sometime?" I asked. "I'm much interested in this subject."

"Of course. Just tell the secretary I sent you."

I hadn't followed through at the time. Now I decided I would. But the secretary looked puzzled when I asked for the letters. "I wonder what he means. We didn't receive any alumni protest."

"None at all?"

"Well, two did come the day after the suit opened, but one was from a crackpot who's always protesting about something. None have come since then."

"Could they have gone to another office?"

"President Darden gets some complaints direct. You might try there."

Without result I talked to his secretary, and then to Mr. Colgate W. Darden, Jr., himself. "I can't recall a single out-and-out protest," he said. "I believe only three people have expressed regret to me, and they all did it parenthetically. I understand that many were received at the Alumni Office though. Have you been down there?"

A sensible guess as to how the rumor started seemed that, arriving so quickly after Swanson's suit was announced, these letters were much discussed and assumed to be only the first of a landslide to come. The rumor well fitted our deeply ingrained conviction that trouble starts whenever the racial issue is introduced, and so the story kept going even though the barrage of protest didn't materialize.

Swanson's own experience, too, indicated that this fear of "trouble" might not be well founded. For several weeks after his arrival persons who wished him well, including most of the University's professors and administrators, had sweated out the suspense. I had sweated right along with them. Even though I knew that the majority of students and faculty were pleased to have him, I couldn't escape my old indoctrinated fear that "trouble" would inevitably result from integration.

The Parker poll, I reasoned, did show that five per cent

of the students objected strongly, and this was enough for a mob. Moreover, they didn't know about the Parker poll, and their conviction that the majority would approve their action might give them an ugly kind of courage.

Would Swanson invite "incidents" by attempting to eat with the other students at the Commons? the University community wondered. Would he try to sit in the student, rather than the colored, section at the first football game? (Surely he would have sense enough not to!) If he did, someone would be certain to start trouble! Swanson did everything we hoped he wouldn't be foolish enough to attempt— and he suffered, by his own statement, no unpleasantness related to his race.

I began to write letters to friends in various parts of the South, asking how they felt about integration in our colleges and how they thought their friends felt. The now familiar pattern again emerged. With few exceptions, each was glad about it himself but thought few others would be. Most of them wrote with deep emotion, displaying raw consciences and depressed love similar to mine. The evidence was growing that I was a typical Southerner, that the situation was based on an evil illusion.

Autumn moved into Christmas. The old year gave place to the new. I was silent but I was hurting. The press continued its negative stand. Politicians lifted their chesty voices on the side of white supremacy. Race-baiting letters to the editor appeared in increasing numbers. Good-willed people were silent. An ugly vision was materializing into reality.

And Sellers had said, "Citizens like yourself are greatly needed." "Keep up the good fight," he had said.

I had excuses for silence. One was that I had two sons, aged eight and eleven. If I entered the fight, mightn't they get hurt? But Negroes had children, too, and their children were getting hurt—and Negroes were in the right.

Winter crept toward spring. "Greatly needed." "The good

fight." But they didn't want me! They didn't *like* me. They thought all whites were the way those editorials, letters to the editor, and political speeches made us sound. Yet why, *why* did they believe that? Wasn't it because people like me didn't speak?

Spring moved over the Virginia hills. In April 1951, my heart drew together, then burst suddenly outward, spilling over the pages in an article addressed to Negroes. Into it I poured the ache of the wound to my faith in an image and an ideal that I loved. All I had learned so far about the thinking of both races mingled with my hurt and poured out in a plea for understanding and for the revival of my dying vision.

Most whites lack experiences which would enable us to comprehend what Negroes' experiences are, I pointed out. When we approach Negroes in the spirit of brotherhood and they take offense where none is meant, new barriers of resentment rise in us to replace our old disintegrating wall of prejudice, and nothing is gained.

"Is it your aim to show us that the patience, humor, spontaneous warmth, and ability to bear and to forgive, which have earned our respect, won our love, and increased our shame down the years, were for you only the necessities of oppression? . . .

"Now that your oppression is ending, you can show us that your soft replies to insults were not conceived in fear but in courtesy deeper than ours . . . Forgive us a little more . . . Patiently and painfully help us to a better understanding of your needs and sufferings. Then you will see our hidden love come forth . . .

"The handwriting is on the wall. Soon you will be with us . . . Long, too long ago you should have been. But let the writing not be on the wall alone. Let it be in our hearts and minds as well. It can be so, if only the love which God gave equally to both our peoples marches with you through the gates which man shall soon open by law."

I mailed the manuscript to Mr. Sellers and awaited an angry note revealing my stupidities anew. But nothing ever happened as I expected any more. He wrote a kind letter thanking me for the "deep and moving sincerity with which the piece must have been written," and said it would appear in the next issue of *The Tribune.* Then he added that, had time permitted, he would have called on me personally to thank me for it. After dark months of failure, once again I had succeeded in communicating across the segregation line.

But in the midst of my triumphant joy, my early training spoke sternly to me again. "Be careful! He almost called on you! And it would have been *your fault.*"

A few months later I recalled my panic with a wry smile. After routing the code I was taught, I made many efforts to get Mr. Sellers to come to dinner, to tea, or simply to come and have a chat. I never succeeded.

"Why?" I demanded at last. "Why won't you come?"

He fixed me with a baleful, bitter eye. "Someone might drop in and you'd be embarrassed. I'm not prepared to be a source of embarrassment!"

Many upper-class Southern Negroes feel so. Few will cross the threshold of a Southern white, beg as he will. Years may roll into many decades before they can forget our public insults and rejections enough to enjoy ease among us. Such is the "black wave" which most segregationists think is rising for the sole purpose of social engulfment.

That was the last time I felt panic at thought of a Negro calling on me, though the code continued to twist my thoughts in other ways.

My success in communication through my article encouraged me to reach out to Negroes, old and young, men and women, for clues to understanding. But only occasionally did one respond and take a turn at removing one of my segregation grooves.

My largest single effort was choosing from the letters-

to-the-editor column in the *Richmond Times-Dispatch* names
of six hard-hitting opponents of segregation who appeared
to be Negroes. I wrote to each, explaining that I wished to
understand the Negro's point of view but had found that I
constantly gave offense. Would he please list some attitudes
and acts of whites which Negroes found particularly offensive, so I would know how to avoid them?

Only one of these letters received an answer. Later I
learned that the five colored recipients who did not reply
suspected me of seeking sport at their expense, whether
sexual or sadistic they weren't quite sure.

John Whetzel of Danville, Virginia, was the one who replied. He said it was clear that I was good-willed and sincere.

Thank heaven! I thought. At least it's clear to one Negro.

He further said that the fact that I asked such a question
at all suggested that I expected a Negro's reaction to be
somehow different from a white's. He advised me to study
my conduct and conversation to see if I didn't behave dif-
ferently toward Negroes, and didn't often imply the existence of a difference.

Truth bells tolled dismally in every vertebra of my spine.
Here obviously was at least one common denominator among
the many angry eyes and sudden silences I had encountered.
Dimly I could see that no matter how cordial, frank, and
open I had been in my overtures of friendship to Negroes I
had never quite, not quite, behaved as I would had they
been white. For one thing, I addressed myself to them rather
as a middle-aged person often speaks to a teenager, with a
condescending, faintly amused courtesy. For another, in my
search for enlightenment most of my questions certainly did
carry the implication of a difference beyond the mere difference of circumstances. This clearly was one of the points
the two colored ministers had tried to get across to me.

And yet my behavior didn't reflect the way I felt. It was

like a suit of armor strapped on me. Inside I was the little girl who had shared my best moments with Negroes and had often been healed in their love. Was there indeed nothing in my talk and manner which revealed this truth to them?

I wrote Mr. Whetzel by return mail, thanking him for his helpful letter and stating that he was the first Negro who seemed to have some understanding of my real feelings.

He replied that he was white.

He also said that he was bedridden and at most had four months to live. A victim of the rare disease popularly called "creeping paralysis," eighteen months before he had been a strong, vigorous man in seemingly perfect health. Now he could not even feed himself or turn on his side without help from his pretty young wife. But his throat was not affected as yet and he enjoyed dictating letters and talking with friends. Would I please come and see him? We could discuss what might be done to improve the Negro's lot.

Of course I wrote that I would—though I dreaded the ordeal. Here, I thought, was a doomed man who knew he was doomed; a once active, independent person, rendered helpless by the terrible, slowly tightening fists of death. A visit to his bedside couldn't be other than a gloomy, horrible experience.

But it wasn't. He greeted me as a charming host, then fell into an easy, interested discussion of the predicament of Southern Negroes. Far from being depressed, I was soothed and uplifted in an atmosphere which can only be described as one of charged peace.

At first I thought that this must be just a brave act. How could a man feel joyous and full of interest in mankind under such conditions? Before I left I knew that here lay a genuine demonstration of a great truth. John Whetzel's interest in others and determination to serve them to the end were the source, the cause of his state of mind. His vitality stemmed from his experience on his deathbed of the greatest adventure of life. He was defending what he believed in, fighting for truth. He was talking and living freedom. By contributing to the lives of many, he participated in a larger life. He did not, in fact, lie bound to his bed. By sympathy, by empathy, he led a vigorously active existence.

"I can't do a thing to help my body," he said cheerfully, "but at least I can improve my spirit—and I have."

"You do much more," I told him. "You improve the spirit of people who meet you. You show us how we ought to live. You're tangible proof of something we all want to believe, that the real man is free of his body."

His smile was happy. "God has made my illness the means of doing His will. I have a lot of visitors, and people who would never listen to me if I were whole and hardy respect my opinions now. They figure that if a dying man says that justice, understanding, and love between men is the most important thing in life, it really must be so."

But the source of his influence was deeper than that. It lay in his demonstration that in dedicating himself to the highest that he knows, a man can lift himself out of the conditions of his life and give to himself a higher dimension. He died before I could visit him again. But in me—and in how many others?—something in him that was eternal called forth an eternal *amen*. Something that was his still lives on in me—an unwavering certainty that the highest that one knows must be loved and served, and that in this voluntary service lies mastery over any circumstance that would make one a slave.

CHAPTER 12

Not a White Lady Slummimg

I APPEALED TO MR. SELLERS TO TEACH ME THE FACTS WHICH had been omitted from my education, to help me bridge my chasm of segregation and knock down my segregation walls. Whether I would take up the banner of brotherhood again I wasn't sure but I was impelled at least to seek to understand.

Characteristically, he replied, "All right—provided you approach the assignment as an objective student of sociology, not as a white lady slumming!"

Indignant that he thought the stipulation necessary (though it undoubtedly was), I agreed, and for many months visited his office weekly for instruction.

In my childhood I would have been warned against him as a "mean Nigra." Not only his attitude but also his appearance would have prompted this warning. He was more than half white, and his skin was a shade of tan lighter than the midsummer tint of many whites. His nose, hair, and the shape of his head were quite Negroid, but his eyes were a clear blue-gray.

Although of medium built, he somehow gave an impression of being burly, and he had a caged-lion quality about his movements that suggested a repressed strength which he assured me he did not have. His face habitually wore an angry, bitter look—at least when he was talking to me— and a small scar on his lip added to the effect of a dangerous man, not to be trifled with in any way whatever.

When young, he had been a public school teacher° and my appeal to his teaching skill awakened in him an insight that elementary, even first grade, techniques were what I needed. He let me move at my own slow speed, gave me easy homework assignments of fascinating books and articles, restated and re-illustrated all important points until I absorbed them, and freely administered praise and encouragement whenever I grasped at last a simple truth which I should have known at first.

Although he viewed my whole tribe with impatience, distaste, and suspicion, when challenged as a teacher he recognized that I meant well and wanted to learn, but simply understood almost nothing about Negroes, the behavior of the South, or the promises made by our Constitution. He patiently set about the tedious process of re-education, helping me to unlearn so that I could learn rightly, and extending to me the sort of kindness one offers an earnest but not bright child.

After the bruised bewilderment I had endured in exchanges with those (including himself) who assumed I knew everything they knew and was therefore being deliberately offensive, his paternalism was like balm. I fell easily into the relationship of a white child under the authority and supervision of a Negro adult. It was almost the only familiar thing in the new world I had entered. Standing on this bit of homeland, I was able to endure the breakdown of a system of beliefs upon which most of my everyday thinking had rested.

For his part, the experience of reversing the paternalistic role with a white adult was obviously a pleasure which com-

° He has now returned to teaching—in New York City.

pensated for some of the trouble and annoyance I caused him.

Under his instruction I learned facts I hadn't suspected existed. More important, I learned new attitudes by becoming conscious of the faulty content of old ones.

It may have been during my first lesson that I commented on his Yankee accent, and asked if he were from the North.

"Oh, no, I'm a Southerner," he said.

If he had thrown a cup of water in my face, I couldn't have been more surprised. A Southerner! Never had I heard a Negro thus designated. Southerners were white. Sellers was a Southern Negro, not a Southerner.

But of course he was a Southerner really, I hastily told myself, proud of my ability to adjust to shocks.

He seemed to read my thoughts. A natural actor, with unerring skill he injected a breath of courtliness into the tone of his urbane voice, and added:

"Yes, I'm a Virginia gentleman."

The cup this time held ice water, but I denied myself a gasp and would not look away from his face. The edges of my eyes noted his faultless, immaculate attire. Measuredly I replied:

"I'm glad, because Virginia gentlemen are getting rather rare."

His eyes laughed at me as with resolutely deliberate speed I took myself off.

By concentration, within a few weeks I was able to compel myself to stop saying "both Southerners and colored people" and to say instead "both white and colored Southerners," though for several years if I used the word "Southerners" alone, I always meant white Southerners, and even now I often slip into the habit. Balking at the phrase "colored Southerners" was obviously—even to me—improper in one who wished to end segregation. But many of my patterns were not so easily recognized as bad. Some—mainly those related to the many nuances of paternalism—I clung to as good.

Mr. Sellers politely expressed regret that *The Tribune* was in no position to pay for the article of mine he had published. I was shocked. Payment from a Negro! What a horrible thought! We were supposed to do what we could to help our Negroes. It would be like accepting fifty cents from your own child for pressing his Sunday suit!

"I wouldn't dream of taking money from you for my writing on this subject," I told him. "It's a debt I owe."

I was proud of my sense of indebtedness and expected recognition that it was generous. Instead I met a stony look and ominous silence. Not for half a decade did I fully grasp the fact that it is the new Negro's right—one he covets—to pay for services from whites. His escape from our paternalism has real meaning for him. He consciously struggles to bring this escape to fruition in himself and others. With knowing self-indulgence he sometimes even patronizes white, rather than colored, taxi drivers for the sheer triumphant joy of tipping a white man.

I was slow to understand. I couldn't bring myself for a long time to accept payment from any Negro who engaged my services as speaker. For even longer, I winced as I forced myself to take a proffered check. But the day finally came when Sellers' implanted wisdom flowered, and I saw something besides love and a sense of obligation in my reluctance to accept money from Negroes. It was clearly related to the old double code of behavior—a cousin of the practice of always tipping Negroes, never whites.

But the first fissure in my approval of paternalism came early in "The T. J. Sellers Course for Backward Southern Whites." I sat one day across from him at his desk. A local Negro had just been convicted of theft and, though there were no extenuating circumstances, he was given the minimum sentence. Sellers was furious.

"If he'd been white he'd have got double that time in jail," he said, his mouth turned down, hard lines below its corners.

Puzzled by his insistence that no distinction be made, even in a Negro's favor, and pained by his failure to recognize that light sentences were given in kindness, I said sadly:

"It's sort of an effort to even things up."

He turned angry eyes on me. "It's insulting. The inference is that Negroes can't be expected to be honest."

This simple, indignant summary of the implications of paternalism in our courts struck through my entrenched parenthood. Staggered by the impact of the thought, and getting my first full look at the Negro's point of view, I saw a world in which the entire fabric of the white Southerner's thinking about Negroes, even down to his cherished tenderness, is wrong. In that world the whole Utopian vision of the South, which for me had been a kind of faith, is set against the harsh facts of the Negro's life, and bitterly resented; and all that I had rejoiced in as noble in our relationship with Negroes is seen by them as mere ego-satisfaction for ourselves.

My sensation resembled those of a bewildered mother of an adolescent, who finds that her little attentions and instructions, which formerly had seemed appreciated, are now resentfully rejected by her child turned teenager. Only months before, he had appeared to know that these were expressions of love. The mother still thinks of them so, but to the youth they seem cruel efforts to keep him a child against his will. I had been raised to think of Southern paternalism as one of the noblest outreachings of the human spirit. I now saw it reacted to as if its intent were to humiliate rather than protect.

T. J. was skilled in storytelling, and presented most of his points in dramatizations. By means of this method, I lived through—not merely listened to—his review of the many frustrations, humiliations, heartaches, and challenges which result from being a superior member of an underprivileged, segregated minority.

I became aware of the difference, which reaches into every corner of one's life, between being a member of the exclusive group and a member of the excluded group in a segregated society. Previously, like most of my kind, I hadn't seen why segregation should be more unpleasant for a Negro than for a white. Why should they feel stung by "White Only" signs if we had no such reaction to "Colored Only" signs?

But now I identified myself with a colored parent confronted with the task of explaining to her child why he could not go to the nearest and newest school, could not eat in the restaurant, drug or variety store, could not enter the larger and better of the two waiting rooms provided in all railway and bus stations, could not sit in the preferable, ground-floor section in a movie theater, or—if there was no colored balcony—could not see the exciting film showing there at all. I found that there is no way to explain these granite facts again, again, and again to a joy- and freedom-seeking child without making him aware that he is judged inferior, and instilling the dark fear that perhaps he really is.

I identified with a young wife faced with the fact that her husband would be crippled for life when that car struck him down because the colored ward at the hospital was too full to admit him, and he had to be treated inadequately at home —knowing that there were vacant beds in the white ward.

I learned that some Southern hospitals do not have a colored ward, that Negro emergency cases have sometimes passed beyond help on a long ambulance drive to a distant hospital because the local hospital had no Negro facilities. I was sure (and still am) that few of the individual admissions clerks, doctors, or nurses involved personally would have chosen to let a man die or be permanently handicapped for the sake of segregation had any one of them had the authority to admit a colored emergency case. I was witnessing an example of the terrible mechanical rigidity which takes possession of our modern institutions, so that the human heart and human will no longer have their say. The segregation robot, once set in motion, controls the segregator as well as the segregated with an iron, mechanical hand which will not be stayed for mere broken bodies, broken hearts, or sympathy.

I identified with a young student struggling his way through college on pathetically insufficient funds furnished him through his parents' heroic sacrifices—sacrifices which would have been unnecessary were he permitted to attend the for-white-only college in his own hometown. Finally graduated, and eager to repay his parents both in money and satisfaction, he made the bitter discovery that white employers do not distinguish between a colored student graduated with honors and a colored illiterate. He was still eligible for only the lowest-paid bracket of manual work.

I became a young mother nursing her child while she scanned insurance statistics to learn that, because he was a Southern Negro, his life expectancy was many years less than if he had been white.

In my very viscera I became sick at these injustices—of which I had known nothing at all before.

Sellers worked not only upon my ignorance and my ingrained attitudes, but also on my unconscious habits. My pronunciation of the word Negro was called to my attention at every lesson, sometimes by his chucklingly repeating it after me the way I said it, sometimes by stories of how Negroes were affected on hearing it said that way.

At first I tossed off his protests as trivial. "You're just trying to undermine my Southern accent," I complained. "Why should I learn to talk like a Yankee? It would be pure affectation, even if I liked it. Anyhow, I think the pronunciation 'Nigra' sounds better. 'Knee-grow' sounds perfectly idiotic."

He persisted until he partially succeeded. "Nigra" began to grate on my ear. It's no easy matter, however, to change the phonetic habit of a lifetime, and after my ear was trained, I still had to train my tongue. It was more than two years before I could say the word Yankee-style without feeling awkward. And nine years later I discovered that *still* I had the word only half right.

Talking to another white liberal, I took the liberty of pointing out to her that she did not throw the accent on the "grow." She hotly replied that I made nothing of the "Knee." Horrified I realized that I had indeed been saying "Nig*row*," and that this doubtless tortured sensitive ears as much as my fellow liberal's version, "*Knee*gra."

Although results of my efforts so far have been discouraging, I hope some day to convince a few people that the white Southerner's pronunciation of this word is not an index to his attitude toward Negroes. We are not accused of contempt toward our distinguished families of Randolph and Armistead when we pronounce them "*Rand*-uff" and "*Ahm*-sted." It isn't assumed that we are trying to be insulting when we pronounce Carolina and Virginia, "*C*'-ah-li-nuh" and "Vuh-gin-yuh." Yet when we say "Nigra" most people who don't say it think we're striving to approach the word "nigger" without actually saying it.

True, if we make a project of it, we can finally come up with Negro as the only two-syllable word in the entire language which we pronounce correctly. There, like a flag of brotherhood, it waves lonesomely above a forest of Southern slur, attesting bravely to the lengths which a Southern white will go to gain admittance to the human race.

CHAPTER 13

Convex and Concave

T. J. SELLERS' RE-EDUCATION OF ME INCLUDED A BREAKDOWN of my habit of dropping the myriad of individual Negroes into a single mold, regarding them as a solid, undifferentiated racial lump. I recall assuming that a man I often saw cleaning T. J.'s office may have been one of the guests at a dinner to which T. J. was invited. Sellers' eyebrows and tone went up in unison, as he softly inquired, "You mean *my janitor?*"

Startled, I saw that my subconscious made no distinction between a Negro editor and his domestic help. Both being colored, to me they were of one social group. This may be one of the several instances in which our stereotype, while condemnable as false to facts, represents a moral ideal which is in advance of the reality.

Another day I asked, "Who will Negroes vote for in the city elections?"

I saw in his eyes the familiar burning which I evoked in so many Negroes' eyes. "The capitalists—of which there are a few—will vote for the same man white capitalists vote for. Each individual will vote for the candidate he considers the best man and whom he thinks may further his particular aims—just as white voters will. Of course if civil rights were an issue in this election, you would see some lining up by race. But there are even some Negro segregationists. Negroes aren't a bag of potatoes, as the white man likes to think!"

Now at last I got the second point that the two ministers had striven in vain to convey. But having got it, I made a comment of my own.

"You're guilty of potato-thinking, too. What do you mean, 'the white man likes to think'?"

I sometimes found other whites in Sellers' office when I went for my lesson. Also, I often brought one along. My intention was to expose them to learning, but I soon found that I learned more quickly and agreeably from observing their blunders and consequent rebukes than from my own. Sellers had a mobile face, and when he politely restrained his tongue—which was seldom—his face became doubly expressive. I found it easy to read his reactions. From observing the unconscious misbehavior of these others, I got an answer to a question which had long bothered me: Why was it that I got along less well with Negroes since beginning to understand their problems than I had before?

I had noticed deterioration in my relationship even with domestics whom I had long known. Were my conservative friends right, and had Negroes little regard for whites who violated segregation conventions? Watching Sellers' other visitors, I discovered that white Southerners are at their very worst when they make their first, fumbling attempts at brotherhood. This is why:

Well-bred whites offer Negroes a quite acceptable relationship within narrow dimensions. They are polite, kind, friendly in all their points of contact. These being limited and rigidly fixed, little room exists for friction and error.

Once one of us begins to respond to the call of brotherhood, however, his inept attempts to move out of the white race into the human race make suddenly conspicuous his many bad habits and misconceptions. He launches splashingly into half-measures which only accent his unwillingness to extend full acceptance. He stops calling new acquaintances by their first names, for instance, but still finding it impossible to call them Mister, Mrs., or Miss, he leans heavily on pronouns.

As I waited for T. J. in his office one day, a young white liberal breezed in and inquired of the secretary:

"Where is *he?*"

She looked up from a letter she was typing and asked sweetly, "Who?"

He swallowed, smiled, then stated playfully, "Now you know who I usually want to see at his own office!"

"You mean Mr. Sellers?"

"Of course. Where is he?"

When Sellers arrived, I listened fascinated while this young white man bounced from pronoun to pronoun in a four-way conversation with Sellers, his secretary, and me, often saying "Mrs. Boyle," but not once able to get out anything better than "he," "she," or "you" with reference to Mr. Sellers and Miss Paige.

I knew how he felt. This block is a queer thing, and really isn't so much related to superiority feelings as to stage fright in that it hangs on self-consciousness. Those whose hearts are involved in tender though conventional relationships with Negroes usually find it more difficult to address them with prefixes than those who are indifferent to them. It is as if you were suddenly required to address your mother, father, sisters, and brothers as Mrs., Mr., and Miss.

Although my block was not quite so bad as this young man's, and I was able always to force the words out somehow, I remained self-conscious in using them for more than two years. Even now under certain conditions the old code briefly stirs, giving me a sense of guilt and making me feel foolish when I use them.

For those struggling with this block I recommend that they clip from newspapers and magazines pictures of

Negroes, then pick up one after another and repeat, "*Mr.* Brown," "*Mrs.* Gaston," "*Miss* McLeash," until at last the inner partition breaks down.

Once a woman about my age fixed Sellers with eyes bright in anticipation of approval, and said: "*I* think segregation in theaters and on buses is undemocratic. I wouldn't mind if they stopped it right now. I mean, I *really* wouldn't. I'm as ready to sit by a polite, clean Negro as by some of these unwashed, loud-talking whites I see around."

"I suspect quite a few feel as you do," Sellers said acidly.

She missed his irony, and departed obviously feeling that she had impressed him with her open-mindedness. When she had gone he said:

"An intentional insult has a more decent feel about it."

Among incipient crusaders for brotherhood one often finds a trying type to which I once belonged, one who seeks Negroes out for conversation but will discuss only the race problem. Every platitude of brotherhood is shiny new to him and it never crosses his burning, eager mind that his colored victim is as weary of them all as a man is of puns on his own name. A member of any oppressed minority appreciates being able to forget his problem entirely in conversation with members of the other group. But to permit this is virtually impossible for the newly awakened crusader.

Worst of all, however, is the righteous-indignation type of embryo crusader, who in hot pursuit of the sufferings and indignities heaped upon Negroes, unhesitatingly pries into their private affairs, asking personal questions—"How much money are you able to earn?" "How much rent do you have to pay?" "How much can you afford to spend on your children for Christmas?"—questions he wouldn't dream of asking a white person. In all objective innocence, one of these inquired of Sellers:

"Are you able to estimate how much white blood you have?"

Sellers looked out of the window silently for a moment, then he turned squarely to him and looking the inquisitor full in the face with his honest blue-gray eyes, he said gently:

"Not a damn drop."

Second only to the righteous-indignation type, and quite like him, really, except that he is less aggressive and more tearful in emotional tone, is the bleeding-heart type. He lifts the Negro from the status of "second-class citizen" only to thrust him aloft as a pitiable wrong to be righted. Even one moment of genuine fellowship with a newly budding crusader of this kind is quite impossible for his "black brother." He tags all colored people as tragic figures struggling in a quick-sand of injustice without any power of self-help, utterly dependent on crumbs of kindness from whites. Had it not been for Sellers' heated instructions, I might have slipped into this pattern.

A frequent visitor at *The Tribune* office was a young law student of this type. Having progressed from thinking of all Negroes as irresponsible delinquents, he now gathered them together in another mass as martyred saints. Criminal convictions of Negroes were almost always frame-ups in his mind. If not that, then at least some white man was the first cause. To Sellers this was paternalism at its smothering worst.

"He segregates as much as a Mississippi politician," he pointed out, "only he separates Negroes as white sheep, from whites as black wolves. Please do one thing for me: Always remember that 'Nothing so much resembles convex as concave.' If you feel obliged to whitewash Negroes it's because you secretly think of them as not being good enough as they really are. Besides, I'm not flattered by a representation of my race as not having red blood enough for its members even to commit an occasional crime on their own initiative."

I must have looked astonished, for he asked:

"Put it this way: The Negro needs, has earned, and **is**

entitled to *equality*. This consists in his being thought of and treated exactly as any other American. Anything beyond that *smells*"—he bore down on the word—"of charity!"

I've heard no other statement which I think summarizes so well what I believe the Negro American really wants. It seems little enough to ask, yet in the South it has been asked for again and again, restated, enlarged upon, explained, reinterpreted, plugged, and reiterated, and still is seldom either understood or believed.

Once I said to Sellers, "I don't understand why Negroes regard it as insulting when whites assume that they are different from us in their outlook. Chinese don't seem to feel that way. They appear quite ready and willing to call themselves different from us."

At this stage in my education almost everything I said made him angry, so I expected to see his eyes burn. Instead they froze.

"The comparison is odious," he said flatly.

I leaned forward, thinking I had him. "Now why is it odious? Do you feel superior to Chinese?"

"No. But when they feel as you describe, they are not yet Americans because they are still identifying themselves with an alien cultural and religious background. But the Negro's memory is wiped clean of all that. Christianity is the only religion he has known, American democracy the only culture he has known. All his hopes are in the blueprint of this nation's charter. This is his country. He wants only the right to share it equally with his countrymen."

Light broke in my darkness. Americans. Of course! I had never before thought of Negroes as Americans. To me they had seemed pilgrims, their native, natural abode, Africa.

Yet they have died for this country in four wars. The first American killed in the Revolution was Crispus Attucks, a free Negro. They were born here, raised here. They live by the same ideals, speak the same language, study the same books, receive the same programs over the air, read the same daily papers. They have no other land than this.

With every tick of your watch some segregationist says, "Send them back to Africa. They'll be happier anyhow with their own kind!" And as he says it, some kindly new-born liberal wonders if indeed they might not like to return to their own land.

Their kind? Their land? Who but us? Where but here? If your great-great-grandparents were Russians, is the Soviet Union your home? Large as are the economic and civic wrongs of the South against her colored citizens, the tallest of our wrongs is our failure to see them as native sons.

CHAPTER 14

Once to Every Man and Nation

EARLY IN MAY 1951, TEN MONTHS AFTER GREGORY SWANSON opened suit for admission to the University, I knew that I must decide, definitely and finally, whether or not I would fight in the Negro's battle for equality. I weighed the factors with care.

My approach was not what it had been in 1950. Then— moved automatically as a mother champions her child—I had taken it largely for granted that I would "defend our Negroes." Also, since *noblesse oblige* was a built-in part of my snobbery, I felt that I must defend less privileged persons or be unworthy of my heritage. Opposing these emotional drives was merely the Southern code of the status quo.

Much feeling but little thought had gone into my decision to stand with Swanson. When my new vision of justice came, I had plunged into the situation without pausing either to study it or to compute possible costs. I had been taught not to count the cost of doing right. That was one of the things "my people just didn't do!" To do right being the most important thing in my life, you naturally did it without calculations. Resultant losses you met one by one, as you would any other disaster.

This is clearly the most sensible and easiest way to deal

with a moral issue. It reduces decisions to one: Is the contemplated action right, or isn't it? Even so, making this one decision is not always simple. My thinking concerning the segregation issue in 1951 was more elaborate, because more informed, than in 1950.

Having learned that Negro leaders resent our possessive protectiveness nearly as much as our snow-blind injustices, I strongly suspected that some preferred to fight for their freedom without the white man's help. Wouldn't it be more wrong than right to help them do a job which they wanted to do alone?

The answer to that, I decided, depended on my interpretation of what the job was. If I wasn't now fighting to help "our Negroes" (having learned they weren't ours) but to defend a Christian ideal and a democratic principle, then it was irrelevant whether Negroes wanted me in the battle or not. The rightness of their fight made it the personal fight of all who believe in rightness.

Also, because as a white Southerner I was partially responsible for the inequities which Negroes suffer, it was my responsibility, and therefore my right, to atone. My responsibility was increased by the fact that other whites were not assuming it, and thus by default had elected me "George."

I cautiously discarded the word "inequity." While of course I was concerned with justice, something more was involved—something as warm and personal as justice is cool and impersonal, something even deeper and more basic than justice, for it is the foundation upon which justice itself rests. The corporateness of man—that was it!—the structural oneness of us all. Within this corporateness, there exists, I saw, a complementary relationship of each to all others, because of our likenesses and because of our differences. As St. Paul put it, we have "many gifts, but one spirit . . . we are members one of another."

For me the issue seen in this light began to breathe and

pulse with renewed life. It concerned not only equal opportunity, but also *shared* opportunity. The choice was not alone between fairness and unfairness to an oppressed people, but also between wholeness and division in the family of man. It was between integration and disintegration in our very hearts, between love and hate—between the highest and the lowest values I knew. This being the case, it was a challenge I must not evade, a goal worth any sacrifice.

But what about my husband and two little boys? It was one thing not to count the cost for myself, quite another to give no consideration to them. I dismissed my fears for my husband. He was old enough to have his own views and I knew on this issue they paralleled mine. Though he might not approve of my crusading, I thought his sense of values close enough to mine for his discomfort not to be too great.

But maternal fear and heartaches clutched me on all sides. I struggled to put them aside. What did I desire for my sons above all else? Wasn't it that always, no matter how costly it proved, they would choose the highest they knew? If so, then by choosing a difficult right against an easy wrong, I would be making them a valuable gift.

I wish I could say at this point that one of the things which rendered my decision difficult was that I modestly doubted my ability to make a real contribution to the cause. But my upbringing had not made this doubt likely. As a member of the best family (well, perhaps just one of the two or three best) in Virginia (the best state in the best part of the best nation in the world) it would have been gross hypocrisy for me to tell myself that I might make a large sacrifice and only a small impression. I expected to suffer but I expected to achieve. I thought I would be yelled at, but I was certain that I also would be heard.

In reviewing my qualifications to be an effective crusader, I characteristically put my membership in the First Families of Virginia at the top of my list. I believed this to be a revolver with at least five shots. I thought it meant that I had the basic character necessary to carry on a thankless struggle for a principle I believed in; that I was a one hundred per cent insider with the needed understanding of the thoughts and feelings of other Southerners; that I was endowed with total confidence in my social status and therefore felt socially secure enough to endure temporary ostracism; that I could claim the right to speak to, and to some extent *for*, other Southerners without being discounted as a meddling outsider; and that I automatically had unquestioned prestige.

Second on my list of qualifications, I put my low quota of fear. Timidity being unpopular in my family, I was raised to feel that even looming danger isn't the least bit imminent, and I characteristically trip with gay stupidity to the dentist's chair—to meet each onslaught of his buzzer with incredulity. Therefore, I concluded, threats and attacks probably would challenge rather than terrify me. I felt disgustingly secure.

Third qualification: I had considerable energy and persistence. I knew that in the beginning at least, this was going to be a discouraging contest. I had never been easy to discourage. I didn't think I would be now.

Fourth was the fact that I was an experienced, even mildly successful, popular-type writer. I knew I had no literary gift, but I had acquired what might, in this case, prove more valuable—a knack for popular presentation. For many years I had been able to place in national magazines about three out of four of all the many manuscripts I wrote. This put me among the fortunate few in the nonfamous writer field. I should be able not only to say clearly what I thought and felt on this issue but also to say it loudly.

Fifth on my list (though had I been confronted with its placement, I would have insisted that it was first) was my faith. I believed that if you did what was right to the best of your ability you would receive all help necessary from Above. I felt adequate to meet any and all contingencies myself, but if something did come up which I was unable to handle despite my heritage, I thought that God would supply whatever I needed until I could take over again.

Just what did I see as my possible role in the coming drama? I saw myself as mediator, peacemaker ("Blessed are—"), restorer of the Southern Utopia of heart- and soul-satisfying interracial relationships, but on a higher plane than before—a plane where equality would rule over all, and each group would accept the other with the self-giving hearts of children. I had taken as my motto, and was striving to live by, St. Francis of Assisi's well-known prayer:

> "O Lord, make me an instrument of thy peace.
> Where there is hatred, let me sow love;
> Where there is injury, pardon;
> Where there is discord, union;
> Where there is doubt, faith . . .

> "O Divine Master,
> Grant that I shall not so much seek
> To be consoled as to console,
> To be understood as to understand,
> To be loved as to love.

> "For it is in giving that we receive . . ."

In giving we receive. I believed this in a literal, as well as in a poetic, way. Not only did I think you could not pour out unselfishly without receiving an equivalent inner blessing, but also—what with man being golden—I couldn't conceive of doing so without receiving some kind of response. I thought that as I lived out the St. Francis prayer in the South, hatred and evil would speedily dissolve in my solution of understanding, faith, and love.

"What about Jesus' own experience?" someone inquired of

me once when I expressed these confident thoughts of the future.

Agilely I replied, "His crucifixion was for six hours, His resurrection was forever." The resurrection and triumph of Southern loving kindness seemed to me assured and not far off.

But although I was naïve as an infant bunny in my theology and in my hopes, I made an astute analysis of what a white integrationist might expect to go through before Utopia was realized. Until the majority of my peers were ready to junk their acceptance of the status quo, despite the fact that they felt much as I did concerning Negroes, they would on that account make me suffer for my activities not less but *more*. I based this conclusion on my experiences while directing a project for the rehabilitation of homebound invalids.

It had been one of those rare undertakings which are above controversy and criticism. It involved aiding helpless people who were public charges to reclaim their independence. Despite its nature, however, I had found that although the majority of people cheerfully lent any assistance I asked for, the few who refused did so with unmistakable hostility. It seemed that this could be only because their refusal hurt their consciences and put them on the defensive. They resented this and blamed me for it, sometimes choosing to defend themselves by sniping at me. Once I was even accused of working with invalids because of a sadistic desire to witness their suffering.

With the raw consciences, fears, and other inner conflicts of white Southerners to deal with, it seemed likely that this type of hostility would tower over me like a cliff. Moreover, confronting them with the injustices in our system would begin an uprooting of their hearts. Furious retaliation might result. I myself still ached where some of my dream roots had been agonizingly torn out. I would be hated as pain is hated.

As for my position with Negroes, where I failed in my

efforts to help, I could expect to be frozenly ignored. Where I succeeded, they probably would enthusiastically congratulate *each other*. I recall saying to T. J. Sellers:

"A white person supporting you in this fight will end up with no friends on either side."

He smiled without comment. In this respect he saw the same picture I did.

But in another respect he saw a quite different one. Lacking my faith in people, especially white people, he didn't see me as marching far before I crashed into adamant resistance—and this, he thought, would be the end of my whole "experiment in brotherhood."

His cynicism infuriated me. I felt he was low-rating not only me but also the whole South. Since everybody was basically on the side of love and justice, determination and persistence in defense of them would insure final victory. Although I could expect overwhelming opposition at first, one by one people would realize that I was only standing by what they, too, believed in, and would lend me their support.

I made my decision on a Friday night early in May 1951, and all day Saturday I was sick within. The Southern code muttered in my ear through the day into the night. I no longer believed in it but I could still hear its voice—and I knew others believed. I was haunted by the feeling that I was being catapulted into outer space, far from all that I had known.

Next day when I went to church, conscious fear so surrounded me with chill, stiff hands that my fingers were clumsy as I sought in my hymnal the number posted for the processional. It was 536. I sang it through mechanically until I reached the last stanza. Then I felt suddenly eased:

"Earth shall be fair, and all her people one:
Nor till that hour shall God's whole will be done.
Now, even now, once more from earth to sky
Peals forth in joy man's old, undaunted cry,
'Earth shall be fair, and all her folk be one!' "

It seemed a benediction on the course I had chosen. More relaxed, I moved through the rest of the service. Number 519 had been selected for the hymn before the sermon. I read it in astonishment. Written by James Russell Lowell in 1845, it sounded as though it had been conceived and phrased for me personally at this moment in my life.

"Once to every man and nation
Comes the moment to decide,
In the strife of truth with falsehood,
For the good or evil side;
Some great cause, God's new Messiah,
Offering each the bloom or blight,
And the choice goes by for ever
'Twixt that darkness and that light.

"Then to side with truth is noble,
When we share her wretched crust,
Ere her cause bring fame and profit
And 'tis prosperous to be just;
Then it is the brave man chooses,
While the coward stands aside
Till the multitude make virtue
Of the faith they had denied.

"By the light of burning martyrs
Jesus' bleeding feet I track,
Toiling up new Calvaries ever
With the cross that turns not back;
New occasions teach new duties,
Time makes ancient good uncouth;
They must upward still and onward
Who would keep abreast of truth.

"Though the cause of evil prosper,
Yet 'tis truth alone is strong;
Though her portion be the scaffold,
And upon the throne be wrong,

Yet that scaffold sways the future,
And, behind the dim unknown,
Standeth God within the shadow
Keeping watch above his own."

The minister, Dr. Theodore Evans,* knew nothing of my problems or intentions, yet as he began and developed his sermon it was as if he were counseling me alone. He said that whenever you chose what seems to you the highest course, you have made the right decision, so you shouldn't fear that later developments might prove it unwise. God is not so much interested in accomplishments as in people, and if you decide on the basis of love for your fellow man and of a desire to do what is right, you may be sure that you chose according to His will, regardless of outward results.

When the service was over I left the church with all my doubts wiped away. They never returned. No defeat has been so complete, no despair so deep that I ever regretted having chosen as I did. Always I have had with me the thread of comfort that I chose rightly at the crossroads of 1951.

* Mentioned in my dedication.

CHAPTER 15

The Semantic Barrier

Now THAT I WAS READY TO ACT, SOMETHING THAT I AT FIRST had only vaguely sensed pushed steadily to the front of my consciousness. This can best be described as the semantic barrier. It was an obstacle to understanding which grew rather than diminished as I talked with a widening circle of educated Negroes. Though not directly related to their suspicions of my motives and intentions, the barrier greatly added to those suspicions because it was built into my very efforts to communicate my sincerity. An improperly constructed airplane when it strikes the sound barrier is wracked apart. The high speed at which I attempted to integrate myself made my impact with the semantic barrier inevitable, and my poor preparation made it severe.

White and colored Southerners both use English terms, but often the meanings we give them are as separated as our lives. The semantic barrier consists of words, phrases, even whole areas of thought, which have for the two groups widely divergent inferences and emotional connotations. Often as a Negro friend and I talked together it was as though we spoke different languages. Worse! For when persons address each other in different tongues, they are at least aware that they do not understand what is being said. But I sometimes said one thing, while he or she heard another, and each of us sustained an illusion that communication was taking place.

I struck this barrier repeatedly in my ill-fated article, "We Want a Negro at the UVA." The title itself was an example. To me it expressed that we at the University not only were willing but also wanted to let down the bars. To Swanson and Sellers it implied that we wanted only this particular Negro, this chosen one, this exception. They were well aware that special concessions of various sorts have always been granted to "Mr. Charlie's favorite Nigra," whom it pleased Mr. Charlie to single out. Soon after The War there was even an influential man who insisted that his former slave traveling companion be seated beside him at dinners. His eccentricity was smilingly humored by his hosts wherever he lodged. Therefore to my colored critics my title failed to suggest a change of heart.

"If you didn't intend this singling out, why didn't you use the plural—'We Want Negroes at the UVA'?" Swanson asked in 1953 when I met him at an NAACP meeting.

I still think it was mostly chance that I didn't. But I also think that what little motive I had was right and sensible. It is the first break-through, like the first olive out of the bottle, which paves the way for easier success in future. The big news was that a Negro, any Negro, was wanted at the University. If a thousand had been wanted, the 999 would have been secondary.

Reading the article over after several months of "The T. J. Sellers' Course for Backward Southern Whites," I was able to identify some of the many elements which I have already mentioned as contributing to its backfiring with Swanson. But what struck me hardest about the article was that throughout it showed no flicker of awareness that Negroes see a *different picture* of the South than her white patriots do, or that they speak of their situation in other terms than those we employ.

My description and interpretations of Swanson's character and behavior presented him, I now saw, in a light which would have directed toward him ire and contempt from many Negro leaders. For instance, eagerly straining to paint him appealingly, and consciously combatting a widespread belief that educated Negroes are rude, overbearing, and belligerent, I said:

"The most disarming aspect of Swanson's character is that with all his assurance and courage he has not a trace of defiance."

Now to members of a minority who have not yet been able to extricate themselves from oppression, "defiance" is not synonymous with boorishness as it is in a long-secure, top-dog society such as mine. Rather, it is identified with strength and courage. I have learned that in describing a Negro to members of his own group, if one intends praise it is well to avoid such a phrase as "quiet and easy-going." Translated into the language of oppressed minorities, it sometimes means "timid, lethargic, and spiritless." In the present-day Negro's struggle there is no place for the philosophical, make-the-best-of-it type of person regarded as so attractive in settled, smooth-running societies.

Another word which has opposite meanings in the languages of minority and majority groups is "privilege." I was raised to feel that a privilege is something special, over and above one's rights which, by contrast, are properly stood up for and insisted upon; that a privilege is something which no socially sensitive person, white or colored, ever asks for, let alone demands. Speaking from this background, I said of Swanson in the article:

"He has a sure sense of where rights cease and privileges begin. He seeks no privileges until they are offered unmistakably and freely to him."

In this statement I was not projecting a stereotype of how a Negro should behave but, rather, my opinion of how any gentleman would behave. Attributing this nice distinction to him was intended as a high compliment, which it seemed to me he merited, judging by his "shyness" in contacting me upon his arrival. My huge blunder stemmed from my ignorance of the fact that in an underdog society if any distinction is made between the words, it is often that privileges are those rights which are controlled by the individual rather than by law. Therefore, since denying or granting them to his fellow man is entirely in his own hands, the individual who denies them should be doubly reprimanded, and the courageous, public-spirited course is to do him this service.

The word "group" has different applications which resulted in many confusions for me before I learned them. To me, "my group" meant my social class or, specifically, the friends and acquaintances which I expected to see at most parties and faculty receptions I attended. But Negroes invariably thought I meant the whole white race. As I glibly spoke of "my group's" willingness to end segregation, I was not thought of among colored acquaintances as the most truthful person they knew.

Sellers somehow failed to inform me, and it was Sam Gandy, then director of Religious Education at Virginia State College (for Negroes), who let me know that the word "race" has crept over the border into the near-offensive classification, and has to be replaced among well-informed persons by "group." The concept of race widens the gap between peoples, Sam said, and I mustn't say "interracial relations" any more, but "intergroup relations," and so on. My first reaction was consternation. I now had no brief means of reference to social classifications! For I had already discovered that the word "class" as a social definitive had fallen into disrepute almost everywhere in America except among aristocratic Southerners.

Dr. E. B. Henderson, then vice president, later president of the Virginia State Conference of the NAACP, was first to inform me that the phrase "you people," when employed by a white addressing Negroes, without exception rouses colored audiences to wrath. As I constantly heard it used by whites addressing whites, I was both amazed and without an explanation. I finally concluded that Negroes must be unaware of its free use among whites and therefore take it as the mark of an inveterate segregationist setting his stage with "you people over there" and "us over here." Gradually I learned to avoid as a deadly virus any word or combination of words which could be so construed.

Slang phrases, I found, often lack identical implications for our two groups. "Keep your neck in," was one I tripped over with Swanson. At the University, the green student was often instructed to keep his neck in, by which was meant that he must be generally unobtrusive and especially have a care not to violate such cherished customs as referring to the lawn and grounds, never to the campus, and calling himself a first year man, never a freshman. But to Swanson my motherly advice to "keep your neck in" appeared to mean, "Be a good Nigra and stay in your place."

In reading a letter to me from a dedicated liberal, Sellers stopped short when he came to the word "negro." "No need to go on," he said flatly. "Anyone who doesn't even regard the Negro highly enough to capitalize the word is merely being hypocritical when he speaks of brotherhood."

But this error is often rooted not in one's thinking but in the age of the dictionary he happens to own. A generation or so ago Webster and others listed Negro with a small n, and if a Southern white has been fortunate enough to inherit a dictionary, it seldom occurs to him to purchase another.

Use of the word "slavery" by whites, as Sellers early let me know, is generally construed by Negroes as an effort to assert the white's innate authority as master. Yet in myself, and I was sure in many others, this reminder that Negroes were once our slaves elicited only a general consciousness that they have a claim on us.

There are many words and phrases, in fact, which filled me with tenderness and desire to serve but which I learned should never be spoken to Negroes. Among taboo items are some fictional characters, of which Uncle Remus is the most familiar; some old favorites in songs, such as "Ol' Black Joe"; and even some real people—your "old Mammy," for instance. To freedom-seeking Negroes they all spell STEREOTYPE and stereotypes are seldom classified by Negroes in terms of the kind of emotion they arouse.

It may be that in this they err. The good stereotype has enormous power over the hearts and minds of white Southerners. It might be set to work as a force fighting on freedom's side. My own good stereotypes drove me into the initial involvement which resulted in my eventual education to their evils. The constructive power of an image is not measured in terms of its truth, but of the love it inspires.

CHAPTER 16

No Ears to Hear

MY DECISION TO OPPOSE SEGREGATION WAS NO SOONER MADE than I had occasion to affirm it publicly. The NAACP had just announced intentions to abandon a forty-year struggle to achieve equality under our separate-but-equal system and to strike for an end to segregation. In response, Ross Valentine (pen name of a feature writer for the *Richmond Times-Dispatch's* editorial page) accused the organization of seeking the "forcible and coercive overthrow of the regional mores."

Being in the midst of unveiling in myself countless ugly evils within these mores, his voice of awe in speaking of them both amused and annoyed me. In a letter published May 17th, 1951, I replied:

"It's too bad about our mores. I know how you feel, because I'm covered with them myself. We remind me of the rhyme: 'One, two, three; Mama caught a flea; flea died; Mama cried; one, two, three.'"

No replies were published, but through the mail I got my first letter from a stranger. Prophetically, it voiced the protest soon to become the chorus of every discussion of integration in the South: "Nonsegregation would lead to the disastrous mongrelizing of the races."

Shortly I submitted a letter which was a summary of my over-all position and a call for the support of other white Southerners. It reviewed what I had learned about the large amount of hidden willingness to end segregation among well-educated whites, then added:

"They don't stop to think that by not speaking out they are dodging their gravest responsibility. Of what use are intelligence and culture if they give one no support in the expression of his convictions? Of what value, if one lacks courage to make into an actuality the democracy of which we boast so unconvincingly abroad?

"Do we want the Negro to think that we are solidly against him in his fight for justice? . . . If the opposition alone speaks, there is nothing to make him hope that many white people silently wish him well.

". . . Negroes are fighting now for their right to human dignity. There is no just and discerning white man who does not feel shame that fellow Americans in the commonwealth of Mr. Jefferson's birth must fight to obtain human dignity.

"Here where Washington, Woodrow Wilson, and Lee were born, are there so few white people who will stand up and be counted for what they believe?"

Times-Dispatch editor, Virginius Dabney, wrote me explaining that he could not print this letter, as it would bring to his page a barrage of protest, with a net result the opposite of my intention. His letter was simply a more effective rephrasing of such weary clichés as "Feeling runs too high on this issue" and "The less said about it the better." But Mr. Dabney was widely reputed as an authority on Southern attitudes and had been on the editorial staff of the *Times-Dispatch* for nearly twenty-five years. A pronouncement from him was entitled to be taken seriously. I weighed his opinion, then rejected it on the ground that if the views currently being expressed were not challenged, they would seem to be endorsed by us all.

Fools rush into territory which scholars skirt, so I sent the letter refused by Dabney to the second most widely distributed morning paper in the state, the *Norfolk Virginian-Pilot*. It was published and was followed by five letters to the paper from white people backing me up, besides some letters mailed to me directly—and *no* protests.

I sent this information to Mr. Dabney, with a similar letter for publication. He promptly printed it at the head of his letters column. No protests resulted. It looked as if I were right, and we were readier for integration than we ourselves suspected.

Armed with this data, I formulated a plan. I would organize a group of white persons who would flood the editorial pages with constructive letters. This just might accomplish the three things that most needed doing: Influence the unconverted, strengthen timid white liberals, and prove to Negroes that many whites were with them.

In a few weeks I had a list of fifteen people who had agreed to submit such letters to Virginia papers, besides a longer list of prospects still to be contacted. Two of the fifteen wrote as well as signed these letters. Two more gave me permission to attach their names to any letters I thought appropriate, merely mailing them copies. Touched by this vote of blanket confidence, I sent in all my best-written letters under their names. The other eleven wanted me to write the letters, then let them make what changes they wished before signing them.

During the next three months we published fifty-one letters in leading Virginia newspapers, most of them appearing in the *Richmond Times-Dispatch*. One after another, I took up various misconceptions current among whites and pointed out their absurdity, being careful always to identify the writer as white. Editorial pages developed a new look, which was promptly noted by Negro leaders. I savored the delectable taste of first success.

But there was a weakness in this project which I hadn't anticipated when I conceived it. I had expected merely to get the writers started, assuming that they would then continue under their own steam, leaving me free to find and train others. I found that while some half a hundred statements had indeed appeared with fifteen different signatures, actually I had written all but five, and had done so under conditions more difficult than if I had been working alone. Thus the limitation of my own exhaustible time and strength was placed upon a movement which I hoped would go forward with geometric progression.

Moreover, my creativity, which had geysered up for the purpose of phrasing points which I hadn't seen made in print, retreated before the grinding hack-job of repeating these points again and again in different words to rub them into the public mind. This was a job for many, not for one. Creeping exhaustion overtook me at the very thought of continuing on as a literary centipede.

I felt only relief when other news of feature interest claimed the attention and space of Virginia editors, and they abruptly ceased to print our letters. In rejecting one signed by me, Mr. Dabney courteously explained that he thought the public was temporarily weary of the discussion and he did not intend to publish more letters on this subject for a while. I joyfully disconnected my ghost-writing mill and turned my attention to other projects.

I never returned to ghosting on a large scale, though I published many letters under my own name, and occasionally wrote one for a friend. The wisdom of this decision now seems questionable. Had I used the lull to build up a stock pile of letters, and to sign up more "clients," the organization might have become large enough to wield noteworthy influence.

In 1957 when tensions were mountain-high and pushing daily upward, I made a weary effort to gather the organization together again. It was too late. Perhaps partly because I lacked my one-time fiery conviction that the public mind was easily swayed by truth, but chiefly no doubt because fear was galloping on great pale horses across every county in the state, I found this second effort fruitless. Signers I once had found so surprisingly plentiful and bold, now were both scarce and careful of what they said. Blank failure where once I had easy success left me almost ill with despair. In the fall of 1951, however, I had no premonition of such a future. There were so many rich, unplowed fields in 1951 and '52 that my feet ached for new furrows. I wrote reviews of books by and about Negroes, hoping to sway the public to read the right ones and not the wrong ones; I wrote articles for religious magazines, hoping to persuade ministers to speak out more often on the brotherhood of man; and I wrote a column for our Negro newspaper, which more about later. I also talked to everybody who would listen to me, white and colored.

What I wished to accomplish was clear in my mind: I wanted, as St. Francis said, to "sow love." I wanted white and colored Southerners to love each other and thus bring the Southern dream true. I saw myself as a catalyst.

I worked hard to get Sellers to accept my thesis that when whites became aware of the facts they would, with the kind graciousness characteristic of the region, fulfill all that was right.

"Ninety-five per cent of the contempt, injustice, and cruelty which Negroes receive is unintended and unconscious," I insisted. "We don't know what we're doing. We're just illiterate in this area of thought. But like illiterate Negroes, most of us lack neither willingness nor ability, but simply opportunity, to learn. We were raised in a framework of white supremacy, remember, without ever having had anybody call it that to us. Naturally we take it all as a matter of course until it's called sharply to our attention."

"It's been continually called to the attention of whites for a little matter of eight-five years," he replied. "Their attention is conveniently occupied."

"It's not like that," I said. "A newspaper account of some far-off incident doesn't get one's attention. When an area of thought has been blocked off, only something near at hand and personal can get through the barrier. We meet no educated Negroes who might break through our block. In school, in church, in social gatherings, even at home, the subject of segregation is seldom mentioned, and then 'delicately,' like sex. Ordinarily nothing comes into our lives to make us question behavior and attitudes we learned when we were very young."

Sellers declined to give this thesis credence. Because I was his pupil, his sharp mind reached into mine, recognizing my abysmal, helpless ignorance as the source of my faulty behavior, and grasping this ignorance as a challenge which it was his job to meet. But other whites were not his pupils, and he wasn't prepared to extend this insight to many of them. It would have let them off the hook of full responsibility for conduct which had flayed and hampered him all his life. My effort to make the educational process a two-way affair left him cold.

"But I concede that you know more about Negroes than I do," I argued. "Isn't it obvious, then, that I must know more about whites than you? You've been segregated just as much as I have. Don't you think you have anything at all to learn from me?"

"No, because I'm a sophisticated newspaper man and you're a naïve idealist," he said. "I'd be a sucker if I listened to you."

"It's worse to be a cynic than a sucker," I countered. "But the point is, whatever I am, there are more like me where I came from. If you know nothing about us, it's past time you learned."

Almost daily I discovered some behavior groove or inhibition in myself which fought on the side of segregation against my heart. I was certain that these were not *me*, but were, rather, something imposed on me from without. I had never invited them, or given consent to their coming into me. But I couldn't convince T. J. Sellers that they were superficial and not necessarily related either to the deep feelings or to the convictions of persons they inhabited. I knew my real living was done behind my conditioned exterior, as though this exterior were a theater curtain drawn between the Negro audience watching me and the pulsing drama being enacted on the stage inside me.

"I'm not alone in this," I insisted. "Other Southerners have this behind-the-curtain drama going on inside, too. And I'm not alone in my childish ignorance of Southern oppression, or in my childish eagerness to learn. We need Negro ambassadors who will come to us and explain the Negro's situation and how he feels about it; and we need Negro missionaries, too, who will make us understand again the ideals of democracy and the spiritual truths of brotherhood. Every Negro who has a chance to contact whites should think of himself as a misisionary."

Sellers looked at me steadily. "Cannibals eat missionaries," he commented.

I laughed angrily. "You see us as white giants deliberately oppressing you through pure ill will. We're really white children, guilty of the awful but unconscious tyranny of children."

"I've got news for you," he said. "If a man slugs me, I'm lots less interested in why he does it than how hard he hits."

"Your analogy is no good," I told him, "because it provides that he hit you intentionally. You're not going to tell me, are you, that if a man bumps into you, it makes no difference whether he stumbled and fell against you or deliberately ran you down?"

For once, T. J. said nothing, sitting on my words as though they were the lid of Pandora's box.

"Before whites can even begin to improve themselves," I went on, "they have to become conscious of what their blocks are. This they can seldom do without help. Don't you see? We don't even realize we *are* prejudiced, so how can we set about learning how not to be?"

He still said nothing. I was gaining momentum.

"The stage curtain may be a tapestry depicting indifference and rejection, but the drama behind it is a love story. Whatever our secondary feelings may be, our deep and leading emotion toward Negroes is love. This isn't because we're trying to be Christian or civic-minded. Our hearts go out to you, whether we will or no. Can't we keep it that way? Can't we start from this and solve our problems outward from it, not start with the problems and press inward until there's no love to work with any more?"

In his eyes I saw no softening. His mobile face reflected a pendulum swing from anger to stoniness, to anger again. When he finally spoke, his voice was impatient:

"What good is a love which has no recognizable results? Did Jesus say, 'By their fruits ye shall know them,' or did I just make that up?"

I was helplessly silent. How famine-sparse indeed were the fruits of Southern love.

He began talking in a low, rapid voice, telling me one of his vivid stories. He created in my mind a graceful old plantation house presided over by a lace-covered, hoop-skirted lady. In her back yard stands a cabin-shack where a great black man with bulging muscles lies on a sickbed, turning, writhing, and whimpering like a small child. None know what ails him and the other Negroes, through fear of contagion, leave him untended.

The creaking door of his shack opens and the perfumed lady-in-lace comes and kneels beside his straw pallet. The sun sweeps in behind her, making her pale hair glow, crown-like. She puts a soft hand under his head and raises it, while with the other she presses a cold drink to his lips. She leaves, but returns again and again, bringing medicine, food, white linen, even warm water and soft washcloths with which she herself bathes his dry, dusty body, leaving it fresh and cooled.

His heart grows large and strong with gratitude and trust, spreading its health to every cell, until again he is the great dynamo of a man he had been before disease struck. He returned to his work with an energy unknown to him before, because now he knows he is working for an angel.

Sellers paused, then added: "The man who told me this experience was ninety-seven years old, and he still wor-shiped the 'angel,' but he still lived in a squeaky-doored shack. He still couldn't read, and he wrote 'X'—like this— if he had to sign his name. He was too old and weak to work, and of course he had no pension. I was just a kid in school but do you know what I told him? I said, 'Lord, man! Don't you know she was just protecting her investment? A good slave was worth two thousand dollars or more!' "

I rose spontaneously to my feet. I don't know whether or not my eyes wept, but my heart did. "Oh, no," I said. "No. I used to hear my grandparents talk about their slaves. They spoke of them with love. It was in their eyes and voices. Money has a different look and sound."

He didn't reply, but his eyes conceded the point. For a moment he believed me.

Only days later, however, his busy belief that no good ever lived in relationships between Southern whites and Negroes was like a swarm of fretted bees about me again. I met its stings one by one.

Then one morning I woke holding in my hand the simple truth that if you don't love another, it's hard to believe that he really loves you, and if you hate him it's nearly impossible

to believe in his love. For then your will is set against thinking good of him, and what higher good can you believe of
a man than that he really loves?

Yet there is a sense in which Sellers was right. While in
the white South the love of many of us reaches out in the
Negro's direction, it's rare that it makes connection with
Negroes themselves. Instead, it surrounds our own homemade image of "our Negroes," and this image is many a
long pace from the real Negro who aches and is angry under
our heel.

Indeed, this loved image extends so high into the world
of wishful thought that it never could find a counterpart
in earthly man. No mere man could be so unresentful, humble, and tenderly loyal as our dream-Negro, just as no
woman ever was so pure and yet so loving as the dream-
woman who ruled man's heart back when he was unchallenged master and tyrant of her fate.

As I became aware of what the walls of my prison were
made of, I could see that Negroes were shut in by similar
walls. To them, as to us, habits of thought had been passed
along which set the races apart, pigeonholing us as though
we were documents instead of beings like themselves.
"Whites feel" thus-and-so, I was often gravely told. "They
believe" so-and-so. These stereotypes were seldom even
recognizable caricatures of any whites I had ever known.

Fascinated, I pointed out this discovery to Sellers. He
was not even slightly interested. I mentioned it to other
Negroes, and was met by the same cursory dismissal. They
were as resolutely blind and deaf in their prejudices as any
contented white supremacist was in his. Just here, I first
became aware that each human soul has vested interests
in not hearing various truths, regardless of how good and
beneficial these truths may be. The modern colored Southerner derives personal satisfaction and balm from believing
the worst of Southern whites, and also it helps him fight

them. I guessed that Sellers would rather lose a leg than his fury at the white South.

Before 1951 sank behind the rising New Year I realized that two great areas of deafness existed in the South: White Southerners had no ears to hear that which threatened their Dream. And colored Southerners had none to hear that which could reduce their anger. The difficulties of my chosen task now confronted me squarely.

CHAPTER 17

Mirrors and Candles

I TOOK SERIOUSLY MY FEELING OF HAVING BEEN ELECTED "George," and if I had learned anything during my eighteen years of professional writing it was that you should never speak out in print unless you are standing on firm ground. So I gave more time to gaining than to dispensing information. Not only did I spend tedious hours with my nose in books and periodicals, running down facts which supported my thesis, but also—and more joyfully—I conducted personal investigations and experiments.

One of the latter was aimed at learning why so many Negroes are convinced that most Southern whites are engaged in a deliberate, conscious effort to humiliate and make them miserable. It was quite impossible that this was so, I reasoned, if only because man's universal sin is his absorption in his own affairs. Few people concern themselves with others enough to bother about making them either happy or unhappy. I decided to pretend to myself that I was a Negro and see if I could thereby catch a glimpse of what the Negro saw.

It was nearing Christmas in 1951 when I began this purposeful game. Taking crowded buses to and from the shopping district, I would move back to a rear seat. When I had to push past a long line of standing whites, sometimes one would look stony-faced and not let me by. As my role of Negro pressed into my consciousness, I found myself thinking:

"They don't even want to admit I'm living—not even long enough to let me get where they say I've got to go!"

Full of excitement, I was sure I had caught one of the thoughts behind the look of frustration—half anger, half despair—I had often seen on dark faces as their owners struggled toward the back of an overloaded bus.

But what was the real explanation of the unyielding bodies and faces of whites? A paranoid chip on the shoulder perhaps? A self-centered conviction that the smallest inconvenience to themselves was not to be tolerated? The one thing it couldn't be was race prejudice, since only to myself was I black.

Once an elderly, courtly man stood in the aisle, swaying pendulum-like from the strap above my head. Nearer the front, two women rocked precariously on French heels. The last vacant seat was beside me.

"They'd rather stand than sit by me," my colored mind cried. "I might as well have leprosy or something!" My own self-rating sagged, dragging at my vitality.

The old gentleman would not sit while ladies stood? (Some survivors of the buried era of Southern gallantry exist.) And his portly bulk hid from them the vacant seat?

I almost **held** my breath. I had stumbled on a factor in the race problem which I had not seen or heard mentioned. Conduct which to a socially secure white person seems merely odd or accidental obviously can be interpreted only as pointed discrimination or insult by one who knows he is sometimes rejected.

No day now passed without my suffering humiliations "because of color." Sometimes they pelted me like hail, and I returned home to my white skin waspish and sore to the touch. Countless little happenings which, as white, I had never noticed, now stood out like racial brands. People who had been cordial to me at small gatherings failed to recognize me on the street. Old acquaintances who talked intimately with me in private, scarcely nodded when they were with a friend—"a white friend," I thought bitterly.

Store clerks, intent on a blistered heel or a breakfast quarrel, skipped over me when I was next in line. Chronic bustlers shoved me aside, a cleaning shop implied that I was lying when they lost my dress, impatient motorists tooted when I exercised my pedestrian's right of way, a delivery boy was insolent, and a salesgirl let me know I was more trouble than my account was worth. Chocolate-skinned, I didn't think of them merely as unpleasant individuals who should have been spanked for bad manners when they were young. To my pretended black self they were typical examples of contemptuous treatment of Negroes by whites.

Once, heavily laden with Christmas packages, I rounded a street corner, and a huge, red-faced man bumped me, knocking my parcels in seven ways. Without pausing to pick them up or muttering an apology, he strode on. I almost cried aloud, "He never would have done that to a white woman!" and such searing indignation rose from my dark depths that I was left weak.

For many days this illusory insult obtruded itself like some horrid disease between me and a healthy relationship with other whites. Even though I knew it was without substance, it had an evil life of its own. In growing humility, I digested the smallness of my soul compared with those of the many colored Southerners who live through countless such mirages, believing them wholly real, and yet retain their inner dignity and outer warmth.

From what reservoir of strength, I asked myself, comes the fortitude and tender, near maternal patience with which some Negroes bear our seemingly unflagging blows? No normally sensitive person could fail to react as they do to the picture they see. To their already heavy load of real discriminatory practices, the larger burden of seeming discrimination is added. White hostility is like a single light reflected by many mirrors, until it glares upon the observer as though it were a hundred lights.

But I failed to note something then which I later learned. Just as you can mistake a reflection for a real candle, you can also mistake a real candle for a reflection. I was to receive many burns as I thrust confident hands into flames while trying to push "mirrors" aside.

For the next three years, I lost no opportunity to gain further insight into minds of both white and colored Southerners. In the winter of 1952, a year and a half after Gregory Swanson's advent, and two and a quarter years before the Supreme Court's decision outlawing segregation in public schools, I made a "spot-check survey" of an area of Richmond which was in the process of being infiltrated by Negroes.

The usual thing had happened when the first Negro bought a house in a formerly all-white section. It was before the era of Southern bombings (though one had gone off in Mims, Florida), and no threats were made. Whites merely hastily met and agreed not to sell another house in the area to Negroes. Then somebody broke the agreement, a second Negro family moved in and, presto! the whites stampeded.

I spent two full days interviewing stampeders. Determined to make this a test of the tenability of my position on Southern good will toward Negroes, I carefully spoke no word of my own feelings to people I interviewed. One of the roving reporters of *Reader's Digest* had by then heard of my offbeat activities on the integration front and had asked me to write a piece about the Southern scene as I saw it. So I could truthfully say, "Good morning. I'm doing a survey for *Reader's Digest* to learn how we Virginians feel when our neighborhoods are infiltrated by Negroes."

Before reporting what the people said, which is baffling in the light of later developments in the South, let me say that, in addition to recognizing that my sampling was unscientific in many ways, I now see two factors as possibly important which at the time I considered negligible.

One was that enormous publicity had recently been given to rioting of Yankees in Cicero, Illinois, over Negro infiltration, and Southern editors were busy pointing with pride to our good race relations: *We* had had "no race riot in the so-called prejudiced South" for umpty-ump years.

The other was that although I did not verbalize my attitude, it may have been implied in my manner. At any rate, the following were the kind of replies I got to questions which were as objective as I knew how to make them.

QUESTION: "Do you *personally* object to having a Negro neighbor?"

TYPICAL ANSWERS: "Why, no. Not personally. Negroes make good neighbors." "Not a-tall. When they get hold of a good home they take pride in it—keep it up better than most whites." "Why should I? If it were up to me I'd stay right here." "Oh, no. They go their way; I go mine."

QUESTION: "Then why don't you stay?"

TYPICAL ANSWERS: "Everybody's moving." "People would think it was funny." "We wouldn't have any friends." "The children would be embarrassed living in a colored neighborhood."

Something that was difficult to explain then, and almost impossible now, is that after two days spent in knocking on doors, I ran into no hostility whatever.

I've already noted that there was no difficulty in finding whites who would sign their names to letters to the editor defending integration, provided I did all the work. It was even easier to find those who would sign petitions pleading for an end to specific forms of discrimination. I delighted in circulating them, and with fascinated journalistic zeal noted down reactions of each person as I requested his signature.

In the summer of 1952, the city bought new buses made in Georgia. Painted on them at the factory were notices that whites must sit in front, Negroes in the rear. Segregation was observed in our local transit system but signs had never been used, and Negroes entering the new buses winced, then burned.

I wrote a petition requesting the transit company to remove the signs, and without difficulty got signatures from white people in every section of town. When I presented this at the company's office, the presiding official seemed positively pleased. The signs were gone in three days.

Reporting this incident in my *Tribune* column, I triumphantly affirmed: "The most valuable unmined raw material in the nation today is the good will of white Southerners. If we look for it, uncover it and use it, miracles will happen in the South."

Another petition I passed was aimed at having the courtesy titles of Mr., Mrs., and Miss extended to Negroes in our local newspaper, *The Daily Progress*. I had learned with joy that more than once white church and charity groups, after being assisted in some special project by colored citizens, had refused to have any publicity on their efforts unless their Negro co-workers also were listed with courtesy titles. The publisher's reply was always: "My white subscribers would object."

Weary of his reiteration, and full of faith in my fellow man, I wrote a petition stating that the undersigned white subscribers requested that courtesy titles be extended to Negroes. A friend and I carried this in our purses, offering it to whoever happened to be present when an opportunity to pass it was found. It was presented indiscriminately in a doctor's office, a grocery store, a library reading room, and a church guild meeting. I then found there were sixty-two signatures, only one man and one woman having declined to sign.

"Where are you from?" I inquired of these two. The man said, "South Bend, Indiana," and the woman said, "Boston, Massachusetts."

Circulating this petition I felt I had learned a good deal about people's thinking. Surprise was the commonest reaction. Most people simply did not know that courtesy titles were customarily not extended to Negroes in the *Progress*, having never noticed. Joy was next. Some reached for the pen with such explanations as, "You bet I will!" and "My, I'm glad you're working on that!" A few revealed fear by refusing to sign until they received assurances that their names would not be published. Only the man from South Bend exhibited anger.

As my views were already becoming locally known, I asked a friend to send the signed petition to the *Progress* with a letter pointing out that virtually no opposition had been met. Prompt and courteous, the publisher's reply thanked her for her interest in the *Progress*, and informed her that the paper's policy would remain the same.

This incident supported my rapidly growing theory that the bottleneck, when not some law, was almost invariably a stubborn official who stoutly maintained, in face of all contrary evidence, that "the people aren't ready for that change yet." I thought I had truly got a cross section of public thinking because of the many different places where the petition had been presented. However, I now note one factor which didn't appear important at the time: It was passed around at the University end of town. Later developments showed this to be more liberal than the other end.

I wasn't the only person in town who circulated constructive petitions. A local Negro had been convicted of raping a white woman, and was promptly given the death sentence. As the date of execution approached, a young white lawyer from Richmond, Howard Carwile,* appeared on the scene with a petition asking the governor to spare the man. And a white student at the University of Virginia passed one he had written asking that the sentence be commuted on the ground that there was a reasonable doubt of guilt. The student told me despairingly that he could get few white signatures:

"They won't believe that he's just being railroaded!"

"Are you quite sure he is?" I asked. "Were you at the trial?"

"No, but what chance has a Negro in our courts?"

I hadn't seen the trial, either, so I appealed to Sellers. "Do *you* think there's a reasonable doubt of his guilt?"

"I do *not*. I've a brief of the trial if you want to read it."

It revealed that not only had the man been caught in the act, but also the woman was mutilated to a degree that made it impossible for her to have been a willing participant. The well-meaning student was following the familiar young crusader's pattern of substituting convex for concave.

But there was need for a petition with another approach, so I wrote one. It stated that in all the time that court records had been kept in Virginia, the extreme penalty for rape had many times been invoked against Negroes but never once against a white; and, therefore, in the interest of equality before the law, the man's sentence should be commuted to life imprisonment.

Even though this is the most sensitive area in race relations, I easily found nine white friends who agreed to get ten signatures each. Thus far, Virginians were behaving as I had predicted. Sellers had stopped jeering at my seat on the topmost billow of a pink cloud, and was watching with

* Now author of "*Speaking from Byrdland*," Lyle Stuart publishers.

concentrated attention, but he had an air of expectancy that was nearly as maddening as his old chuckles.

I undertook to get twenty signatures myself to help make up for those who probably would not get their allotted ten —for residence on a cloud had not separated me from knowledge of human lethargy. To get twenty signatures I had to interview forty people, some known to me, some not. I was fascinated by the discovery that only a scant handful knew that Negroes often suffer a special penalty for interracial rape. This supported my contention that innocent ignorance was a chief factor in the South's prejudice.

Most of those to whom this discrimination came as news were shocked and incredulous. Some were indignant with me for false charges against their South, and were only partially placated when I assured them that it was my South too, by birth and heart.

Note that this was my first taste of the resentment and fear which I had originally expected. I also met my first large percentage of closed ears. Their owners wanted neither information nor arguments for signing. I understood how they felt. Knowledge of this discrimination was a threat to their Dream. I was satisfied, even surprised, that half of them signed.

Also, I was gratified that only one refused on the ground that a Negro who crosses racial lines in rape *should* have a heavier penalty than a white man who does it. This one man expounded his position:

"In all unbiased justice he deserves it, because to force a white woman to lie with a Nigra is a terrible defilement of both her flesh and her spirit—enough to ruin her life. Women kill themselves sometimes afterwards, you know. It's about like sodomy. Well, that's just what it is—sodomy."

I foolishly asked, "Do you really think it's much harder on her than on a young colored girl raped by a brutish white?" I should have known what he would think.

He chuckled unpleasantly. "Are you joking? A Nigra girl is always a little bit willing—especially if the man's white."

I hastily left this repellent character, but felt slightly soothed when his wife followed me to the door and silently signed the petition.

The other nineteen who refused offered a variety of reasons, shorn entirely of race prejudice. They said that they thought all offenders, white and colored, should be executed for brutal rape; that if this man's sentence was commuted, with our present parole system, he might be released to strike again; that they trusted our courts, and if death had been ordered, the details of the crime must have been such that death was warranted.

I took them all at their word, not yet having learned the glibness of the human tongue in making its owner appear blameless. But I've little doubt now that many rooted their refusal in the subterranean river bed of a belief voiced by that one frank person among them. Indeed, such a line of thinking is evinced by the *un*blindfolded "justice" in Southern courts. Surely few judges would deliberately punish a Negro more for the *same* crime! But they are conscious of no bias in exacting a worse punishment if in their estimation the crime itself is worse.

My activities were not confined to surveys and petitions. Being by nature prone to action, and by faith convinced that Southern prejudice was mostly a mirage, I stepped forward whenever unproven prejudice was assumed to be in operation. It was rare that resultant experience failed to give my thesis support.

Once the student president of an interracial fellowship group gravely assured me that the only place in town they could have a supper meeting was the Unitarian church.

"Have you asked the other ministers?" I promptly inquired.

"Well, not point-blank, but they made it clear there wasn't any use."

I got permission to ask "point-blank," then telephoned the Episcopal minister. Having explained the nature and aims of the organization, I requested permission to hold a supper meeting at his church.

"Let me see if that date's open," he said. It was.

The Presbyterian minister said stiffly that the Session had to pass on permission to use church facilities. "I'll present your request at the meeting tonight."

Like the student, I felt there was little hope here, and was tempted not to call back next day. But setting my jaw, I followed through. In the same chilly, hurried voice he said: "We voted unanimously to welcome the gathering. I thought we would."

The Baptist minister said, "Why of course. We like to encourage such things."

Satisfied, I investigated no further, but I haven't a doubt that our Lutheran, Methodist, and several other ministers would have made similar responses in this year of 1952. Consciences were stirring on the segregation issue, and there were no organized penalties for brotherhood at that time.

With my beliefs youthful and militant, I could draw only one conclusion from my accumulated data. To the student president I triumphantly carried the good news, appending this pompous comment:

"I've concluded from many experiences and researches that the bad images of each other we carry in our minds give us a lot more trouble in the integration struggle than real live Southerners do. I think our racism is just a bogeyman. It's power lies entirely in our own belief in it."

Possibly the most astonishing fact I have yet recorded is that it was over two years before I had to eat any part of that statement.

CHAPTER 18

Facts and Figures of Good Will

MY GROWING CONVICTION THAT SOUTHERN PREJUDICE WAS just a bogeyman was supported by data which for nearly two years had been dropping into my lap like ripe plums. Whether or not social scientists would consider this data statistically significant, it was overwhelmingly convincing to me. I still think it represented the feelings of a substantial number of my compatriots at that time, and that had there been strong and effective liberal leadership, this data probably would have represented a majority.

I discovered that a local Negro dentist had nearly as many white as colored patients, the number of the former having risen sharply when he moved his office from a highly visible location to a quiet back street. I located a Negro physician in Clifton Forge, Virginia, who had a large practice with 70 per cent of his patients white, and I also found many others scattered throughout the South, whose percentages of white patients were nearly as high.

Mississippi is reputedly the most prejudiced state in a supposedly rampant South, yet a Methodist friend told me of an incident there which made me question this concept:

The national Woman's Society of Christian Service held their annual meeting in a Mississippi town graced by two

Methodist churches. The minister of one was asked if its facilities might be used for meetings, including meals. After cordially agreeing, he backed down when told that there were colored delegates. Not he, but his people would object, he said.

But the other minister answered: "How can we send missionaries abroad and not do this at home?" Thus challenged, his parishioners treated their colored dinner guests as daughters of the King.

A college girl told me of a secret ballot taken by a teacher in her Mississippi school. After passing out scraps of paper, this teacher asked each pupil to state, unsigned, whether or not she would be pleased if her school accepted Negro students. Nearly all scribbled "yes," but none avowed such sentiment openly.

Buried in the pages of a tiny religious publication on the library shelves I found a notice that forty-five out of forty-eight white Mississippi students at a conference had signed a letter to their bishop urging him to do what he could to end segregation in churches and schools.

I launched into an effort to find records of similar incidents and polls which had occurred recently anywhere in the South. My findings exceeded my hopes.

The first Negro student admitted to the University of Texas, after a long fight in the courts, had promptly been elected by his fellow students to the chairmanship of the social committee of his class. And at Wayland College, Texas, a poll showed that 98 per cent of all the students wanted an end to segregation there.

The first Negro student admitted to the University of Oklahoma was placed in the beginning—unbelievable as it sounds—in a little penned-off area to preserve the letter of segregation. But indignation against the pen had risen so high among white observers that a poll was taken. It revealed that 76 per cent of the students and 100 per cent of the faculty wanted the removal of *all* segregation signs on the campus.

In 1951 the Florida Student Government Association, composed of leaders from all the white colleges and universities in Florida, had unanimously approved a resolution calling for the abolishment of segregation in state-supported institutions of higher learning.

Ninety-five per cent of the students at Baptist Seminary in Louisville, Kentucky, voted to admit Negroes, not only to classes but also to dormitories.

Students of five white colleges in Louisiana published a protest against segregation, stating that integration was not only inevitable but *also welcome* (this was the position which I wanted all who felt as I did *openly* to affirm); and the Student Federation of Louisiana voted 78 per cent in favor of having Negroes participate in their programs.

In Georgia 87 per cent of the students of Columbia University stated that they would not object to having Negroes attend that school, and 95 per cent of the theological students at Emory University voted for admission of Negroes there.

In Missouri representatives of seventeen colleges passed a resolution urging the governor to support legislation to end segregation in state-supported colleges. In North Carolina more than twenty student organizations demanded that segregated seating in their stadium be discontinued. And throughout the South the Southern Baptist Church, which is considered highly conservative, had lowered racial bars in every one of its seminaries.

The Southern Conference Educational Fund, Inc., after polling faculties of 143 white colleges and universities in Southern and border states, finding that 70 per cent favored "nonsegregation" (reported in Chapter 6), had polled physicians in these same states. Of nearly 6000 white doctors who returned ballots, 71 per cent favored admitting Negro doctors to their county medical societies.

I found that in the last two years five Negroes had been elected to city councils in various towns in North Carolina; that a Negro who ran for the Louisiana State Board of Education had carried more white than Negro precincts; that in Tennessee a Negro physician was appointed to the Knoxville City Planning Commission and a Negro lawyer to the Nashville Board of Education; that in Florida a Negro minister was appointed to the Miami Welfare Board, and a Negro was elected by an all-white vote to the Dade County Medical Association. And, although our theaters are segregated, a Negro was elected president of the South Eastern Theater Conference by a 90 per cent white vote.

In Virginia, a Negro lawyer had been elected to the Richmond City Council, and another was serving on the Planning Commission. And a Negro had just been unanimously elected president of Augusta County Ministerial Association, with 90 per cent of the voters white.

Testing my theory that it was the "lower" (uneducated) classes who made all the trouble in the South, I wrote to state directors of the CIO and AFL in several Southern states and was delighted to find that those who replied gave no support to my theory whatever. Not only did whites and Negroes work together without friction in plants and union meetings on an unsegregated basis, but also Negroes were often elected to important offices by a majority white vote. On the executive board of the Alabama CIO there were at least five Negro vice presidents, although white delegates outnumbered Negro delegates four to one.

I noted a great deal of what I called "bootleg nonsegregation" going on everywhere. One of our largest railroads had made little pretense of segregated seating for years; white and colored teachers often had illegal integrated conferences following publicized segregated ones; and certain lunch counters all over the South quietly served both white and colored patrons with no complaints being heard.

Moreover, laws against integrated public assembly were openly got around by designating any meeting "private." Soft chuckles rolled from the three corners of Virginia when Adlai Stevenson spoke to the people of Virginia, September 20, 1952, and Richmond officials decided that, as he "would be speaking to a Democratic party meeting and not to a public gathering," it was quite all right for the audience to be mixed. More than 5000 persons, white and Negro, crowded through the wide-open doors of the city's largest auditorium.

All this data and much more like it went into my column in *The Tribune*, the weekly Negro newspaper of which T. J. Sellers was Charlottesville editor and manager. Into this column I threw all the young zest of one who imagines that you need only point to an obvious truth and you will be believed. My plan was to publish the series of articles locally first, then rewrite them for a Negro syndicate—for this was before I was fully convinced that most Negroes have no ears for the news that large numbers of Southern whites silently wish them well. Indeed, one of the things which convinced me was the manifest boredom of Negro editors when I approached them about running these articles.

My column comprised two series of features, running alternate weeks. Statistics appeared biweekly under the title "Facts and Figures of Good Will," and the other weeks I used a question-and-answer series called "From Behind the Curtain," signed, "A White Southerner." The latter always began with the following paragraph in italics:

"Segregation is America's iron curtain. Its greatest evil has been that it prevents us from understanding each other and from being conscious of each other's growth. On both sides of the curtain we are about fifty years behind in our interpretations of the other. Write in questions concerning racial attitudes of the educated white Southerner of today. (Names will be withheld.)"

While I made in this column an occasional idiotically optimistic statement based on my high-reaching faith in mankind in general and in the South in particular, much of what I said was solidly based. Although my present phrasing would be far less pat and smug, and qualifications would be more in evidence, with minor changes I would stand behind most of my answers today. The following excerpts are examples of statements which I think are substantially true.

"QUESTION: How can white people reconcile their feeling that it's all right to have us come into their homes and take care of their children with their feeling that we would contaminate them if we sat beside them on a bus?"

"ANSWER: This is like replying to the question, 'When did you stop beating your wife?' I have never known anyone who felt 'contaminated' by sitting beside Negroes. Undoubtedly there are cases of this feeling, just as despite vaccine there are cases of smallpox. But it is a mistake to figure these into your everyday thinking.

"With few exceptions, we avoid sitting beside Negroes because to sit with one would make us *conspicuous*. The very same people who in the South stand rather than sit beside a Negro are perfectly happy seated beside one in Washington, D. C., and points north. Since mixing up the races is contrary both to law and custom in the South, only a potential crusader will be party to it. The rest of the white population would as leave board a bus in a bathing suit, and for approximately the same reasons.

"The answer to your question is that *custom* is the common denominator between these two apparently irreconcilable attitudes. We are used to having Negroes nurse our children; we are used to having them sit separately on buses. It's as simple and as stupid as that."

"QUESTION: Is it pure sadism which makes whites so unkind to Negroes?"

"ANSWER: Yes, it's often pure sadism—by a small sadistic

minority. And remember there are three times as many mean white people in Virginia as there are mean Negroes. This isn't a confession of racial inferiority. The percentage of sadism is about the same in both races, but 75 per cent* of Virginia's population is white.

"To make matters worse, since the Negro belongs to a relatively helpless minority, he is a natural target for the sadistic white man. One such man can be mean to an awful lot of Negroes, thus creating the impression that a lot of white people have been mean. However, if it's any solace, I've never known a white man who treated Negroes with contempt, who didn't also treat with contempt any member of his own race of whom he could safely take advantage. I know of not one single exception to this rule. . .

"There's another aspect of the 'mean white man' problem. Warmhearted white people often wound Negroes without even suspecting that they've done it. Segregation has so far separated us that we have an entirely different set of sore spots. This is what baffled me most when I first began to have Negro friends. I had to learn a whole new keyboard of social tact."

"QUESTION: If many white people are as kindly disposed toward Negroes as you claim, why don't more of them do something about our problems?"

"ANSWER: Well, we're certainly kindly disposed toward ourselves, and we have plenty of pressing problems of our own which we aren't doing anything about. Not doing anything about problems is a universal human failing. . . . Also, I'm afraid that people of all sizes, colors and degrees of intelligence are even less inclined to do anything about other people's problems than about their own, no matter how kindly disposed they are."

* Actually it's about 80 per cent or four times as many. I inadvertently quoted the number of white compared to Negro school children. But young Negro graduates leave the state in large numbers to escape the handicaps of segregated employment.

"QUESTION: Since a member of another race can seldom be congenial in the little ways that we all look for in choosing a permanent mate, why do whites think that integration will certainly lead to frequent intermarriage?"

"ANSWER: I'm afraid that the white man's private sins are largely responsible for his sloppy thinking in this area. Viewing the steady stream of mulattoes in the South, he feels sure that many of these would have resulted from legal unions had it not been for the segregation law. He fails to note the fact that segregation is responsible for the chief factors in the perennial increase of mulattoes. Here are a few of these factors.

"1. The lure of forbidden fruit. Just as the prohibition law encouraged drinking, the segregation law encourages interracial sexual intercourse.

"2. Many white men, feeling nostalgic for their childhood associations with Negroes, struggle against a deep and persistent desire for their company. Being prevented by law and convention from expressing it in friendly companionship, they resort to a sexual outlet.

"3. Because of economic pressure resulting from segregation, there is a larger and more attractive choice of purchasable ladies in the colored group.

"4. Because segregation separates the groups so completely, a white man's misdemeanors are less likely to come to the attention of his family if he crosses the color line.

"5. Ruthless men feel secure in the law, since in case of error they cannot be made to marry the injured lady . . ."

"QUESTION: When white people discuss Negroes privately, what is their main criticism?"

"ANSWER: My answer will have to be divided into two sections: (1) Criticisms of what they (so aggravatingly!) refer to as the 'typical Negro,' and (2) criticisms of the modern, educated Negro.

" 'The typical Negro' is criticized for unreliability . . . and for personal untidiness.

"Actually, both these faults are related to social level, not to race. That we are really aware of this, whatever we may say, is proved by our preference for Negro servants over white. Sometimes we even say it. We are fond of pointing out to Yankees, who frequently prefer white help, that our preference is based on the fact that 'Negroes are both cleaner and more dependable than the Southern domestic class of whites.'

"The chief criticism of the 'modern Negro' is a lack of courtesy. It is said that while demanding acceptance as a right, he assumes an attitude of discourtesy which would make any white man completely unacceptable to his own group.

"While, like all generalizations, it is untrue of a great many, it can't be denied that an uncomfortable number of modern Negroes can be fitted with this glove. It's only natural that in reacting against servile courtesy, Negroes by and large should confuse it with courtly courtesy and brand all courtesy as servile . . .

"The difference between servile and courtly courtesy is almost entirely internal. If we offer it reluctantly, it is servile. If we offer it graciously, it is courtly. If it is a bribe for good treatment, it is servile. If it is a gift of human warmth, it is courtly. Since these distinctions are above the grasp of the majority of both races, I'm afraid that true courtesy will remain a grace belonging only to the spiritually aware few."

"QUESTION: Anyone reading your feature, 'Facts and Figures of Good Will,' would gather the impression that prejudice is just a myth. Is that what you are trying to make us believe?"

"ANSWER: Far from it. I am merely trying to show that prejudice is only a small part of the picture. I want people to realize that while prejudice certainly does exist and must be dealt with, there also exists an enormous amount of good will of which too few of us are aware.

"Almost our whole effort has been directed toward fighting prejudice, publicizing atrocities, exposing discrimination. In consequence there has grown up in our minds a one-sided picture of the situation which is a serious hindrance.

"This concentration on the negative has had three nearly disastrous results:

"First, it has disheartened many superior Negroes and filled them with a sense of futility. After all, they feel, if the majority of the majority group regards them with aversion, what's the use of even trying to combat such overwhelming odds?

"Second, it makes members of the white good-willed majority imagine that they belong to a helpless minority who will only be regarded as traitors to their own group if they defend the Negro's position.

"Third, it gives such aid, comfort, and encouragement to the ill-willed minority that they are not afraid to say— and until recently, even to *do*—anything they want to . . .

"Protests and legal action against discrimination should not be reduced. On the contrary, I should like to see them become more widespread. But they should be made and taken in full knowledge that they are approved by a vast army of white Southerners, many of whom would be openly batting on our side if only they knew how.

"It is my conviction that the time has come when the most effective attack on prejudice is to recognize and publicize the existence of this army of allies. We have thought too much about the strength of the enemy. Let's turn our attention to the constructive, creative forces in our society. In these lie our real strength."

Lest you gather the impression that I spouted only enduring wisdom and good counsel in my column, let me quote the following:

"QUESTION: How will whites react if the Supreme Court ends segregation in public schools?"

"ANSWER: They will react the way Americans react when a president is elected after a bitter campaign. That is, the opposition will shut up and the support will begin to function. There will, of course, be some grumblings but these will be in undertones, and the large majority will immediately lend their support to the new interpretations of the law."

Once in a resounding burst of faith in everybody I said that I thought the snowball of integration had reached the brow of the hill and would soon go speeding down, and regardless of what the Supreme Court decided, all facilities would be voluntarily integrated within five years. This, remember, in the year 1952.

My Southern Dream had been so braced by statistics and encouraging personal experiences that I was ashamed of my earlier fear that I would be heavily penalized for raising the banner of brotherhood. After waving it feverishly for more than a year, I had received virtually nothing but applause from my peers. Southerners, I concluded, were even better than I had thought. Not even the sea of misinformation which lay across their path to the Promised Land could impede their progress toward fulfillment of that summer-evening way of life they had envisioned.

But there was one discordant fact among the pleasing harmonies of my picture of the South—a fly as big as a horsefly in my smooth ointment of belief. There was no denying that vicious attacks were made on some people for carrying this very same banner of brotherhood which I had for so long brandished unscathed. If I couldn't find a way to get rid of that horsefly, I would have to chuck the whole lot of ointment out. I found a way that was both smug and unkind.

I had written to native Georgian, Lillian Smith to inquire how she was faring down in the pine woods after many books, articles, and speeches attacking segregation. She replied that she was regularly asked to serve on local civic and welfare boards, and so on; that she ran a fashionable summer camp for Southern girls, and following the publication of her most controversial book, *Strange Fruit*, there had been only four withdrawals from her camp, with forty new applications to fill the vacanies.

I had also studied the career of Mrs. M. E. Tilly, likewise from the deep South and likewise widely known for pro-integration activities. She had been voted "Woman of Achievement in Social Welfare" by a large group of Southern women's societies, to mention only one of many similar awards.

So I put one, one, and one together and came up with the whole South. In an article earmarked for a national magazine, but mercifully never printed, I made this statement:

"Before indicting a community which seemingly persecutes a crusader for his ideals, one should look into what other causes he has espoused and what other customs he has attacked. If he has also shocked and outraged conventional citizens on some issue not related to race, their resentment of him isn't a reliable gauge of their bigotry. Many times the situation can be summed up as it was neatly expressed with reference to a well-known crusader of the deep South: 'If he were defending orchids, I'd be up in arms against him.'"

Thus, ironically, in my effort to make the Dream believable, I joined the seething army of attackers who bring earthly hell to those who strive to make the Dream come true. With immutable justice I was to learn one day that a whole city full of frank enemies who shout threats and insults cannot tear one's heart out as can one liberal who turns his back on a molested brother in the name of faith in the South. Because I had once welcomed and thoroughly explored this whole area of interpretation, I was not to be mercifully spared knowledge of one barbed arrow or one spent B-B shot which came from this direction.

At year's end 1952, girded with good statistics and glib explanations for whatever didn't fit them, I felt justified in making these statements in an article which appeared in *The Christian Century*:

"The capacity for democracy of the average Southerner is far ahead of the restrictions imposed by our laws and our leaders . . . Everywhere in the South segregation is far more active on paper than in practice, and far more active in practice than in the hearts of white Southerners . . . Much of the South's failure to realize the democratic ideals for which our nation stands can be attributed to a false assumption that everybody else is prejudiced . . . A few courageous leaders in key positions could take what appears to be a rock-like tradition and crack it like a shell."

Strange as it may seem to those who read the rest of this book, I still believe that in 1952 good leaders in key positions could have accomplished this. But the incontrovertible fact is that, whereas I expected thousands to step forward at the challenge, in all the South not a firm fistful of such leaders were found.

CHAPTER 19

Jeffersonian Americans

As I MOVED CONFIDENTLY INTO 1953, I BELIEVED THAT THE white half of the Southern Dream was true. We really did love "our Negroes," and appearances to the contrary were just an evil illusion. Although the "Sellers Course" had taught me that our expressions of this love often were offensive, I didn't question the high quality of the love itself.

I believed, too, that the other half of the Dream had been true and could be true again. Negroes had once loved us.

Since the deepest desire of every heart was to love and be loved, I reasoned, it was impossible that two peoples could live side by side, interwoven as we were, and not love each other. Once I would have added, "Especially two peoples like us, that are as complementary and supplementary to each other as are men and women." But that would have been before I suddenly realized in the early summer of 1951 that Negroes and whites are the same.

For a long time I had been saying that they were alike —and thinking that I thought it. But one day something in me tangibly dissolved, and afterwards I knew it was a partition which had made me feel that Negroes and whites are *alike* without feeling that they are the *same*. I had had a "we" and "you" feeling which now was gone.

Some immediate rewards followed the dissolving of this barrier. I felt as you feel when you have knocked out a wall between two small rooms in your house. The result isn't just one of the little rooms made twice as big, nor is it simply the two little rooms brought together. It is a new and altogether different room. When the partition between two races comes out within yourself, you haven't just got two races brought together. You've got humanity. If segregationists realized this, they mightn't mind the idea so much. It's the "brought together" concept which seems to distress them most.

I felt whole. This filled me with wonder, for I hadn't known I was divided. I felt relaxed, not having known that I had been tense. I felt co-ordinated and was surprised to discover that I had been confused and torn by feeling one way, thinking another, and behaving still another.

The change probably wasn't as visible to others as to me. Outwardly I continued for a long time to move in my old patterns. Probably I still move in some of them. Even inside me, the change wasn't as clear-cut and permanent as knocking out a plaster wall. My race partition reappeared and vanished like the point of a busy knitting needle. But my over-all view of people showed noticeable alterations from that day.

Some penalties went with the rewards. I saw Negroes more accurately but I saw them unadorned with raiment which once I had found lovely. Their weaknesses became for me merely those of any people subjected to their history— their strengths likewise. They were separated from the blanket virtues, as well as from blanket faults, which I had attributed to them. "They" were no longer lovable. Only some were. There was nothing special about "them" any more. They had just the same old tedious faults and virtues that all the rest of us have.

My relationship with them was realistic—and shorn of

magic. Gone was the distinctive flavor which had made it fun just to be with them; gone the mysterious magnet which had drawn my heart toward the whole group. Once sight of a Negro either in the distance or near at hand—any Negro or any number of them—had made me feel tender and flowing, as the sight of any child does to some people.

In one sense, the wall in me which had separated us was a garden wall. I had looked over it to them as a child might look over a stone wall into a forbidden garden of some mysterious neighbor. In that other garden he sees more beauty and lure than in his own. He may long to be rid of the wall, but if it is removed, mystery and lure will go, too. The garden now runs right into his own. He misses the dramatic reaches of good and evil which his mind had found in the forbidden garden. The witch and the fairy who had lived there are really just a sick old woman and her pretty granddaughter—and where is the fun in that?

Just so, my heart had lost the garden that my feet had gained.

The importance of a lost romantic vision should not be underestimated. In such a vision is power as well as joy. In it is meaning. Life is flat, barren, zestless, if one can find one's lost vision nowhere.

Most of us realize the loss we all sustained when the wall went down between men and women. Our discovery with the aid of science that psychological differences between men and women are not as great as they were once thought to be represents a fact, a truth, which we would not consent to replace with old errors. It is not true that man is brave, strong, aggressive, just, objective, and so on, while woman has a set of different and complementary virtues, such as tenderness, humility, purity, compassion, patience. We all know that the most physically feminine woman is likely to come up with the "masculine" virtues if placed from childhood in circumstances which call for their cultivation, and the same is true of a man.

Yet wasn't there something sweetly wild and stirring in the belief that a great chasm of difference forever separated the sexes, bridged only by wide reaches of the soul? How satisfying to be able to look up to members of the other sex for heightened merit in areas where you believed you could claim little. Your heart went out and up to them because they could supply so much that you lacked, and still you knew that you could fully repay them because you, too, as their other half, had much to give. The whole relationship was one of exchange on many levels in which each completed the other and in doing so gave and received joy.

Facts are facts, and as we learn them we creep nearer to a larger truth, so we can't wisely regret having learned how little different men and women are. Yet we want to think of the other sex in these special ways. We are not complete without chasms across which we can soar only on wings of love and worship. We need the distant as well as the close at hand, the mysterious as well as the familiar, the mountain as well as our level front yard.

So I lost magic and found wholeness when my inner wall went down. I lost the Negro race and found the human race. I was sad but I was healthy. I was willing and anxious to go on from there.

My understanding of what I had gained was much clearer than of what I had lost. I only very vaguely grasped at this time how great and varied is the unconscious exploitation of Negroes by Southern whites. For not only have we exploited them physically and economically to bring ease to our bodies and our purses, but also we have exploited them emotionally to bring us many sublimated satisfactions. Our relationship with Negroes is a many-stringed instrument upon which we play melodies to replenish all the empty places in our hearts.

Or you might call our relationship with Negroes a gigantic psychodrama, in which we act out satisfactions for all our basic drives. Whites who live in realms far above carnal exploitation, nevertheless play a sublimated sex role in the "complementary exchange" with Negroes—which in our imagination is mutually satisfying, because satisfying to us.

The parent-child relationship is almost consciously acted out, with the obedience, seeming respect, and acceptance by "our Nigras" going far toward soothing heartaches for the rebellion, arrogance, and rejection we must endure as our real children seize their own lives from us in adolescence. Even the reverse, the child-parent role, is sometimes filled, as we play the part of babyhood helplessness, satisfying immature longings to be waited on and taken care of.

Finally, we constantly act out the role of the noble-hearted, with a minimum cost in sacrifice and moral effort.

But my need to keep as much of the Southern Dream as I could made me skirt any such analysis as I've just made. To sustain what was left of the Dream, I had to search constantly for the most golden motive I possibly could squeeze between the facts of everybody's known conduct.

In carrying on my crusade to bring the Dream fully into fruition, my primary job among whites was, I thought, to help each realize that he wasn't an isolated, helpless liberal, but a member of a great, silent fellowship of good will. My secondary job was to educate them concerning the modern Negro's character and needs.

In addressing Negroes my primary job was to make them see how we really felt about them, and my secondary job was to give them whatever aid and moral support they appeared to need.

In my efforts to do my primary job with Negroes my motives were even more misunderstood than I realized at the time. In all my articles and speeches addressed to them I stressed assurances (1) that they were not abhorred or regarded with contempt to the extent they thought, and (2) that far from being singled out for such treatment, they were only one of many victims of a universal human yearning to feel superior.

My purpose in this was clean-cut and single: I was trying to increase their sense of belonging, to undermine their unconscious fear that just maybe the loud-voiced segregationists were right in their accusations of inferiority. But with hardly any exceptions, they interpreted my words as efforts to defend whites and—worse!—to belittle their own problems and burdens.

A large part of the misunderstanding certainly can be laid at the broad door of semantics, for many words, phrases, and concepts still had strictly white Southern overtones for me, far different from those they had for Negroes. But undoubtedly, too, an important part was played by the Negro's psychological stake in believing the worst of whites. My more convincing points sometimes created real fear, I now feel sure—for many Negro leaders felt that belief in the good will of whites would reduce their own striking power in the fight for freedom from the white man's rule.

My task would have been easier had I not begun it several years before the Montgomery bus strike and Martin Luther King's historic appeal to Negro intellectuals and simple folk alike to love their enemies, since in this lay both their own spiritual salvation *and their best weapon.*

Until Dr. King marshaled and dramatized the irresistible forces of brotherly love, the trend among thinking Negroes —at least those I knew—was to identify loving the white man with Uncle-Tomism. Uncle Tom, of course, was the chief character in *Uncle Tom's Cabin.* He symbolizes the "good Nigra" who is loyal to his "masters" and thinks it his duty to bear, rather than to combat, oppression. Uncle Toms are about as popular with the new Negro as good, loyal Tories were with American Revolutionaries.

This comparison of Negroes with the Fathers of America is no casual analogy. In Gregory Swanson first, in T. J. Sellers especially, but also in almost every educated Negro I contacted, I was confronted with a Jeffersonian grasp of the American ideal of liberty, justice, and equality for all which made me feel like a visiting tourist talking to a native citizen who is proud of his land.

In the past, references to "our founders," "our great freedoms," "American democracy," "the great ideals of this nation," and so on, had reached me simply as clichés, reeled off by the yard in political speeches in election years. When small, I had learned our important historic documents by rote, and in daily conversation since, it was rare that anybody in my circle said anything about our form of government except to complain about its wastefulnes in action or about how much it had gone down hill since the wrong political party had been in power, or how hopeless it was for the right party to try to get the mess left by the wrong one straightened out in one short administration.

But Negro leaders talked often about our founding fathers, our ideals, and our democratic principles, and although they used the same familiar phrases, these were comparable to what I was used to hearing in the same way that a man is comparable to a figure in a wax museum. I came alive inside with the realization that in the Negro's mouth these phrases were not clichés or excess verbiage, but straightfoward expressions of vibrant, living truths. Breathlessly I listened and felt rising in me an undreamed of response to, and understanding of, what our nation is supposed to be.

In the fall of 1951, when I attended my first Virginia State Conference of the National Association for the Advancement of Colored People, I was confronted with a virile idealism, an awareness of what man must have for manliness, dignity, and inner liberty which, by contrast, made me see how easy living had made my own group into childishly unthinking people. The Negro's struggles and despairs have been like fertilizer in the fields of his humanity, while we, like protected children with all our basic needs supplied, have given our attention to superficialities.

The average white American of today never thinks about the innate dignity of man because he has never had his dignity challenged. He probably has never known even one man who has. Since such a thing is outside his experience, it cannot be for him a living issue.

Against the unmolded clay of my inner American citizenship, I now felt the impress of those for whom the dignity of man was a vital truth. It was the same with the principles of freedom, equality, and the right to chosen pursuits. I had never been aware of the rich nature of these fulfillments, because my experience had never included a lack of them.

I think it was during a speech by the Rev. Francis L. Griffin* of Farmville, Virginia, that I suddenly saw how the situation of Southern Negroes in many important ways resembles that of white Americans before the Revolution. England oppressed and discriminated against us in some instances much as whites now oppress and discriminate against Negroes. And the result has been the same—a fierce awareness of the dignity of man, of the rights of every individual, and a certainty that brotherhood is the destiny of the human race.

It was this awareness, born of oppression and hardship, which gave to Jeffersonian Americans the spiritual brawn which made our nation great. But it has grown weak among us. As our memory of oppression faded, the awareness faded, too. Only in our minorities, oppressed as our colonies were once oppressed, does it still have the powerful thrust

---

* The perceptive Negro minister in Prince Edward County whose parishioners were the plaintiffs in the original suit against segregated public schools which resulted in the historic Supreme Court decision of 1954 outlawing segregation in public schools.

which originally drove its expression into our constitution. Our minorities alone are in a position to know what the fathers of our democracy were talking about.

I looked at the dark, intent faces around me, and I heard old phrases made new because they were understood, believed, and lived by. Here was an America more real, more alive, more lovable, than the country I had always vaguely and complacently called my own.

Part 2

BLOODLESS DESTRUCTION

CHAPTER 1

"I Will Not Run"

ON MAY 17, 1954, THE SUPREME COURT ANNOUNCED ITS
South-rocking decision, outlawing segregation in public
schools. The news came in two parts, the first a simple announcement that this decision had been made. I drew a long
sweet sigh. I felt wonderfully free.

Later, when details were broadcast, I was shocked to learn
that no date for implementation had been set. Everything
I knew about the South, both from intuition and observation, screamed that this was a fatal error.

Voices all around me said, "How wise!" "How fair!" "Now
the South will have time to adjust."

"Adjust!" I cried. "It's as though, after an election, people
were left to decide wranglingly, without rules, when the
new president would replace the hotly supported incumbent.
It delivers the South, like a gift-wrapped package, to the
rabid race baiters."

Disapproval greeted me from other white liberals. They
wanted to rejoice. One even hinted that I was among those
who prefer trouble to success. "There're plenty of other
aspects of segregation you can work on," he said.

I felt justly rebuked. What a time for me to join those who
gave reality to the Southern bogeyman by assuming his

existence! I must be infected with the very defeatism about integration I had myself been fighting! Yet I knew such defeatism was rooted in two illusions—belief that everybody else is prejudiced, and belief that prejudiced Southerners can't be changed short of the grave. I had collected nearly as much data disproving the latter hypothesis as the former.

For instance, according to the latter, the twenty-one per cent of our faculty who opposed integrated graduate schools in 1948 should still be opposing them. Yet four years later, when a student, Thor Anderson, polled our faculty under the auspices of the YMCA, selecting at random 89 professors, all but three per cent checked "no objection" to integration, even at the undergraduate level. But my favorite story of dramatic switch concerned the University of the South in Tennessee.

In June 1952 the board of this institution met to debate whether Negroes should be encouraged to enter its theological school. Encouraged was the right word since none had yet applied. Privately owned by 32 dioceses of the Episcopal Church, the school was not subject to Federal rulings, so any move would be voluntary. After heated discussion it was decided that "the time was not yet right for integration." The board voted against it 45 to 12.

So far no surprises. But when the decision was announced, protests began to pour in from Episcopal white Southerners. Eight of the nine members of the theology faculty announced that they intended to resign. The students polled themselves and reported that ninety-seven per cent favored admission of Negroes. Letters and petitions arrived from the Women of the Church. Church papers published editorials urging reversal of the "unjustifiable decision," and a transplanted Southerner, Dean James Pike, later Bishop of California, refused an honorary degree on the ground that he didn't wish to be associated with "white divinity."

The board decided to spend a year studying the pros and cons of the situation and to vote again in the light of what they would learn. What pros they unearthed is a matter of conjecture, but it is a matter of history that they met as agreed in June 1953 and voted 78 to 6 in favor of integration.

I thought this incident demonstrated the readiness of white Southerners to change once they were aware of the facts and issues involved. I also had statistics showing that in newly integrated units of the armed services, almost invariably it was Southerners who made the first overtures of friendship to Negro members.

Actually, common sense argued that the attitude of normal white Southerners toward Negroes would be easy to change. Negroes have always been kind and courteous toward us, and our happy childhood recollections of them ensure good feelings upon which right thinking could be speedily built. Everywhere in the South, partly from natural warmth, and partly no doubt from expediency, Negroes have made a point of being agreeable to white children.

Thus our prejudices for the most part are rooted, not in feelings of aversion, as outsiders think, but simply in a relatively shallow misconception that all Negroes are child-like intellectually and unacceptable socially, fifty years of segregation having prevented us from contact with those of another caliber. Each of us has known many who seemingly never lift their minds above the simple chores they live by, and most of us have not known even one whose cultural opportunities have been comparable to our own. Therefore, until something happens to shatter this misconception, despite friendly feelings, we can't imagine equality relations with them.

Wasn't it inevitable, I thought, that for those of us who were normally flexible, only a few good object lessons would be needed to start an inner vibration which could shortly result in this shattering of the misconception?

I tried to accept my heartening collection of examples of what had happened as conclusive evidence that more would happen. I partially succeeded. Total success was prevented through my being often asked to speak to small groups of white students and adults about the integration issue, as well as to large ones of Negroes. Both because of a life-long terror of public speaking, and because it seemed an effective way to deal with such a topic, I conducted these meetings with a short talk followed by a long question period. This put my fingers on the pulse of current thinking and feeling, and by midsummer 1954, despite my best efforts to see only the good, I was aware that a dark cloud was descending on the mind of the white South.

Something deep in me insisted that the changes I noted must not be attributed to chance or run-of-luck in the nature of my audiences. A developing pattern was emerging. There was a new all-of-a-pieceness about what our Southern politicians and press had long been saying and the type of response I was now getting from my discussion groups.

Individual thinking and open-mindedness were retreating. The Southern Code was being reaffirmed, whereas a few months earlier it had been critically examined, often even challenged. People had listened to me with keen attention, had weighed new information and arguments in support of changing old customs. Now their ears were closing.

They were speaking less from the heart, conforming, becoming wheels in the machinery of "the Southern way of life." When Negroes were being discussed the leading emotion was no longer a free and creative one of love. It was the rigid, mechanical one of fear! People still claimed love, but their eyes, tones, questions, and answers belied them.

My conscious mind rejected this information. Love, I assured myself, would soon come forward again. I must therefore thrust my finger into the dike until strong men of the South brought sandbags to hold back the dark waters of hate.

Hate? What was I saying? Normal upper- and middle-class white Southerners had never hated Negroes—that is, not good Negroes. Suddenly the wild insight caught me that propaganda machinery was pushing forward the image of the "bad Nigra." People were forgetting the good stereotype, and turning to the bad.

By force of will I thrust this realization into the well of my subconscious. My public utterances followed the pattern laid down by my conscious faith. Yet the contents of my dark well influenced my private thinking, and I asked myself questions I had not asked since 1951: Which of my convictions was I prepared to be martyred for? Which should I verbalize, act on, and which hold quietly until the climate of opinion was more temperate?

In talking with those who differed sharply with me, I began editing my words in an effort to achieve a comfortable semirapport. Many liberals, I told myself, thought this the only way to influence people, the distance between you and your intended convert being otherwise too great for real communication. Back in 1950 I had concluded that you can't hope to undermine an evil institution if you let it appear that you don't really oppose it. Yet those safe arguments of silent liberals seemed temptingly persuasive now.

Then one day as I made a doctored presentation of my convictions which brought me within "listening distance" of a ninety-nine-and-forty-four-one-hundredth-per-cent segregationist, something in me screamed an agonized protest, and my thoughts hurtled back to an incident in my childhood.

When I was about eight, a physician had prescribed, as was current custom, a horrid-tasting tonic. I dreaded my daily dose. One morning my mother prepared it and set the glass on the sideboard, saying as she moved toward the kitchen, "Drink it down quickly, darling, so you won't taste it!"

A cunning scheme took me. If I dumped the medicine and

put back the empty glass, mightn't she assume I had taken it without asking?

Grasping the glass, I sped toward the front door. My father chose that moment to enter. Guiltily I thrust the glass behind me (he probably wouldn't have noticed it if I hadn't) and said in a bright, false voice, "Oh, hi there, Daddy."

"What are you hiding?"

With bent head I fetched the glass forward.

"You were going to throw it out!"

He was a short-tempered man, not given to gentle rebukes. But today he sat down and lifted me onto his knee with a gentle calmness ominously out of character. From long experience, I knew he thought my crime too great for indignation.

"Promise me never again—as long as you live—to do anything sne-e-a-ky." He pronounced the word with terrible slow emphasis which made me see my deed as the essence of moral cowardice. "Always either take your medicine or openly refuse it. Never pretend to have done what you haven't done, or not to have done what you have done. Honesty is more important than anything that can happen to you. Never forget that!"

He kissed me, lifted me down from his lap, rose and walked away without looking back. His action said that he had told me what was right and trusted me to do it.

I stood motionless for a moment, then drank the medicine.

It was clear to me four decades later why I had remembered this incident. I claimed to be using "good strategy to win converts," but my subconscious knew I was just being sneaky about my unpopular convictions.

A few months after this insight, Irene Osborne, of the American Friends Service Committee, stated the principle of personal honesty in a form appropriate to current history. She was touring the South for the Southern Regional Council in an attempt to organize people of vague good will into effective action groups. I rounded up about thirty concerned persons, white and Negro, for her to talk to at a dinner meeting. Her good sense plus her calm, assured manner comforted and strengthened us. She said in part:

"You're probably wondering, 'What should my public stand be? What are the helpful things to say?' But if you merely try to say the effective thing, you'll soon be tangled in contradictions. The most effective thing you can say is what you really believe. State openly your honest beliefs. Your position will be stronger, simpler, easier to hold. You'll be spared many fears and conflicts."

In following this formula, I have found that a minimum of doubt and confusion results. Also, it forestalls that initial fatal step of flight before an advancing enemy—a flight which, once entered upon, has no pause. For when you run from danger, it ruthlessly pursues. Both fear and flight increase until, first dignity, then self-respect, and, finally, even common humanity are jettisoned, and you and your fear dash on, beastlike, caring only to save your increasingly worthless self. If a large number of Southerners had taken Irene Osborne's advice, a shameful page in our history would not have been written.

In this mechanical age, we seem to confuse animal psychology with mechanical processes. To stand one's ground in the path of an advancing machine is certain destruction. Not so, however, with living creatures. In nature, small animals who will not take flight but are prepared to fight till death, often are undisputed masters of larger, potentially more dangerous ones who habitually run when the battle gets rough.

If you are country-bred, you may have seen a dog—whose long-enjoyed, matchless sport has been pursuit of a barnyard cat—suddenly one day dash yelping from the woodshed, the cat in hot pursuit. What changed the dog's character so drastically? Nothing. He was just what he always had been, but *the cat had kittens.*

Boys in tough neighborhoods early learn that to fight it out, even if beaten, is to be respectfully let alone next time, whereas to run is to be forever chased. A historian once told me that in many big battles surrender took place on the eve of what would have been victory had the defeated army held out one more day.

I was raised to believe that flight is cowardice, cowardice self-destruction. The simple adage, "If you run from anything, it will pursue you," was so consistently acted on in my family that I can't even put a face on the chief actor in a scene from my childhood which dramatized this truth. It may have been my Confederate scout grandfather because he did things quite like this to detachments of Federal troops.

I probably was about five, walking with him (or my father, uncle, or cousin) through a neighbor's field when we saw a notoriously dangerous bull. He began a sort of prance toward us, lowering and tossing his head and bellowing.

I caught my companion's hand, and made what I thought was a sagacious suggestion: "Let's run!"

He replied evenly, "Oh, no. That will make him chase us. The safest thing is to go right on."

He squared his shoulders and swung into a marching rhythm which suggested incarnate power. The bull stopped prancing and faced us, head down, ready to charge.

Whimpering, I clutched my companion's hand with both mine, but I didn't pull back. I sensed greatness in this moment. Irresistible force was bearing down on an obstacle. Eternity was in its rhythm.

The bull stood motionless—waiting. I wanted to shut my eyes but I didn't. As I stared, the great black beast gave a short, frightened bellow, threw up his tail and fled.

My companion said calmly, "See what I mean? You can't

be chased if you don't run. Besides, if you don't run, you don't get scared."

"I got scared," I said.

"No, you didn't. Getting a little weak in your stomach doesn't count. If you're really scared, you act scared."

Often since, I've been glad to remember that getting a little weak in the stomach doesn't count.

This demonstration may have sired another experience which prepared me for the 1950's. My mother constantly warned me not to wander far from the house alone because I might meet a mad dog. She may have used mad dogs as a bogeyman to keep me within sight, but probably rabid dogs were her own single-shot fear which she automatically passed on to me. I grasped this sole terror of my childhood, made of it a recurrent nightmare, and lived in dread of bedtime.

The dream was slow torture. I am alone on a hill in sweet content. Then, far away, comes (though actually I think mad dogs utter no sound) the faint howl of a dog. I start to run, feet weighing tons, legs weary. Slowly the howl grows louder. Panic clutches me. Frantically I climb a tree. But as the beast—foaming jaws, red, blazing eyes—comes closer, the tree shrinks until it bends with my weight to meet the leaping dog. Or, dashing into an empty cabin, I bolt the door, but it slowly shrinks, the crack widening until the snarling muzzle pushes through. Whatever the details, the animal's teeth always met my flesh at last, and wildly screaming I woke.

One night as I lay fearing sleep, an inspiration came: The dream obviously hung on the chase, ended when I was caught. "I can't be chased if I don't run!" I whispered. "*I'll never run again.*" In the first quietness of soul I had known for many months, I fell asleep.

The familiar scene began. Alone on a peaceful hill I stood —then the distant howl. "I won't run," I said. It grew louder. "I can't be chased if I don't run!" The howl rose, grew thunderous. The ugly, foaming face came toward me. I clenched my teeth so tightly in my sleep that next morning my jaw muscles were sore. My heart pounded. "I will not run!" The dog sprang. His teeth sank in.

I woke, shaken but triumphant. This dream was as preferable to the old one as a bullet through the heart is preferable to death by torture. Moreover, I had *chosen* what I would do. With a peace which only conscious freedom knows, I returned to sleep.

Once again on the hill, I listened. No howl. I searched the distance. No black speck moved on the amber fields. I held my breath. No dreaded rustle came from the green woods behind. As fear and defeat had formerly risen in me, matchless ecstasy now rose. This was *my* world, not alien earth across which I fled.

The nightmare never returned.

In the summer of 1954, I thought often of the lesson this experience taught as across the South a specter of horror moved, coming closer. There in my beloved Southern meadows were those who crouched, thirsting for a chase. "I will not run," I vowed.

Because of that resolve I have a story to tell.

CHAPTER 2

The Public Education Hearing

BY AUTUMN, 1954, MY PUBLISHED WRITINGS ON INTEGRATION were close to a gross. Something over five dozen articles had apeared in Negro newspapers, chiefly *The Tribune* and the Norfolk *Journal and Guide*. About six dozen others—book reviews and letters to the editor as well as articles—were aimed specifically at Southern whites. Except for five published in religious magazines, these had appeared in Virginia daily papers, mainly the *Richmond Times-Dispatch* and the *Norfolk Virginian-Pilot*. I wanted now to try again to deliver my message in a top-circulation national periodical.

I wrote a piece reviewing reactions in the University community when Gregory Swanson was admitted to our Law School. I added the story of the switch in votes at the University of the South, some impressive opinion polls (like the one showing that most of us wanted our local paper to use courtesy titles for Negroes), some examples of how misled persons in key positions create an appearance of a whole community being prejudiced, and I included from my own experience several heartening stories of good will. Entitled "We Are Readier Than We Think," this piece was mailed out.

About the same time, Virginia's Governor Stanley appointed the thirty-two-man "Commission on Public Education" to study the school situation and to determine how much, and what kind of opposition Virginia should offer to implementation of the Supreme Court decision. With mixed emotions I learned that the Commission had decided to stage a public hearing. Persons with definite views on the school issue were invited to express them at this hearing. The Commission would, it said, study and weigh these views "impartially," after which it would present a plan of operation representative of the people.

Just how it was to achieve impartiality with neither a Negro nor a white liberal on the Commission was not crystal clear. Indeed, it was whispered in some quarters that every man on the Commission was a segregationist, these being the only persons in Virginia assumed by the administration to have common sense.

But even though biased, they were the appointed decision-makers for the state, and anyone with convictions on the issue had a clear duty to testify. That meant me. I felt as soldiers probably do when their officer requests volunteers for a suicide mission, but I felt this less because I feared the opposition than because I had a deep terror of public speaking.

When small I had loved doing recitations. I thought of my renderings as communications from soul to soul, and I assumed that my family's applause, praise, and frequent requests for more meant that others enjoyed them for the same reason—until one day I overheard my mother and uncle discussing them with laughter.

"I think the cutest thing is how she pronounces 'equipment'," Mother said. "On that high note of emotion, when she comes out with 'all the field cowhitment he could find' I wonder if I can keep my face straight another instant."

Listening, and afterward, as I wandered dazedly around

the house and yard, I felt as though a board was pressing into my chest—stiff, unyielding, cool. That evening I quietly refused to recite. I never recited again. I couldn't even read aloud to a small group after that.

The damage included oversensitivity to the almost universal gap between what people say about you to your face and what they really think. In 1955 this added to my punishment as I grew raw with public flayings.

But early in 1951 I realized that a person undertaking the role of "George" in the integration struggle must speak publicly as well as publish writings. So in the summer of 1952 I had taken a public speaking course at the University. Each day before class I said to Fear, "You shan't pursue me for I won't run." But it did not vanish like the childhood nightmare. Slowly over a period of years its power did diminish, then become intermittent. But even now, ten years later, though I have made hundreds of speeches to audiences small and large, friendly and hostile, and talks on radio and TV, the old fear still sometimes rises, wiping my mouth dry and my mind blank.

On the morning of November 15, 1954, the day set for the Hearing, it was less than two and a half years since my first frozen efforts at public speaking. My terror of audiences was still great and to it was added a new conception of the Dixie I loved—a nightmare specter of her angrily pursuing her human misfits. I slipped into my seat about midway in the enormous auditorium of the Mosque Theatre in Richmond, in my hand a brief speech urging immediate integration, and in my middle the cool, unyielding board.

The Commission sat on the stage, chaired by state Senator Garland Gray. Gathered in the auditorium were approximately 2000 people, white and Negro, ironically unsegregated. For the Public Education Hearing had been placed in the category of "private" to permit what once I called "bootleg nonsegregation."

Senator Gray announced that 143 people were scheduled to speak, and when he called a name, its owner must come quickly forward, mount the small platform at the Senator's right, and talk into the microphones which ringed the lectern. My board grew colder, harder.

The marathon began. Of the first five speakers, three were Virginia legislators, one a state senator. They all proclaimed that their constituents stoutly opposed integration. One said that only "chaos and confusion" could result from obeying the Supreme Court. Another urged closing public schools and setting up private ones—the suggestion which four years earlier had shocked me into writing my first letter to the editor. One stated that he doubted that there were enough members of the National Guard to force integration on his county.

Helpless rage saturated me. I had never grown used even to reading such insults to Negroes. It was worse to hear abuse flung in the faces—often kind, noble faces—and living hearts of those present. And these were Virginia's lawmakers who advocated flouting the law! I soothed myself with the reminder that it was well that this infamy was displayed at the beginning, since now every decent person present would be roused, and appropriate rebukes follow.

The next two persons called also were legislators—and these, I knew, were liberals. Praise God! I thought. Now we'll have an answer!

But my soaring thanksgiving, like a burst balloon, fell flaccidly back. Protesting neither against the public insults to Negro citizens nor the blatant recommendations that Federal law be defied, our liberal delegates mildly urged local option so that "communities willing to comply" with the Court order could do so "without being hampered" by those "unwilling." It was like saying, "It might be well not to force everybody to cheat whether he wants to or not, but just to allow him if he likes." And this came, not from Virginia's worst, but from her *best* leaders!

I now realize that courage was needed for career politicians to deviate even this meager degree from the popular position. Nevertheless, history will record, I think, that our liberal legislators were flung a challenge that day which they by no means met. Not only our Southern tradition of kindness and courtesy, not only the ideals of our nation and our professed religion, but also even minimum standards of civilized citizenship were desecrated by Virginia's elected representatives that day, and those whose duty was to oppose them blandly implied by tone and words that it was all quite allowable and that the desecraters merely held "different opinions" from their own.

For me the structure of our public morality crashed to earth. Above its grave a tombstone read, "Be tolerant—even of evil." Logically the next step would be to say to our commonwealth's criminals, "I disagree that it's all right to rob and murder, but naturally I respect your opinion." Tolerance is only complacence when it makes no distinction between right and wrong.

Enormous disgust rose in me. Across my mind marched the words from Revelation, ". . . thou art neither cold nor hot . . . I will spew thee out of my mouth." There was something morally nauseous about this timid half-lifting of a tiny, limp flag of decency when the need was for a trumpet call and a dramatic unfurling of the banner of professed faiths.

This failure of our liberal "leaders" went deeper than mere timidity. Not even a coward will allow the pillaging of what he holds most dear. If he lets his best be ravaged, he does not value it as his best. Something else is treasured more— his own safety. The shame of Virginia was deeper even than cowardice: Her sons and daughters did not care enough about those inner glories which once had made her great.

The Hearing lasted fourteen hours. I didn't stay for it all, but I heard sixty-eight segregationists, many of whom echoed the first five, and —other than myself—I heard only six white integrationists (of whom, incidentally, three were protestant ministers, and one was a woman representing church women) and six white "moderates." The moderates at best advocated minimum compliance or some method of keeping schools open no matter how much law evasion was involved. Of this pitiful, mixed dozen, half were from Northern Virginia—generally considered more northern than Virginian.

I also heard thirteen Negroes who, risking reprisals, without exception called for immediate compliance with the Court order. In quiet dignity and calm strength most of them ignored the insults, and pointed with steady fingers to the unimpeachable principles of justice, freedom, and brotherhood. Sad to the point of pain, I knew that they spoke and behaved as we all should have done, and as once I had believed most of us would. White adults in Virginia outnumbered Negro adults five to one, but only four individuals stood unequivocally with our colored brothers that day.

A sharper pain also stabbed. Who could more properly speak for freedom and equality than professors at Mr. Jefferson's University. Who could more justifiably speak concerning the future of Virginia's schools than the educators at our highest institution of learning? I knew how the majority of them felt about both issues, yet when the future of Virginia's schools and her allegiance to Jeffersonian principles were being decided on the basis of statements made this day, how many of our faculty were here to voice what they believed? Not one.

Still waiting to speak myself, I thought of Germany and the Nazis' easy strides to power, unopposed by those who could have halted them had they rallied in time. I recalled lines from the letter I wrote in 1951 which the *Richmond Times-Dispatch* declined to run and the *Norfolk Virginian-Pilot* printed with gratifying response:

"Of what use are intelligence and culture if they give one no support in the expression of his convictions? Of what value, if one lacks courage to make into an actuality the democracy of which we boast so unconvincingly abroad . . . In the commonwealth of Mr. Jefferson's birth . . . are there so few white people who will stand up and be counted for their beliefs?"

In a ghastly flash of foreknowledge I saw that the ugliest evils of our region would be allowed to revel unchallenged, while we stood by without emotion enough even to wring our hands.

As the opposition towered higher and higher, and I saw the piteous sagging of my side, within me the cold board pressed relentlessly. Would I, too, remain silent when my name was called? I thought of all the formulas I knew for conquering platform fear, and one by one they failed me.

Like most Christians, I tried everything else first, then as a last resort, prayed. My tension eased, my mind opened and the thought came: Concentrate on loving these people. Then you won't be afraid. But how could I love people I didn't know? The answer: Think about their troubles and their virtues.

So I thought, Everybody here has been in pain—some of them in pain worse than any I've known. And all have felt great fear, remorse, doubt, sorrow, and numbing depression. Some are feeling these even now. Then I thought: Everybody here loves someone, and seeks some light, and a better way of life, and has some virtue which I don't have.

A feeling of freedom, detachment, and wholeness stole through me, displacing the cold board.

"Mrs. Sarah . . . Patton . . . Boyle," the voice called measuredly. But my mouth and throat were not dry, nor my hands cold and damp, nor my knees weak. I rose, walked to the platform and stood among the bristling microphones with the ease of one chatting with friends.

I made no great speech, but I said what I longed to hear others say—that integration was not a vile dose to be drunk

϶ welcomed be-
re worthy, and

ould prefer in-
ϸthing we often
applaud those
rts involved in
be as great as
ʋays liked and
ιothing in our
ʋe get a little
ɔf our people
be willing, to
_____ ....ian ideals. I speak for all these
when I say to our leaders, 'Give us a *chance* to demonstrate
the ideals which we all profess!'"

My love lingered as I left the platform and walked up
the aisle. Suddenly a woman, white around the mouth with
anger, stepped out and confronted me, barring my way.

"You!" she said in a low, grinding tone which was soon to
become familiar to me as the voice of hate. "People like you!
Why—tell me *why* you're trying to mongrelize our race!"

Her face was full of fury, loathing; her eyes flat and
glazed. I had never been looked at like that—a look to
horrify, to freeze. But beyond my control, unbidden, up in
me surged compassion. Enveloped in it with her, I felt a
fellowship which outreached my desire or will. She was dear
to me. I knew how heart-torn and desperate she felt. I
wanted only to help.

Love your enemies. I saw this admonition now as simple,
sensible advice. I knew I could face an angry, murderous
mob without even the beginning of fear if I could love
them. Like a flame, love consumes fear, and thus makes
true defeat impossible.

CHAPTER 3

The Power of Positive Thinking

FOLLOWING THE PUBLIC EDUCATION HEARING, I STRUGGLED TO restore my sagging faith in the South. I reviewed encouraging facts, battled for the best interpretation, repressed negative thoughts. Reviewing the Hearing, I stressed the constructive.

How courageous was Mrs. A. J. E. Davis, who represented the Arlington (Northern Virginia—but don't think about that!) Council of Church Women. And what a brilliant, practical suggestion was made by the Rev. Carroll Brooke, urging that an educational program be instituted to prepare school officials, teachers, and children to meet the special problems of integration. The Commission should act on it! (Small chance they would—but don't think about that.)

How heartening that the Presbyterian Synod sent a representative to urge full support of the Supreme Court decision. (Too bad those Presbyterian laymen immediately repudiated the Synod's stand—stop such thoughts!) Remember how the representative of the Norfolk Ministerial Association rose after the depressing array of resolutions from various organiza . . . —(Stop it!) And remember how Ross Wheaton (of Northern Virgin—) urged that we move into integration "fully and without delay."

True, there were five times as many segregationists as white integrationists and moderates together, but this, I told myself, was a mere mathematical figure, and deep truth is found only in the hearts of men. I repeated approvingly, "Deep truth isn't found in figures, but in the hearts of men."

True, the right people had mostly been silent, but now would see they must speak. (They didn't see it in Germany —but that couldn't happen in the South!) As for the University faculty, they probably expected many liberals to speak up at the Hearing and thought their own voices wouldn't be needed. It was good, I thought brightly, that Virginia had had this awakening experience in time. Now her wise and kind majority would know their voices must be raised.

As for the ghastly array of resolutions from Parent-Teacher Associations and other groups begging for continued segregation, I knew better than to take them at face value. I had been present when one such resolution was passed. This was at a meeting of our county board of supervisors, where officials had blithely made up the people's minds for them. The chairman simply read to the assembled audience a resolution stating that "the mixing of races in public schools" would be against the best interests and contrary to the wishes of both races. The board instantly adopted it, and *only after that* threw it open to discussion.

Next day our local paper stated that the resolution had been adopted unanimously "at a meeting attended by 160," the implication for a casual reader being that it was approved by that entire number. Yet actually a prominent local Negro leader, The Rev. Benjamin Bunn, had at once risen to deny that integration was contrary to the wishes and interests of Negroes, and I had backed him up by denying that it was contrary to the wishes and interests of the majority of whites that I knew. As many white people then spoke from the floor in favor of integration as against it—sixteen white people spoke, eight for, eight against—but the resolution was already passed, and was duly read at the Hearing as a unanimous resolution representing our county. This was a typical example of how belief in the Southern bogeyman propagates itself. For action of this kind creates opinions of the sort it claims merely to support.

I eagerly scanned editorial pages for a flood of protest from institutions of higher learning, when their faculties had had time to read the declarations voiced at the Hearing. If even a few such letters appeared, I missed them. Incredulous, I decided that they must think it wasn't any use. My thoughts swung back to my article which a few weeks before I had mailed out. It contained, I thought, enough data proving widespread good will among silent Southerners to convince most open-minded people that firm leadership could pull us out of this moral tailspin. Summing up my points in the closing paragraphs, I had said:

"I do not claim that the whole story of Southern racial prejudice is a myth, but I do stoutly maintain that it is vastly exaggerated . . . A few emotional individuals bellow threats and hatred, a few sensation lovers join them in the din, and the large majority, composed of good-willed but easy-going and peace-loving citizens, cower back, mistakenly assuming that there is nothing they can do about it because their 'number is so small.'

". . . If from this good-willed majority a few firm leaders would step forward in each district, I think you would see an altogether different South emerging from behind the fog curtain of misconception and fear. Our chief need, I think, is for the realization that if we believe in justice and equality for all, we are not only on the side of right but also of the majority, and that we shall suffer no loneliness in our community if we stand up to be counted for what we believe."

These solid affirmations were well supported by little-known but well-established facts which might, if widely read, stimulate our leaders to come forth. I waited, and watched the mails. November 30th, two weeks after the Hearing, I learned that provided I could produce sufficient documentation for some debatable statements, the article would be published by one of the most widely circulated magazines in the world, *The Saturday Evening Post*.

I was dizzy with joy. My files were bristling with such documentary data. Proudly I sent off a batch calculated to knock the last eyebrow twitch out of a congenital skeptic.

Elated by the prospect of helping to bring out the best leadership in the South, I carried on with *Post* editors, none of whom I knew, a frivolous correspondence which shows how self-assured and at ease I was in my golden-hearted world. Asked by associate editor Ralph Knight to write details of my family life for his department "Keeping Posted," devoted to *Post* authors, I replied with a two-page run of foolishness telling all my most choice family secrets. He used it as the basis for a feature which said in part:

"Sarah Patton Boyle—who, by the way, is a cousin of the late General George Patton— . . . reports on how they have the darnedest way of living all around the clock. Professor Boyle, who teaches drama . . . , rehearses The Virginia Players evenings, then, being a photography addict . . . works in his darkroom—and often goes to bed just as his wife is getting up. This isn't *quite* as mad as it sounds, for Mrs. Boyle rises at 3:30 a.m. to work on her writing . . . She loves having people in for dinner, but at nine she pops off to bed, and the guests, taking this in stride, just sit around . . . until they feel like leaving. The only unhappiness in this family results from Professor Boyle *always* being in a good humor; this upsets Mrs. Boyle, who thinks a wife is entitled to an excuse for therapeutically blowing her top occasionally— 'but blowing my top at Roger simply leaves me feeling guilty.' Guess it's one of those burdens a woman just has to bear."

The reference to General Patton came about like this: When asked to write about my family, I casually, Southern-style, let drop the information that "Ol' Blood-and-Guts Patton was my second cousin." Mr. Knight came back with, "Was General Patton your cousin? When relationships get beyond first cousins, nobody can get so completely confused as I can."

Unable to resist pulling his leg, I replied:

"Dear Cousin Ralph: Now I thought I was giving such courteous consideration to your Yankeeness when I made the oversimplified statement that General Patton was my second cousin. Actually he was my first cousin once removed . . . It's like this:

"He would have been my first cousin if our fathers, rather than our grandfathers had been brothers. If our great grandfathers had been brothers, he'd have been my third cousin. Thus, my son, Patton and General Patton's children are third cousins, but Patton was General Patton's second cousin once removed. My grandchildren and General Patton's grandchildren will be fourth cousins, but my grandchildren will be General Patton's second cousins twice removed. It's a matter of keeping the generations straight, you see. If you were a Southerner and somebody said to you, 'I'm John Jones's fourth cousin twice removed,' you would calmly inquire, 'On your father's or mother's side?' Then you'd have all the dope.

"Do you grasp your lesson, Cousin Ralph? (For naturally you can work out a relationship with almost anybody you choose to claim. Maybe even we're 'kissing cousins.')"

I signed it, "Cousin Patty."

He replied: "Dear Sister Patty once removed: Thank you for the relationship lesson. Now I am so completely befuddled that I'll know better than ever to ask anybody about cousins again . . . Fraternally yours."

Shortly I received something sobering. It was the galley sheet of my article for me to proofread. The title, "We Are

Readier Than We Think" had been changed to "The South
is Ready for Integration"! My gentle, dignified marshaling
of unfamiliar but indisputable facts was thus presented as a
fanatical declaration of an untruth, followed by an inade-
quate effort in support of it—for no attempt had been made,
of course, to prove any such thesis.

Unfortunately, editors reserve the right to choose titles,
and use them as eye-catching headlines, while readers, on
the other hand, almost universally assume, not only that
titles are the authors' expressions, but also that they are
either keys to the theme or summaries of what follows. In
vain authors complain that the "headline" clouds their meaning and distorts their logic. But harmful to the theme as an
inappropriate title always is, never is it so deadly as when
the theme is controversial.

By return mail I pleaded for my old title. *Post* editors
were firm. It lacked reader appeal, they said.* After letters
and phone calls, we finally compromised on "Southerners
Will Like Integration." The editors were happy. I was not.
But though it had little connection with my thesis, at least, I
thought, it was true. When finally they got around to integration, they would indeed like it. Like Christianity everywhere, integration in the South had "never been tried."

Publication date was set for February 15, 1955—the February 19th issue. As it approached, I felt little apprehension.
Even the new title couldn't neutralize the facts I had set
forth, I believed, and if taken seriously by the *Post's* approximately seventeen million readers, knowledge of these
facts could change the darkening mood of the South. I confidently asked friends in many social categories to watch for
it, joking about its world-shaking importance. "Oh, you'll
know when it comes out," I quipped. "There'll be banners
on all the stands."

This was said as one might say, "You can tell which house

* For the record, Mr. Knight was not in the title-editing department.

I'm visiting by the red carpet and the brass band." But on publication day, as I eagerly headed for the nearest newsstand, I could see from almost a block away that banners really were there. They'll think I knew and was boasting, I thought, and all the jokes I had made marched before me sounding silly and conceited—quite different from when I had made them.

I parked, and studied the banners as I walked toward them. They said something like, "Southerners Will Like Integration, Claims Virginia Housewife." Friends to whom I had made my banner cracks included many I briefly but pleasantly brushed against in daily errands. Some—postal, and grocery clerks—I saw more often and viewed with more affection than I did most of my faculty and professional friends. Thus my embarrassment over my boner extended wide.

The first friend I contacted that morning naturally was the young man who worked at the newsstand. I grinned at him sheepishly and asked for several copies of the current *Post*. He handed them over with hard eyes and cool silence, so I retreated to my car before looking at them.

The article was headlined on the cover. You couldn't miss it. With the *Post's* normally large circulation, plus aid from the banners, readers might number twenty million. That was good. Or *was* it? I turned to the article quickly.

The title leaped from the page, "Southerners Will Like Integration." Underscoring "like" gave an effect similar to the title I had vetoed. A picture of me walking through the University with two Negro medical students was blown up large and placed under the headline title. *Post* editors probably intended no such implication, but I could guess how amalgamation-minded segregationists would interpret it. The fact that I was more than old enough to be the students' mother wouldn't hamper the imaginations of these segregationists.

The whole presentation of the article made it clear that
The Post hadn't seen it as the dignified plea for better intergroup understanding which the actual wording set forth, but
as "a spectacular." I knew better than to feel exploited. It
had often happened to me—as to most professional writers
—that publication of my writings revealed a big gap between my interpretation of my work and that of the pur-
chasing editors. But heretofore it had mattered less.

I drove to the University Post Office for my mail. There
were seven letters in my box from subscribers who got their
Posts early. Three were of the cheers-for-you variety, the rest
were attacks—based entirely on title and picture, no reference to my data.

Back home, I handed Roger the magazine without comment. I wanted his reaction uncolored by mine. He looked
at it and flushed. Neither of us said anything.

The rest of the day I stayed home and kept busy. Toward
evening two faculty wives phoned. One said she had been
hoping for a long time that some such analysis as mine would
appear, as it confirmed her own observation. The other was
bursting with enthusiasm:

"It's the best thing that ever happened to the South.
People will see the whole segregation issue in a new light."

Neither woman seemed to see anything amiss in the title
and picture, and my optimism returned with a bound. Obviously only the rabid few would fail to respond constructively to my forthright call for support of the highest Southern
Tradition! Would I never learn not to torture myself with
negative thinking?

At one-thirty that night I received a phone call from
Atlanta. The man said he represented the Georgia White
Citizens Councils—the White Citizens Councils being
cousins of, though milder than, the Ku Klux Klan. He wanted
to know whether I was sincere in what I said or was merely
trying to exploit the South's plight. He was courteous, al-

most gallant, and fitted my sterotype of the nonpsychotic Southern segregationist. We argued gently for an hour and fifty minutes (he said the real estate business was good and he could afford it) and as the conversation progressed, I thought I made some impression on his prejudices.

Once, though, he issued a grim warning: "Don't ever come to Georgia. We'd run you out of here!"

"No," I replied, "you'd be gracious and cordial—as Georgians always are to strangers."

When he chuckled and said amiably, "I guess you're right," I wasn't surprised. To me it was just another proof that when you appeal to people's best, they respond with it.

After he hung up, I slept peacefully, and rose looking forward to errands in town. They would afford an opportunity for a spot survey on reaction to the article. Before leaving the house, I got another long-distance call. It was from a reporter in a Virginia town where I had recently spoken at a meeting of the National Association for the Advancement of Colored People. I answered his questions with cordiality and frankness. Pleased with the interview, I asked him to send me a clipping of what he wrote. Then with eager anticipation, I set out to do my errands and get my mail.

CHAPTER 4

The Middle of the Pyramid

EIGHTEEN LETTERS WERE STUFFED IN MY POST OFFICE BOX THAT morning. I read them in my car. Eight were applause, ten attacks—ranging from well-argued opposition to threats and obscenity.

As I read each letter, I made notations on the outside of the envelope so I would never have to read the bad ones again in order to classify them. When I had finished reading and sorting them, I sat trying to push back the bad, and pull forward the good ones in my mind. I felt rather sick. After a time, determined to answer all letters of support, I went back into the post office for stamps.

My favorite mail clerk was at the window. We had often exchanged jokes, sympathy, and other social treasures. I smiled at him more cheerfully than I felt, and said:

"Good morning. My mail is rather heavy today. Now I wonder why!"

He neither smiled nor replied.

My fingers trembled slightly as I opened my purse and put three dollars on the counter. "Fifty twos and fifty threes, please"—for cards were two cents then, letters three.

Silently he laid them down with my change. I picked up the lot and left.

The shoe repair shop was near a newsstand, and a copy of the *Post*, open at my article, lay on a chair as I entered. Looking at my friend behind the counter, I knew that even if I could manage a cheerful greeting, it would be unfitting. His expression didn't resemble that of the postal clerk, who had looked as though I had a running sore on my face. The shoe repair man's eyes were hurt, incredulous. You would expect a man to look that way at a respected neighbor caught stealing.

I offered my ticket and he went for the shoes. "That will be one seventy-five," he said in a low, flat voice.

Back in my car, I sat for a while without starting it. There was no need to wonder what these men were thinking. The letters told me. I wanted to go home, creep into my room, and shut the door. But when you start hiding, where do you stop? I rested a few minutes, then threw the car in gear and drove to the grocery.

A man worked there who once had owned his own store. When he grew too old for responsibility, he still wanted contact with the public so he accepted in a friend's store a tiny job advising customers and making price cards. Though he had little formal education, his brilliant mind was fed with good reading, and down the years I had enjoyed discussing with him a variety of issues, including segregation, on which we saw eye to eye. When I learned my *Post* article had been accepted, I showed him a carbon copy, and he expressed delight, calling it "a real eye-opener." Later he had commented that he couldn't wait for it to appear.

This morning I flew to him like a homing pigeon. Then I was sorry. His eyes avoided mine. He fumbled clumsily among impersonal comments. I moved away, puzzled even more than hurt. He was an individualist, and he had liked the article when he read it. Could other people's reactions

make so much difference to such a man? My stomach felt
as if I were descending in an old-fashioned elevator.

The manager, checkout girls, and clerks were as polite
as they would be to a stranger, but a shade more distant
—all but one. This young man looked at me with sad sympathy. He pointed out the day's specials with that little
dip in his voice used in addressing very ill loved ones. I was
grateful.

As I paid for my purchases, a senior faculty wife of slight
acquaintance approached. She saw me, yet was smiling. I
pushed up the corners of my mouth. Before she reached me
her clear voice rang out:

"Just let me touch you. Never was I so proud of knowing
anyone!"

I felt as if something messy and clinging had been wiped
away. To her my article was a call to high, not low, values
in man. Once more I felt clean.

Looking into the gentle eyes of this delicate-featured,
white-haired Virginia aristocrat, I thought for the first time
in a long while, "Blood will tell!"

Readers from other parts of the country may wonder why
I instantly identified the behavior of this one individual as
a class reaction—especially since outsiders usually assume
that it is the Southern "aristocrat" who is most disdainful
 of his dark brother. But in the South I think it is fairly well
known that the greater part of our race prejudice is vested
in the lower classes—also, that in general their prejudice has
an uglier emotional tone.

Class characteristics are always hard to pin down because
of many exceptions and much overlapping, but despite these,
there is an easily distinguishable dividing line in attitudes
toward the Negro in the white South's topmost class and
in her lower classes. In addition to the educational factor,
the chief reason for the dividing line is simple and obvious:

Until wages took their first big jump following World

War One, virtually all upper-class Southerners had Negro house servants who raised or helped raise their children. Naturally these children tended to grow up to become, like me, what our lower-class brother derisively calls "nigger lovers"—even though their love usually took a paternalistic form. Moreover, this attitude is often passed along—not too greatly diluted—for a least a generation or more to children who themselves had no Negro nurses.

Although fifty years ago every white family above the poor-white class at times had some Negro help for the heaviest work, this was not like having a colored girl live in your home the year-round, as the top class did. But even so, families who had occasional Negro help tended to feel friendlier toward all Negroes than did those too poor for any.

The latter had even to contend with the Negro as a hated economic rival, whose very existence kept wages down. Socially, bottom-rung whites had also an emotional stake in imagining a great social and moral gap between themselves and Negroes: It gave them pleasant status feelings. Sometimes they delighted in lording it over Negroes and humiliating them in all possible ways. The type of hostility that outsiders usually expect of all Southern whites is commonly found in this lowest group.

In short, paternalism is largely a phenomenon of the upper class where prejudice is only shallowly rooted—chiefly in the Southern Code. But in the lower classes, prejudice tends to be more firmly set, often deep in repressed and frustrated emotions. Many of the bewildering contradictions which daily meet the observer's eye in the South become understandable once you know that the same general pattern of daily behavior can cover reactions which are as far apart as tenderness and contempt.

If I knew all this, why was I surprised when my middle- and lower-class friends turned against me? Because by 1955 I was confused by my own accumulated data and a deep desire to believe in it. In 1950 and '51 I knew the above facts well enough, and even put them in an article addressed to Negroes published in *The Tribune*.

Later, as I ran down data for my "Facts and Figures of Good Will" series, I kept coming upon bits of evidence that perhaps the lower classes, too, were readier for integration than we thought. Just at this time my growing consciousness of the oneness of all mankind began undermining my social, as well as my racial, inner walls. Barriers of both race and class—distinctions which once had made me feel secure in my own superiority—now only made me feel lonely and limited. Wanting so much to believe that against brotherhood for all there were no barricades except the lifeless ones of habit, custom, and law, I just *did* believe it.

After a few hours of lower- and middle-class rejection, when my aristocratic friend swept up to me with an attitude so familiar and welcome, my heart leapt back to an earlier type of thinking and I found myself whispering, "Blood will tell!"

In the days which followed, I was sustained by applause from all "the best people"—well, nearly all. An old acquaintance did walk straight past me, without greeting, looking me over carefully as one might appraise an animal of known species but unknown breed. Three others reduced their nods to a two-fifths-of-a-second head-bob, and their smiles to a now-you-see-it, now-you-don't flash.

I got one phone call like that. With a stiffly frozen note in her usually lush tones, a woman answered my "Hello" with a hurried, "I enjoyed your article. It was well done. Good-by." I still don't know whether she thought she was being nice or knew she wasn't. But the fact that she called me with questionable heartiness took the edge off my trust in other calls. Unable to accept them any more at face value, I weighed voice inflections and choice of words for reassurances of sincerity—and sometimes I wondered.

But on the whole, for nearly a week persons who were distinguished either for family background or acquired culture (and these included most of the University community) approached me from all sides —on streets, in stores, at organization meetings, at parties—with apparently honest words of corroboration, appreciation, or praise. More than two dozen others let me know by telephone that they were with me from sole to topknot, reiterating how true my statements were and how much they needed stating.

A stream of acquaintances confided how they always had loved Negroes, how cheerfully they looked toward integration, and how glad they were to learn that many others felt as they did. Some even told me that since reading my article, they had been investigating for themselves and had discovered among their friends many unsuspected liberals who had carefully kept their opinions to themselves.

My highest hope for my work seemed justified: By revealing how many Southern whites were agreeable to integration, I was indeed encouraging each to declare himself. A chain reaction might result which would break the individual liberal's paralyzing sense of isolation.

Not since 1950 had I uncovered more convincing proof that "the best people" were ready for racial equality. Some whom I had been sure belonged to the opposition now stepped forward with expressions of sympathetic agreement.

For example, two days after the article appeared, I received a letter from an aristocratic old lady who had always carefully skirted mention of my integration activities— except once. That once, she gently warned, with the ludicrously contorted logic characteristic of the old regime, that truly "self-respecting Nigras" would think poorly of me for "lowering yourself to associate with them."

The letter she now sent me was written in a delicate hand, shaky with age:

"I hope, Patty dear, you can spare a moment to read these

words from the heart of your old, old friend—words of
gratitude for your article which I have just read: Gratitude
that you are giving us the leader we have needed to right
the wrongs so long endured by our Negro fellow citizens.
This leadership you have won by wisdom and patience,
overcoming the lack of sympathy and courage in those of
us whom you so justly describe as 'good-willed but easy-
going, peace-loving citizens.'

"Mrs. B—— found she could get the *Post* yesterday and
got copies for Mrs. S—— and Mrs. P——, who have always
admired your work—so sincere and so convincing. But until
now we never realized how criminal we have been in not
doing more to second your efforts to win justice for all.

"Pardon this wretched scrawl, Patty dear. You know I'm
too ill to rewrite it, and my ninety-two-year-old fingers won't
write as I want them to.

"Your old, old friend,

Laura D."

When I went to thank her, she said she had sat up late
writing, fearing she might die with her declaration of
support unmade.

The three old ladies she mentioned in her letter bore some
of the South's most distinguished names, and the youngest
of them was above seventy-five. Lifted by such proof of
love and loyalty, and surrounded by evidence that my own
stratum of Virginia society at least was all I had believed
it would be, I strove to bear philosophically the fact that
overnight most of my valued nonsociety relationships had
grown chill.

From the deepest reaches of my family tree I tried to
draw up the old sap of social snobbery, but my five years
of broadened contacts had cut the taproot. Qualities and
sensitivities which I had been taught to look for only on
ancient family trees, I had found plentiful on young shrubs.
My taste for exclusiveness was lost. Congeniality based

merely on similar advantages was not what I wanted any more. I didn't want "my place" in Southern society. I wanted only that new kind of fellowship I had tasted, which leapt easily across barriers of race and culture, background and occupation, mental capacity and education, poverty and wealth, handicap and privilege—which so lately I had thought possible for every human heart.

Traveling from a different direction, I had arrived shoulder to shoulder with Gregory Swanson when he said he wanted to be "just one of the fellows," not for any reason whatever set apart. Seeing myself as a scion of a small, exclusive group of the "best people" made me feel desolate now.

I had thought of the social structure as a kind of pyramid, its many strata cemented into a united block by mutual golden-heartedness and love. Negroes had been at the bottom socially, but also structurally: They were the most important to my heart. The middle section of the pyramid had been the great multitude of white "rough diamonds" who also undergirded my heart. "My own set" formed only the tiny top—a forlorn little thing without the love of the rest.

Was I really only a customer, a readily rejected outsider to so many whom I had thought of as friends? I concluded that likely I was. Resentment, similar to that of Negroes, probably was felt against those "on top" by all less educated or less socially privileged persons. To them it would be an agreeable belief that one of us "high and mighty" ones had done something reprehensible. "They think they're so much, but they do things we wouldn't do!" Indeed, yes, such a thought might seem pleasant.

As in 1950, I saw what I had believed was a lovely picture window become a cheap, painted backdrop. Again my heart ached. When it began to ease, it wasn't because it was consoled, but because part of it was numb.

CHAPTER 5

"Set Not Your Faith in Princes
or in Any Child of Man"
PSALM 146

ON THE THIRD, AND AGAIN ON THE FOURTH DAY AFTER MY
article appeared, between twenty-five and thirty letters
came. The number pro and con were about equal, and since
human tendency is to write protests more readily than
applause, I knew that much approval was indicated. But
my chest and stomach responded little to this calm knowledge. A large, heavy stone seemed lodged there.

Of course I had always conceded that our opponents had
some valid points. This could be taken for granted, since
numbered among them were some who were both intelligent
and kindly. And by all means we should give the devil his
due. But it was hardly minimum common sense to harp,
as some of these liberal letters did, on our opponents' shreds
of rightness to a degree where our own fundamental rightness was buried in verbal confetti. Suppose a defense attorney lent himself to proving how fair he was by reviewing
the prosecutor's case instead of setting forth his client's!

Again, as at the Public Education Hearing, I sensed a
deep sickness which sapped the moral vitality of our side.

Spiritually healthy people rally to the call of the highest they know. These liberals wanted to rally but seemed uncertain about what was the highest. They talked about being rational, fair, open-minded, about carefully looking at all sides, about tradition, strategy, caution, faith in man. Without definite conclusions, their minds went round and round, weighing, measuring, weighing—wheels turning in wheels, like an overcomplicated mechanism.

Mechanism. The word troubled me. It suggested a process by which one could be caught and held.

The opposition, too, was confused but at least it had an emotional power which our side lacked. It burned into one's attention. "What gets your attention, gets *you*." Fascist and Communist know this. But Southern liberals seemed to think it a virtue to be unobtrusive. It was ominous that they described themselves as moderates, ominous that they showed less concern for prevalent injustice than for appearing reasonable. They seemed mortally afraid of taking what the opposition called an "extreme stand," even though, since the issue was common justice, what they would really be accused of was *extreme goodness*. If there's merit in being temperate about wrongs inflicted on others, how easy to be meritorious!

Their attitude tied in with the current fear of being called do-gooder or "nigger lover." What sense did such fear make? Both epithets are really compliments! People seemed to turn now this way, now that, as if they had no inner moral compass and were obeying directions shouted by strangers.

Segregationists had a simple, clear-cut position which they held as a body: "We want to keep the Nigras out!" To be effective, we liberals also must take a firm position, without qualifications or apologies: "We want to let our brothers in!" This would have impact, and was so clearly right that we could march unafraid. For fear is a lonely feeling, a feeling of isolation. When one is right he is aligned with the central structure of the universe, close to the heart of Creation, and safe from the estrangement of fear.

In the larger sense, segregationists, although numerically strong in the South, were structurally weaker than we integrationists. They represented exclusion, separation, isolation, *dis*integration. We represented inclusion, wholeness, unity, brotherhood, integration. But most of us seemed to draw little sturdiness or certainty from the strength of our position. Some of my support letters, and most of the conversations I had with new-found liberals, were three-fourths justification for the person's failure to avow his or her convictions publicly. These explanations all pointed to one thing: Their exponents felt too alone to speak out.

Yet actually they were *not* alone—not in the above larger sense, and not even in the smaller sense, as my article had tried to show. In every community there were enough of us to form a vital, living body which could defend the South's greatest treasures if only we would stand up, able to count each other and be counted by those who had not yet chosen sides in the conflict.

Studying the letters, I strove not to see what I did see: That hardly one in twenty of the whites who cared enough to contact me revealed firmness of character or conviction necessary to spearhead a drive against an evil status quo.

I pushed my thoughts toward the few letters which were not tentative or timorous. Some of those who had applauded on the phone and face to face sounded bold and sure. I pointed out to myself that even a few persons of unyielding conviction can alter an era. The Apostles were twelve.

Toward the end of the week, our local paper featured a letter from a man in Florida saying I was merely one of a few left-wingers and crackpots. "The article and the accompanying photograph are most revolting," he went on. "It is greatly to be regretted that the female author found herself in a position to bring such discredit upon the name of the University of Virginia which I had the honor of attending."

This was my first experience of public attack. I found it astonishingly embarrassing. It was like being sassed by your child before guests, or being openly rebuked by your husband at a dinner party. I didn't want to see people after I read that letter.

Yet surely, I told myself, anyone I knew would greet it either with loyal indignation or healthy laughter. Only a fool would take such a fantastic expression seriously.

In a couple of days two more letters appeared. One from Portland, Maine, said that in spite of my "honeyed phrases and doctored statistics," I couldn't convince him that I was working for the best interests of the South or the United States. I was, he said, working for my own pocketbook.

The other letter, from a prominent local man, gibed that my article had "made of the *Post* a funny book."

As I read those letters I thanked God that next day I was scheduled to be in Richmond at the charter meeting of the Virginia Council on Human Relations, offspring of the Southern Regional Council, the most widely respected of the organizations working for a solution to intergroup problems. Its method was educational, its staff composed of well-informed, well-trained people of both races who were painstakingly careful in gathering facts and making judgments. Bold in their stand, uncompromising in adherence to principle, they seemingly feared only misstatement and factual error. Operating now on a Ford Foundation grant, they were creating state chapters throughout the South.

The meeting surpassed my fondest expectations. Among the thirty-some men and women gathered there as our first board of directors, I saw bishops of three denominations and other prominent ministers, social scientists from several colleges, Ph.D.'s in many fields, and community leaders from several professions—most of them people distinguished by strong, calm faces and an air of authority. Here were both intelligence and character. A quick glance round the room was sufficient refutation of the segregationist's favorite tag for integrationists, "crackpot." Here was a nucleus round which liberal Virginians could confidently gather.

My article was often referred to at this meeting as having "struck the note needed at this time." All seemed to agree that our chief obstacle to integration progress was less prejudice than the white liberal's feeling of isolation, and that this feeling was seldom fully justified. The new state councils would go far in removing it, we hoped, and my article was thought to be a fine prelude to their launching.

Strengthened, I returned home to find in my mail a letter from a local stranger:

"What I have just read in *The Daily Progress* has made me see red. . . I just want to say that I'm so glad you wrote the article . . . I am very proud that we live in the same town and everyone here should be. More power to you. If I can ever be of help, please call on me."

Moreover, the paper featured that day a letter to the editor stating: "Mrs. Sarah Patton Boyle's splendid article . . . serves to remind me anew of a policy of your newspaper which I have long deplored . . . withholding courtesy titles from Negro citizens. . . I wish to go on record as one white reader who would NOT object to a change in your policy —in fact I STRONGLY urge it." It was signed and gave a local address.

Now, I thought, our side is mobilizing. Here was forcefulness to match that of our attackers. True, this letter specifically supported only one small step in the move which the challenge of integration called for. But no matter. If each one demanded the small next step which to him seemed most important, the army of justice and good will would march. I went to my rest that night in peace. Just citizens were becoming aroused. They would route the forces of disintegration.

In the days which followed I looked expectantly for a flotilla of letters in the paper calling for these many steps. There appeared only more attacks on me. Some were by local people, but South Carolina, Ohio, North Carolina, and Mississippi also were represented. Indeed, no lesser personage than the secretary of the (white) Citizens Councils of Mississippi wrote a lengthy piece implying that I was a Communist.

On my side one more brief letter appeared, its author firmly disassociating herself with me in general but declaring herself in favor of courtesy titles for Negroes. This was the last defense of my position to appear.

I still view with incredulity what happened. Apart from the two letters urging use of courtesy titles, no one publicly supported the principles—or any form of their implementation—for which I was being attacked. That persons could sit quietly and watch another clubbed for maintaining what they themselves believed, and not feel impelled to step forth and say, "Now, look! I'm in this, too!" was far from what I had been taught to expect of man.

Following the worst of the attacks, two friends did come to me with burning indignation. They both had high skill in expression and shared with passion my aims and principles. They were people to be reckoned with, so when they told me that they could no longer be silent, I was very thankful. That they would make powerful, forthright defenses of those great, warm truths to which we bowed equally low, I did not doubt. When at last their letters appeared, I was stunned.

One consisted of two lines pointing out the lack of logic in attacking me instead of "the issues dealt with in Mrs. Boyle's article." Had I not known, I could not have guessed on which side the writer stood.

The other letter was long, but even more than the first it disassociated itself from all that I was fighting for, and had I not been otherwise aware, I would have assumed that its author sided with the polite opposition.

"I am not going to discuss the rights or wrongs of Mrs. Boyle's article," it said. "Personally I felt she drew some very large conclusions from some very small premises." It then went on to an impassioned defense of freedom of speech, and ended thus: "Let us, rather, reflect on Voltaire's noble touchstone for such situations—'I disapprove of what you say, but I will defend to the death your right to say it.'"

This type of support from two of the most burning liberals I knew did more to break my spirit than all the letters of attack. A part of my shock lay in their evident unawareness that what they had done was not helpful and was one hundred per cent safe. I tried to concentrate on their *desire* to aid me. My gratitude only stuck in my chest and hurt. These letters were a terrible prophecy—one I was not yet willing to hear—of what could be expected of people when the final crisis struck.

As public attacks persisted, claiming that the facts I reported were half tommyrot and half lies, and no voice defended their truth or affirmed the principles which they illustrated, even those who privately expressed corroboration became silent. The warm social pond in which I bathed suddenly froze.

At church, at parties, and at other gatherings I found symptoms of embarrassment like those of my old friend who worked in the grocery store—and this time there was no clear voice which reinstated me with cleansing words of reassurance. Everywhere people avoided looking at me, talked faster than normal in addressing me, feverishly steered conversation along strictly impersonal lines, at the first opportunity latched onto someone else to talk to.

I was bewildered as well as humiliated. Where were the

many who in private had affirmed that they stood four-square behind the thesis and principles my article set forth? They had disappeared like smoke. The wave of approbation, I realized with a sickening thud, was individual reaction. It reflected only how each person felt as he read the article in his own home. Group reaction, like mob psychology, is not merely the sum of individual reaction.

I now discovered a fact which grew familiar in the years ahead. True feelings and motivation are discerned not by talking to individuals but by observing large numbers of people acting out a situation. Probably none of my intelligent acquaintances was conscious of being influenced by these manifestly irrational and unjustified attacks on me. Each would explain his or her behavior toward me on innocent grounds: She had a headache that day; he just then saw another friend he had to talk to; she was just preoccupied with personal concerns. Individually, each explanation would seem quite valid. But there was no explaining away the fact that there was an abrupt change in the social climate, that my contacts in general ceased to be a chain of pleasant little incidents and became a chain of small wounds.

Moreover, there are always a few who verbalize what others merely act out. These were some of the same vocal people who, clapping loudly, had voiced approval of my article before the public attacks began. They now let me know from behind stiffened faces that, after all, on some points they did disagree with me sharply.

Silence began to obtrude itself into nearly all my social contacts. The topic of integration was taboo when I was near. No one referred to the almost daily assaults on me in the press. Perhaps they thought it tactful, but I felt cut off. Unless I knew him well, I had no way of knowing whether the person I was talking to agreed with me or my attackers. Even if I knew him well, I could not be sure that a specific criticism did not make sense to him. In vain

I reminded myself that while mentally and emotionally playing the part of a Negro I had discovered how deceptive a seeming snub can be. The contrast between my social experiences last week and this week was so blatant that "positive" interpretations became mere caricatures of truth.

Often there arrived in my mail clippings of editorials and other features from distant Southern newspapers, attacking my article as a pack of lies and me as an opportunist. If kind comments were anywhere printed in the South my "supporters" failed to send them.

Among the undermining feature stories was the one by the young reporter who had interviewed me by long distance, and whom I had thought friendly. He twisted my every statement just enough to make me sound brazen instead of frank, silly instead of humorous, cheap instead of high-principled. For instance, where I said I joined the National Association for the Advancement of Colored People because I believed it was the *right* thing to do, I was quoted as saying I did it because it seemed to be "the thing to do."

I wanted copies to send as a warning to fellow crusaders. Writing to the reporter, determined to be both kind and a good sport, I told him that I knew he could have made the story worse if he had wished. I added, "Any time you'd like data from me, I'd be most happy to supply it. I've no secrets from the press, and I know what a tough job it is to gather data." I visualized him as repentant upon its receipt. Shortly I received both the clippings I ordered and a new one. He had written another scathing story, based on my letter, which he interpreted as final proof that notoriety was all I wanted.

I was stunned. I had held before me only faith in his basic goodness. Even after his unkind story, I had turned the other cheek. His response had been to haul off and slug it! But if people were basically good, they *must* respond to faith and gentleness!

That afternoon a local radio reporter phoned, wanting an interview. I was understandably hesitant, but consented to discuss the possibility. After frankly explaining my reluctance, I agreed to grant him one in a few days. Five minutes later, my radio being on, I heard him reporting our conversation as an interview. Apparently reporters regarded me as fair game with whom both ordinary courtesy and professional ethics could be suspended. I began to feel hunted.

Deeply bruised, I was still trying to pretend I wasn't. Tension was rising in me but I wasn't ready to admit it. Never had I needed so desperately to uncover my wounds to someone who would understand. My whole being called out for a listener to whom I could pour out my bewilderment and pain—someone who shared my belief that evil was just a bogeyman and that human goodness was real and full of power. Only such a one could grasp how it felt to make discoveries which could not be reconciled with faith in man.

I crept to my best friend and tried to tell her a little of what I had been going through. She drew back, eyes hurt and disapproving. Goodness always comes forth at the call of goodness, she said. I must always expect the best of people, and I must expect the best things to happen; then they *would* happen.

I attempted to explain that the shocks I wanted to talk about, far from having stemmed from negative thinking, had been a direct result of my expecting of people goodness which they failed to manifest. If my original childlike faith in their worthiness had not brought it forth, how could I hope that a pretense of faith in them, which was all I could now produce, would be likely to prevail?

To my amazement, instead of confronting the problem with me, she reacted with anger. I was "wallowing in the negative," she said. I must lift my thoughts.

With pain I realized that she didn't want to hear anything I had to say. My unhappiness was a threat to something more precious to her than my welfare—her own faith in the dream which was being destroyed for me. A feeling of desolation swept me. Though I didn't know it, this was only one of many future lessons I was to have in the hard truth that seldom does either the degree of your own need or the strength of the bond between you and another person count with him for much if anything so important as his own dream, fear, or ego image is involved.

As if I hadn't learned enough for one day, I now fully grasped the over-all flaw in my belief that positive thoughts were the key to destiny. Faith in them led inescapably to the conclusion that any time I ran into trouble it was my own fault, for had I held the right thoughts, logic insisted, nothing could have gone wrong. In times of deep distress, therefore, when I would most need a consoling faith to turn to, I could expect from this faith only to be confronted with an accusing finger pointing at myself, thus adding guilt feelings to my other pain.

In short, I saw that although there is a proper time and place for positive thinking, when perhaps nothing else works so well, used as a central faith, it has a *negative* result. Like all shallow philosophies, this contains the seeds of its own negation.

I felt weary and lonely as I took my departure from the friend whom I had never before turned to futilely. "Remember faith can move mountains," she said confidently as she kissed my cheek.

I remembered that Jesus had said, "Oh, Jerusalem, Jerusalem . . . ye would not!" If positive thinking was the skeleton key to hearts and wills, how was it that one of Jesus' own twelve——?

To avoid the negative, I saw, I would have to shut out many simple facts. Among these, that I had got over 125

letters from segregationists, many of them official condemna-
tions from various organizations, but from Negroes I had
got only a handful of letters, one phone call and two wires
—all from scattered individuals, speaking for themselves.

Although eventually I received full support from Negro
organizations and press, at this time not even their newspapers offered a clue as to what colored experts thought
of my article. A news story in the big Norfolk Negro weekly,
The Journal and Guide, contained long excerpts from the
article but no evaluation or other comment whatever. Had
I indeed, I asked myself, "only stirred up trouble," and in-
curred all this personal misery without bringing aid or
comfort to those for whose rights I fought?

"You're feeling sorry for yourself!" I suddenly accused.
"And whatever is true or false, whatever is right or wrong,
I know you shouldn't do that." After all, hadn't I known
from the start that opposing the status quo would not be
easy? Well, it wasn't easy. Just accept that, then go right
on opposing it.

I felt calmed. I had been running from evil by pretending
it wasn't there. I wouldn't run any more!

CHAPTER 6

The Wall

ABOUT TWO AND A HALF WEEKS AFTER *The Saturday Evening Post* published my article, the editorial page of our local paper featured a thirty column-inch attack on me reprinted from the Raleigh (N.C.) *News and Observer*. It was by a regular columnist of that newspaper, who was an expatriate of Virginia and definitely a part of our top social cream, her family being both aristocratic and distinguished. The following excerpts will give you an idea of her feature's impact:

"I am informed by . . . my brother, . . . former Dean of the University of Virginia . . . that so far as he knows, the reaction of Charlottesville people to Mrs. Boyle's article has been 'most unfavorable.' 'Revolting' is the word applied to it by some, with whom I agree. . . Thousands of readers of her piece outside the South, ignorant of conditions here and mistakenly assuming that she knows what she's talking about, will be grossly misled. . .

"She states that of 89 members of the faculty at the University of Virginia, 'selected at random' who were polled in 1952 . . . only three per cent objected to integration. . . . That's quite an odd figure, by the way, since three per cent of 89 faculty members is two faculty members and sixty-seven one-hundredths of another faculty member. . .

"Mrs. Boyle, so sensitive to injustice and all, says that when Swanson, the Danville Negro, was refused admission to the University of Virginia law school, she 'felt a twisting pain.' I assure her that the pain which twisted her then was as nothing compared to the excruciating one I experienced upon reading her piece. . .

"The smug assumption of superiority on the part of the author, evident in this piece made me blush, not only for Mrs. Boyle, but for another half-baked reformer, the one I used to be, . . . though never along this line. As they grow older, self-constituted reformers often gain insight into the basically neurotic nature of their ailment. And Mrs. Boyle, it would seem, is now quite old enough to know better. . . But, still, it's so satisfying—isn't it?—so pleasantly inflating for the ego, to lift high the torch to enlighten one's be-nighted fellow-countrymen; to be the inspired and inspiring herald of a bright, new day, a shining Dixie Joan of Arc . . .

"Publication of her piece undoubtedly netted Mrs. Boyle considerably more than 30 pieces of silver. For now's the time for the Southern 'liberal' to cash in! Northern publica-tions . . . ever eager to get in a whack at this region, should handsomely remunerate Southerners sanctimoniously super-ior to their regional mores. . . Practically any literate person in the South . . . should be able to turn a pretty penny by writing . . . pieces designed to sell the region down the river —an inspiring transaction, indeed!"

The humiliating effect of this kind of public insult is hard to exaggerate. You know it will produce malicious laughter, not alone among your foes, but even to some extent among those who might be classified loosely as your friends. Yet what tormented me most was its sheer venom. I had not realized that people in my own social group might feel so poisonously about me. When others had misunderstood, those in my own group had seemed so fully to understand that until now I had been able to believe total rejection of me was limited to members of other classes.

But now—just as the obscene and accusing letters I got in such numbers interpreted for me the frozen voices and faces of my less educated friends, this feature interpreted the abbreviated nods and smiles I sometimes got from faculty and professional friends.

I had maintained a dignified silence through all the other attacks but this I had to answer. In a letter to the editor, I wrote that since the statement of this columnist seemed to summarize most of the arguments I had heard against my article, perhaps this was the moment to reply. Those who disagreed with me, I said, seemed to be victims of certain false assumptions. These were that the title was the article's summarizing sentence, that I was a novice in this field and didn't know what I was talking about, that the article was a mere effort at sensationalism, that my data were meager, and that my data were inaccurate.

After each heading, I made a simple, factual refutation. Then I added that it was to be hoped that this columnist was not "entirely serious when she implied that reformers are basically neurotic, as this would rule out all our great political and spiritual leaders since the beginning of history. In closing I shall say that I'm sorry she has ceased to be a 'shining Dixie Joan of Arc' at a time when every armored arm is needed. For I think she has a good arm, and I have no doubt that once she used it well."

Later I learned that many people, even among the opposition, thought well of this reply. It is significant that at the time I did not get one phone call telling me so, and that only two close friends even mentioned it to me—so effective was the wall of silence that had risen.

Though I tried, I could not interpret this wall as mere misguided tact. I had often sadly observed that in times of turmoil and tension, people's images of each other become very mobile. Also, that a drastic change in one's image of a friend makes inner loyalty to him quite impossible, for he appears not to be the same person one had thought him. It is even possible that this is what happened to Jesus' disciples after declaring that they would die for him. Indeed they would have died for the Messiah. But when the highly respected temple officials treated him as a common criminal, the Messiah image of Him vanished, and suddenly he seemed just another crackpot rabbi claiming Divine annointing. For such a one, they had never promised to die.

I knew that to many people I didn't look the same after the attacks as I had before. They felt silly, even guilty, for having acclaimed me. One woman let me know that she had accomplished what many probably wished they could: From her memory she simply erased her rash acclaim. I chanced to meet her in a drugstore, and not having seen her since her congratulatory call of two weeks before, I warmly thanked her for it. She stared blankly, then said with an embarrassed little laugh, "Oh, *that*! I'd forgotten I did that."

A segregationist organization in Louisiana about this time made reprints of my picture in the *Post* strolling with the two Negro medical students. They clipped it to another sheet, headed "Segregation or Degeneration? The choice is yours," on which were printed pictures of white women dancing, drinking, and cuddling with Negro men. Although the price printed on this little gem was "$7 a 100 copies" it was distributed to members of the University faculty, the local Department of Health and Welfare, and elsewhere. One fact stood out: Some person or group in my community was ready to invest heavily in order to hurt me.

It became my common experience at parties, large or small, to meet at least one other guest who thought it jovial to needle me audibly about my views. At first I welcomed these incidents as well-meaning breaks in the wall of silence. But it soon became apparent that the needlers intended, not to laugh *with* me, but *at* me. And there was no break in the wall because anyone listening to the heckling merely jumped in with a new topic. On no occasion did anyone join me against a heckler. Sometimes a few people would be pointedly friendly after such an incident, but I was given no clue as to whether their behavior stemmed from compulsive good manners, common charity, or the sympathy of an ally.

The wall between me and others, which relentlessly grew taller and thicker as days passed, was not constructed entirely from their side. Indeed my own altered images of them, my own shocks and disillusions, were separating me from them more than their behavior. Nor was the barrier merely local in origin and operation. Letters pouring into my mailbox from all over the South, even from all over the nation, dovetailed with local experiences, supplementing and explaining them.

To share the view of humanity which I was now being shown, you must have a look at my personal mail. I said "personal," not "private," for offensive post cards were often sent me, and jibes and insinuations commonly appeared on the face of envelopes. A mail clerk seeing a card addressed to "Sarah Patton (nigger lover) Boyle" would be tempted to turn it over and read—to quote an example—"Your article in the Post is rotten! . . . I still think you are a *bitch*." Sorting my mail after taking it from the box, on finding such a card I once saw through the stamp window smirking glances exchanged between clerks I had thought of as friends.

The more than one hundred and fifty letters of opposition which by now I had received on my *Post* article can be roughly classified as discussions, insults, and threats. Clippings, leaflets, reprints of speeches and articles, and other literature were often enclosed to supplement the letter-writers' points. Favorites among these enclosures were features and editorial comment from various Southern newspapers blasting my article. After reading several of these, my long-flourishing faith in the integrity and responsibility of editors of large newspapers was gravely impaired. For example, after a lengthy assault on my article, the editor of one of South Carolina's most widely read newspapers made, without qualifications, the following incredible assertion:

"The NAACP, operated by white men with a few Negroes for front, has forced Northern papers to swindle the public by suppressing the pertinent, material information that a fugitive or a criminal arrested for some horrible deed is a Negro."

Now not only does that one sentence contain several statements which are untrue, but also they are puerilely and naïvely untrue, and moreover they are easily verifiable as untrue. One has only to look in on any NAACP meeting or visit a state office or the national office of the organization to see that it is run by Negroes with an occasional—*very* occasional—white helping. True the national president is white, but his function is primarily that of liaison officer. The real head of the organization is the executive secretary, who has invariably been colored. Even in the North the NAACP's white membership is small and in the South is infinitesimal—roughly ten per cent in the nation as a whole. I have attended eight Virginia state conventions in the last decade and have never seen more than a handful of whites among hundreds of Negroes. Very rarely is a white person offered a position in the NAACP—local, state or national— which carries any real responsibility.

As for forcing Northern papers to suppress news, even if it were possible for any organization to do this, the NAACP certainly could not. It has no power except that of an enforced United State Constitution, which its able lawyers insist shall not be ignored. That a voice like the *New York Times*, which the editorial went on to mention.

specifically, could be silenced by an organization of the proportions and assets of the NAACP is so patently ridiculous that one blushes to realize how many people harken to the paper that made this and similar statements.

Another editorial closed its abuse of me with this comment: "The publication of her articles, we believe, puts *The Saturday Evening Post* into the pamphleteering class with *Time, Life, Collier's* and other propagandists. . ."

Disturbing as were loose, wild comments from widely respected sources, I was even more disquieted by the writings of editors who tried to, yet could not, understand— like the writer of this editorial from a Virginia city:

"I happen to know the above Mrs. Boyle. She came to Danville once and stayed several days. My impression of her was that she was a person who sought to do good. . . How anybody who appeared to be as reasonable as Mrs. Boyle appeared at that time could get as far off bounds as she got in the *Post* article is more than I can understand. What she wrote in the *Post* didn't sound like the words of a person trying to do good."

Here I saw the wall between myself and other Southerners built with stones so firmly lodged that there was little hope of breaking through. I did not think I could state my case or reveal my intent more clearly than I had done in the *Post*. If after reading what I had said there, a friend—and I had thought of this editor as a friend—could not even believe I meant well, it didn't seem that words were of much use between integrationists and segregationists in the South.

CHAPTER 7

"Discussions"

THE ARGUMENTS AGAINST INTEGRATION WHICH POURED FROM my mail were based, directly or indirectly, on an assumption that Negroes were so far inferior to whites that association with them would be culturally, morally, and physically perilous to us. Disease, rape, and murder were believed to be ever-possible results. Starting with this assumption, the paranoically inclined imagined the existence of a terrifying "integration plot," supposedly instituted by Communists and/or Jews and/or Roman Catholics, with a view to weakening now, later taking over, the United States. Some made little distinction between these three groups of "subversives"!

Others had a list of subversives which was even more inclusive. I received one circular which listed as Communist fronts The National Council of Churches, United Church Women, YWCA, YMCA, Catholic Committee of the South, Community Chest, Red Cross, United Nations, and Supreme Court, besides (inevitably!) the AFL-CIO, Anti-Defamation League, National Urban League, and NAACP.

Pondering this list of organizations and groups whose purpose and dedicated effort are to implement the principles for which we as a people stand, I wondered uneasily how many of my countrymen were influenced by the accusation that all these were Communist. The implication was that Communists were the chief people in our nation who were seriously concerned with other people's welfare.

Though claiming to be anti-Communistic, such propaganda so strengthens the Soviet cause that it is hard to believe that Soviet leaders are not using, even if indeed they did not instigate, this means of undermining us from within. Here in America, where ideals of equality and brotherhood are held before us from childhood upward, what could more effectively prepare our people to accept Communism than to "accuse" the Communists of being behind every effort to implement these ideals?

Some of the enclosures I received were newspaper clippings and reprints headlining Negro crimes or quoting statistics interpreted with an anti-Negro bias, if not invented altogether. Some were so-called "conservative" periodicals which had no good to say about anybody who wasn't an Anglo-Saxon-Protestant-Southern reactionary. Some were reprints of speeches building the white racial ego, and leaflets and booklets containing "exposés" of assorted minority groups, immigrants, liberal government officials, social scientists, educated people in general, and any individual or organization that subscribed to the one-world concept or to the practice of the brotherhood of man.

This material was printed and spewed into the public lap by a variety of segregationist organizations, some national, some South-wide, others restricted to states or even communities. Besides the Ku Klux Klan and the rapidly multiplying White Citizens Councils, some of these organizations were The American Nationalist, the National Citizens Protective Association (very active in printing and distributing literature), the National Association for the Advancement of *White* People (italics mine), the Federation for Constitutional Government, the Southern States Industrial Council, the White Race Club, the (God help us!) Southern Gentleman's Organization, the Defenders of State Sovereignty and Individual Liberties (in Virginia), and the North Carolina Patriots.

One leaflet tried to prove that every recent liberal in the United States Government was a Jew, even claiming that they had all changed their names from stereotyped Jewish appellations (Roosevelt's "real" name was Rosenfeld, as I recall) in order "to carry forward subversion more effectively." A personal letter to me, signed by a segregationist club in Louisiana, had this to say:

"You're obviously a paid tool of Jews. . . Jews are working like vermin in dark recesses. Like jackals they sneak around and get fools or knaves to do their dirty work for them. . . If they can get the obviously inferior Negro race mixed with whites then the Jews can dominate the situation."

From Arkansas I received this "information" which seems to sum up the views of the worst foes of the National Association for the Advancement of Colored People:

"The NAACP, a communistic inspired hate organization, has authorized all black preachers to encourage all black females to bear all the children possible, legitimately or illegimately, to eventually out-number the white population and ultimately uprise and massacre the white race. . ."

J. Edgar Hoover, however, has repeatedly stated a very different view.

In a letter to the NAACP's national office, which he gave them permission to print, Mr. Hoover said: "Equality, freedom, and tolerance are essential in a democratic Government. The NAACP has done much to preserve these principles and to perpetuate the desires of our founding fathers." And in his book about Communists, *Masters of Deceit,** he says in the section headed "Communism and Minorities": "The NAACP's national leadership has vigorously denounced

* Published by Henry Holt and Company. Also published in paperback by Pocket Books, Inc.

Communist attempts at infiltration," then goes on to relate a technique used by the NAACP to foil Communist efforts which he calls "one of the most effective anti-Communist measures I have heard of."

But since unfounded scurrilous accusations and insinuations against opponents of segregation come constantly into the hands of Southerners who never see the refutations, they are read, and believed—often reluctantly—by some who are both intelligent and well-educated. Of course they reach maximum deadliness when expressed—as they often are—by persons whose positions lead one to hope that they would not make irresponsible statements.

The effectiveness of these attacks lies partly in the simple psychological fact that most of us remember conclusions more readily than we do either a train of reasoning or the data which support it. Therefore, when a demagogue proclaims in ringing prose that some organization is "said to be a Communist front," a few hours later most of his listeners think that a specific authority was quoted. They don't expect to be able to remember the authority's name. Even among intelligent people the phrase "it has been said" often has nearly as much propaganda power as an authorized quotation from a reliable source.

Few people realize that a statement taken from the Congressional Record need not necessarily be true, that, indeed, under Congressional immunity statements can there be made which would immediately incur a damage suit if made under other conditions.

Here are some verses from a twelve stanza "poem" circulated by the National Citizens Protective Association for two cents a copy.

> "Nine traitors to the white man's race
> Sat in our Court Supreme,
> And all agreed that whites and blacks
> Must join their mongrel scheme . . .

These 'nine white men' in Washington
    Would mongrelize our land.
They even have the gall to think
    We'll fall at their command . . .

The time has come, sure as the night
    Flees from the rising sun;
For white men to protect their own
    If need be with a gun.
A hundred million white men cry
    That they will not obey
This 'traitor-law' which would destroy
    The white man's U.S.A.

I laughed amusedly when I received this poetic diamond in 1955. Nothing, I thought, could help the liberal cause more than this revelation of the mental and moral caliber of the advocates of segregation. Later, I reluctantly held a different view. Couched in oratorical prose, during the next few years every thought expressed here was offered by duly elected representatives of the Southern people, including state governors and United States senators, and was implicitly endorsed at the polls by large majorities in subsequent elections.

Often my eager hope was that a speaker had gone too far and that, in large numbers, outraged consciences or enlightened minds would rebel. In no case did I see such rebellion. After five years of incredulous, tearful observation, I concluded that no idea is so degraded that it cannot be voiced in such a way as to render it acceptable to civilized people. We joyfully respond to any evil disguised enough to free our consciences.

Adolph Hitler was nearer the facts when he said that the greater the lie, the more readily it is believed. He came quite close to having a world conquest as proof of it. A startling lie gets your attention, and is remembered. Then sufficient repetition will dull its incredibility and at last make it acceptable—unless a clear-cut, unyielding standard in one's heart renders it forever incongruous.

Watching one ridiculous lie after another pound its way to acceptance in the South, I had disquieting musings on people's trust in one another, and on the conquering power of evil. I saw that until we have learned from sad experience to do otherwise, we automatically judge others by ourselves. Observing an action, we ask, "What would prompt me to do that?" then attribute the same motivation to the other person's act. Thus, truthful people, with no training in the earmarks of falsehood, more readily believe a lie than those who are liars. I was jolted. This gave evil an advantage I had not anticipated. I had always assumed that when lies and truths were placed side by side, all normal people could pick out the truths. From observation I now learned that, on the contrary—perhaps on the theory that truth is stranger than fiction—most people choose to believe the most spectacular lie.

In the same way, I learned that reason has little appeal, even for quite rational people, when its alternative is excitement. That was why I abruptly ceased to whisper, "Thank heaven, now they've gone too far and the decent Southerners will rebel," when a leaflet like the following would come into my hand:

"When in the course of human events it becomes necessary to abolish the Negro race, proper methods should be used. Among these are guns, bows and arrows, sling shots and knives.

"We hold these truths to be self-evident: That all whites are created equal with certain rights; among these are life, liberty and pursuit of dead niggers.

". . . We have been oppressed and degraded because of black, slimy, unbearably stinking niggers . . . If we don't stop helping these African flesh eaters, we will all wake up and find Rev. King in the White House.

"LET'S GET ON THE BALL, WHITE CITIZENS."

This leaflet was distributed to an audience of 15,000 people, February 10, 1956, when Senator Eastland addressed the Alabama White Citizens Council. The "Rev. King" referred to was twenty-seven-year-old Negro leader Dr. Martin Luther King—he who had stood on the torn porch of his freshly bombed Montgomery, Alabama, house, where his wife and baby had just narrowly escaped death, and soothed from the hearts of a seething black mob all thought of rioting by gently repeating newly living words:

"Love your enemies . . . pray for them . . . forgive them . . . and may the Father forgive them, for they know not what they do."

CHAPTER 8

Insults

SOME OF MY INSULTING LETTERS WENT TO SUCH INCONGRUOUS lengths in unconscious humor, that in the midst of feeling grisly I could sometimes laugh.

"Almost the whole Yankee press is composed of a bunch of sadistic South haters who will stoop to any depths," proclaimed one. ". . . Pack your bags and move to Yankeedom. The South doesn't need your sort. Your article is downright sickening . . . Your frequent reference to prejudice is insufferable. I for one am not prejudiced."

Another said, "Your article disillusioned me. I did not believe that there was another American white woman with a principle as degrading as that detestable Jewess, Eleanor Roosefelt [*sic*]."

And, of course, I heard this familiar note struck: "Respectable colored people are contemptuous of whites who lower themselves to mingle with them."

Accompanied by a clipping reporting an assault by a Negro man, one letter castigated me for wanting to "force association" with such people, then gravely stated: "You have never in all your life read in any paper nor have you any evidence that white boys ever assaulted or raped a white or colored girl."

Referring to the Supreme Court and Chief Justice Warren, one snarled: "Why don't you join the Earl Warren Minstrels where the propogation [sic] of mulattoes is the chief thing?"

Another stated tersely: "We have read your nauseating article in the Jewish propaganda magazine."

Many of my addressers were so angry or disgusted that they had difficulty with salutations and closing phrases, being unable to bring themselves to begin with "dear" or end with "yours." The latter problem usually was solved simply by breaking off suddenly after a final invective and signing their name—or, more often, some selected pseudonym.

Salutations showed more variety. Here are only a few, culled from many:

"Mulatto Boyle:"

"Nigger-lover Boyle:"

"Scalawag: your insidious, repulsive article . . ." Etc.

"You old fool: We don't want to mix with you or the Negroes."

"Dear Boil: Your article was the rottenness [sic] thing I ever read."

"Mrs. Boyle: You slut. You should be ashamed!"

"White trash: You're more repulsive than the worst Negro . . ." This last was signed "The Southern Gentlemen's Organization."

Some of the more shameful vituperation is as follows:

"When a white woman will sink to your depths for the cheap price of a magazine article, then the most charitable explanation is that you have reached that period in your forties which makes some weak women irresponsible."

"We—a chartered organization dedicated to fighting communism and mongrelization—were discussing your fanatical attitude, and we decided unanimously that either you are a Northerner or a Southerner with Negro blood."

"You are a disgrace to the South. You are a yellow-belly and a scalawag. Go North, nigger lover, go North."

"Of course a lot of old women have to fall back on niggers when they can't get white men into bed with them any more."

"You white trash! People sure will do anything for money, won't they? The only people who believe in integration are the people who get something out of it and the people who are crazy. I don't think you're crazy."

"It is plain that you have Negro blood or you would help whites get ahead instead of kissing the back sides of Negroes. Drop dead you dirty nigger lover. I mean every word of this."

"Trouble makers like you keep the colored people stirred up. If such as you would keep their mouths shut, there would be no trouble between the races."

"You stinker! I hope you get all the Negro men to rape you that you seem so anxious for other people to get. You're no better than the lowest and dirtiest of them. You have worked hard to get the Negroes to attack white ladies on streets, in the home, bus, school, churches and everyplace, you stinker. I heard a man say of you 'that—low trash can write anything!' That's the way you are thought of. Get out of our nation and go to Africa with your buddies. There's where you belong."

"How much did the NAACP pay you to write this?"

"In the picture you're standing as close as you can get to that nigger ape."

"Real Southerners are ashamed you're white."

"I think your article is a pack of damned lies."

"Why don't you leave Virginia?"

"I'm ashamed of having gone to the University of Virginia since it contains such as you."

"You're a perverted homemade Yankee and scalawag."

"You're probably ostracised by society and take this means of getting even."

"Your article is unfair and contemptible."

"Your article is disgusting, untrue."

"May God have mercy on your soul."

"I hope your daughters soon climb in the arms of black, stinking, greesy [sic] Gigger-boos."

From Palm Beach, Florida, came this brief note: "Sarah P. Boyle: Re: Your article in the Saturday Evening Post. You dirty, lying, nigger loving slut, I hope the nigger [obscene word] and nigger lice adhere to you. Drop dead you dirty slut."

From Maryland came this one:

"Perhaps your husband is impotent and cannot satisfy your desire and you have heard the reputation of negroes as boudoir bandits and how they handle those black poles of theirs. Some perverted women like it that way."

And from Brooklyn came this:

"Mrs. Boyle—like other over-sexed whores who can never get enough you turn to sucking nigger [obscene word]. Go to Harlem (NY) and see the hundreds of white whores pecking for niggers. Few white men, very few, doubt that when a white woman comes out for niggers that she gets the belly [obscene word] ed off her. In your picture in the Post (Sat. Eve.) the look on your face *proves it* . . . A white *MAN*."

It was after reading mail like this that I had to look into the faces of those who had always seemed the great middle section of my pyramid, upon which my heart rested. When I saw eyes and mouths grown hard, disillusioned, coolly speculative, lewdly amused, or even just sadly aloof, what could I think of except what I had read?

Looking into the faces of these middle-class segregationists, I saw not merely respectful hostility, but incredulous contempt, and I knew that these degrading pronouncements were not just empty accusations, hurled to shock and to wound, but a struggling effort to put into words what the people really thought of me.

Dressed for this contest in the highest principles I knew, I was not prepared for eyes that could see me garbed only in filthy rags.

CHAPTER 9

Threats

THE EVENTS DESCRIBED IN THIS BOOK, AND THE RESULTANT changes in my attitudes, so far have been set forth almost chronologically. But for the sake of continuity of ideas, in this chapter and in many others which follow it seems best to organize my material in a more subjective way. My first threat was received near the beginning, my last near the end, of the decade which my story covers, but we shall now examine them all together, arranged according to their type.

In 1951 when I resolved to brandish my banner, I expected a deluge of threats, and assumed that they would challenge, rather than terrify me. This deluge never came. With superhuman cunning, evil refrained from launching its chief attack in a form which I was qualified to use constructively, and the deluge which actually descended was one of contemptuous jeers and obscene insults. However, I did receive a few threats—about a score—most of them between 1955, when my *Post* article appeared, and 1958, when Virginia's "massive resistance" to integration began to crumble.

It developed that I was quite right in believing that my psychological factory could convert them into stimulation.

In fact, even though it may sound strange to some modern readers, I enjoyed many of my threats. Since in the mid-twentieth century, when security is vaunted above adventure, this is an unusual—even censured—reaction to danger, my feelings need explaining.

If someone attempted to scare you and failed, you probably would have a sense of triumph. Almost anyone would. The further your tormentor went, provided he didn't succeed, the more triumphant you would feel. It's like a game or a contest in that the greater the odds against you, the more exhilarated you are when you win. So it should be understandable that after successfully confronting extra-vicious threats, I felt an upsurge of energy, strength, and determination which sometimes lasted for weeks. Indeed, the challenge and stimulation of occasional threats helped me to continue a struggle which in other respects was a weary, monotonous drizzle of steady losses.

With only two exceptions, threats (or "warnings," as their perpetrators perferred to call them) were anonymous, and the majority came by letter. But the phone was not entirely neglected, and occasionally "visual aids" were used. There were a few that I found quite distressing because, if carried out, they would have hurt my husband more than me. They referred to getting him fired on the grounds that reluctant taxpayers shouldn't be burdened with the salary of a man who supported a woman working against the welfare of the commonwealth.

Once I was sent a clipping of a signed letter to the editor urging like-minded persons to join the author in his effort to have Roger dropped from the faculty of the University. Twice I was sent, without comment, carbon copies of letters to Governor Stanley and the University's President Darden, demanding that Roger be fired. Once I was told of an organization which was working along this line. And once, even, I was informed that a bill was being introduced in the Virginia Legislature, the privately stated purpose of which was to rid the taxpayers of the Boyles. Happily, it was killed in committee.

Threats such as these contributed to the nightmarish atmosphere which crept like a dark cloud across my starry vision of the wondrous beauty of man. But most of the others did challenge me personally. Some were vague, consisting of anonymous warnings, couched in such gangster-hackneyed phrases as "if you know what's good for you," or "if you want to stay healthy." These were accompanied by instructions to shut up, or leave the South, or both. It seemed unlikely that anything so nebulous would result in action, but still they gave me a clear focus of evil against which I could pit myself.

Once when I was scheduled to speak to the all-Negro Independent Voters League in Suffolk, Virginia, where the Negro population is high, I got an angry note advising me to stay away. With enormous satisfaction I ignored it. Nothing happened—except an ovation from the Negroes I addressed, who apparently appreciated my coming to an area so hostile.

Several times I received phone calls which gave ominous inflections to words like "You just *better go* North, my girl!"

The vibrant note of malice which these unknown voices often held was disturbing, and the frequency with which they came when my husband had just left town gave me a weird feeling of being spied upon. But it was fun to reply sweetly, "I understand your point and appreciate its wisdom, but I've decided to stay and work toward improvements in the South."

One ingenious telephone threat provided me with the usual triumph plus comic relief. It was a version of the famous "All is discovered—FLY!" technique. As I remember the original anecdote, a practical joker scribbled those words on scraps of paper which he thrust into the mailboxes of a

number ⟨…⟩ reproachable citizens,
then cyn⟨…⟩ them left town.

In my ⟨…⟩uthern accent stated
over the ⟨…⟩t only did its owner
"know all ⟨…⟩ "prepared to publish
document ⟨…⟩ I didn't immediately
get out o⟨…⟩

Now I ⟨…⟩self as having "lived
a blameless life," but a quick glance back over my fifty
years of terrestrial habitation did reassure me that the hate-
heavy voice was lying. So I said:

"Thank you for telling me about this, though it's a compliment I don't deserve. To think that you would go to all
that trouble to gather data about li'l ole me—and then even
plan to publish it in my lifetime!"

The receiver clicked as the man hung up, and I chuckled
for days.

Another amusing one which, knowing who sent it, I was
sure was intended to be dead-serious, was in the visual-
aid classification. It took the form of a neat, famous-make
greeting card which delightfully depicted a person dripping
tar and bristling feathers being ridden on a rail. The in-
scription said, "I hear you're leaving town!" It was signed
by one of the most active and angry leaders of our local
White Citizens Council. I usually ignore opposition letters
of all kinds, but this stirred me to reply:

"Thank you for the Hallmark card," I wrote. "I'm touched
that you cared enough to send the very best. However,
your sending it was prompted by wishful thinking, I fear,
as preparations for integration next fall keep me too busy
to contemplate even a short trip out of town. But should
circumstances beyond my control render such a trip necessary, I think my sentiments would resemble those of the
man in the story who when taking a similar ride was heard
to remark: 'You know, if it weren't for the honor of the
thing, I think I'd rather walk.'"

I felt positively renewed as I mailed this note. A cheerful curtain had been dropped for a while between me and my undermining awareness that I was passionately despised.

The need to laugh in combat is fully understood by seasoned Southern liberals but seldom by tyro liberals who have never known protracted, tension-building attack. It is because of this need that we are all so deeply indebted to P. D. East, creator and editor of *The Petal Paper*, which from the depths of Mississippi sends out biweekly across the South a fresh, cool ripple of chuckles at the conservative Southerner's expense.

In the fall of 1954 I wrote a letter to the editor urging our leaders not to limit us at the outset to a program which we knew in our hearts was wrong, and to base their plans for Virginia on a higher estimate of our ethics, our stamina and capacity to recognize and respect the humanity of other human beings. It was not unusual when I appeared in print to have my mailbox disgorge angry missives in reply, but this time there was something special with a local postmark:

"I think we have heard just about enough out of you and if you want to be a nigger lover dont try to tell everyone to do the same thing. If you keep on running your big mouth you may get a something like a big egg planted under your house like they are getting in Norfolk. WATCH YOUR STEP SISTER."

In Norfolk a bomb had just ripped away part of a building.

Now this letter voiced more than the vague wish that some misty disaster would overtake me. It expressed a definite visualization of an act which might stop my mouth. The difference between the more common vague threats and this statement was like the difference between an angry man saying "Some day you'll get your deserts!" and his saying "Careful! or I'll knock your teeth in!" In the latter case, more care on your part is indicated.

But in August 1959, just before our local schools opened

for the first time on an integrated basis, I learned that a threat can get closer to action than the one I just described. My phone rang one night a few hours after Roger left for a week's trip. From the receiver issued a man's voice with that grinding, mechanical quality suggestive of absence of both reason and feeling which I had come to associate with my worst calls.

"You'd better be out of your house in fifteen minutes," the robot voice said, "because in fifteen minutes we're going to blow it sky high."

His voice conveyed his message to my stomach, chest, and joints. I could hear him breathing hard on the other end, awaiting my reply.

From my own experience and that of others, I had concluded that nothing so wet-blankets predatory emotions as friendly indifference. Perhaps, even, instinct warns the aggressor that intended victims who register no fear may have a deadly means of defense. So I said:

"Now why do you waste your good time trying to upset me? If I scared easily, don't you know I'd have left town long ago?"

"You'd better get right out of the house," he repeated. "We'll be there in fifteen minutes sharp."

"Good enough," I said, stressing inflections of Southern hospitality. "You and your friends come along on out. I'll be real glad to see you."

When he hung up without replying, I felt good. *He* had retreated, not I. It was my theory that one should never hang up on a threat call—for this in itself is an admission of defeat. Moreover, I was sure it was good psychology to let your enemy talk himself out. That way, he loses impetus. His hostility is spent in making the threat itself, and the likelihood of further action is reduced.

I felt as though I had drunk a magic potion and multiplied my size. The man really had sounded dangerous, yet I had not run. I wasn't sure that I had vanquished him. He and his friends might possibly call my bluff. But I was sure I had vanquished a moment which could have vanquished me, and the knowledge made me feel resilient, strong, and adequate to meet whatever other challenges the night might bring.

It brought none.

Of course I don't know, but I suspect that my foes felt quite unstarched about the whole idea of heckling or punishing me. Haven't you often seen "unstarching" take place in a dog who goes leaping forth, barking furiously at a stray dog, only to have his visitor, instead of taking flight, keep trotting calmly along, or perhaps pause and wag his tail?

At any rate I know that another local integrationist let her fear and indignation at a telephone threat be communicated to her unseen assailant, and the result was that threat followed threat far into the night. She was told she would be dragged from her house, thrown in the river; that her house would be burned down around her ears. It proved to be such fun to torment her that a carload of hoodlums drove back and forth in the street outside her yard between phone calls. I may be wrong, but I think that had I shown fear I would have received similar visitors on the night of that threatening call.

Visual-aid threats have more emotional impact than either spoken or written ones. Even the funny little tar-and-feather card stimulated me to reply. I'm sure I simply would have ignored a letter stating flatly that I would be tarred and feathered. True, the voice can convey feelings hard to project pictorially, and there's always something rather eerie about an anonymous letter, but the verbal threat, after all, is a human contact of sorts—a direct engagement with another human mind. The wordless threat, on the other hand, is a cold, dehumanized design for your inner destruction. Its message leaps over the mind, goes straight to the senses. One such threat is still, after several years, imprinted under my eyelids. It was a large photograph of the bloody, slumped body of a lynch victim chained to a tree.

A startling visual-aid threat was used in Tennessee to teach me a lesson about visiting in Negroes' homes. I was to be guest speaker at a big Negro church on some special occasion, and the address of my colored hostess for the week end inadvertently got into the news release in the paper. So word quickly spread that I was down there "socializing with niggers."

That evening during a charming reception in my hostess' home, a telephone barrage began. The phone rang every couple of minutes until my harassed hostess left the receiver off the hook. Bravely she said nothing to me about it until after the climax later that evening. If she had only told me, I could have warned her that closing the outlet our tormentors had chosen for their animosity might drive them to worse expression of it. But at this time I thought the many phone calls merely had reference to preparations for the celebration next day. My first inkling of trouble came when I was roused about midnight by the insistent pealing of the doorbell, and the sound of hurried footsteps and excited murmurings from my host and hostess.

Pulling on wrapper and slippers, I stumbled sleepily into the hall. Through the double plate glass of the storm door two men in white coats, bearing a stretcher between them, could be seen just outside. I learned that my host had phoned for the police and would not open the door until they came. When at last the siren could be heard, he cracked the door and asked the men what they wanted.

Bewilderedly, one answered, "The ambulance is here, sir."

"Ambulance! What for?"

"Isn't this the house? We got a call to come to this address and pick up the mangled or dead body of a Mrs. Boyle."

The presence of the two businesslike hospital attendants in white coats exuding a faint odor of antiseptics, the narrow, neat stretcher, the dim hulk of the ambulance poised in the dark driveway—all conveyed more clearly than any verbal threat the fact that there were people nearby who wanted to see me mangled—or dead.

But while ambulance sending may have the merit of some freshness (though my case was not unique in the history of the integration struggle), I know of no visual aid so effective as the more familiar burning cross. I got mine after John Kasper, nationally known rabble rouser and organizer of White Citizens Councils, made his third visit to Charlottesville and held a series of rallies which whipped the worst element of white supremacists into a frenzy. A feature of these rallies was the names and telephone numbers of all known local liberals printed in large letters on posters and held aloft for loyal members of the White Citizens Council to copy and use as they thought best.

On the night of August 29, 1956, I crept into bed about nine o'clock after a weary day of telephone insults and ugly letters which brought to my quiet, country dwelling an atmosphere of mob violence. I did a little devotional reading, then switched off the light. The expected blanket of darkness did not descend. An eerie, flickering light filled the room, and I now noticed a crackling noise, almost like dry leaves being raked, issuing from the open window. "A brush fire?" I asked myself. I rose quickly and looked out.

There it stood below, six feet tall and not a slipper's toss from the house, the flames stretching eastward in the light breeze like banners of evil. The soft hiss and crackle was a fitting voice for live malice, and the odor of burning, oil-soaked rags a fitting miasma of human moral degradation. Little blasts of dry, scorching air, made soulless by unholy heat, beat at my face. Here was an expression of hate which shocked four senses with the forceful thrust of evil.

Again I felt the magic potion of inner triumph slip through me, making me feel tall and strong. This flame had been set to throw terror into my heart and spine and feet, but it could not conquer me if I did not cower or retreat. I lifted up my being to the cross's wild beauty—like sky-rockets and Roman candles—and suddenly I laughed aloud at the irony of an attempt to torment me with a blaze of loveliness formed in the symbol of eternal love.

The only other person in the house was my thirteen-year-old son, Patton. Wanting him to share the best of the experience, I called him from his room.

"Look!" I said. "They're burning a cross for Mother. Isn't it beautiful?"

He peered out, cried "Yes!" and dashed for his camera.

Together we ran into the yard and he took half a dozen pictures—probably with the setters of the cross watching from a distance, thinking no telling what dampened thoughts. Then we doused the cross with water and brought it, only slightly damaged, into the house.

Later, I hung upon it a framed motto, the gift of two liberal friends. I understand it was originated by General "Vinegar Joe" Stilwell. It says, "Illegitimus Non Carborundum," which freely translated from Vinegar Joe's "Latin," means "Don't let the S.O.B.'s grind you down."

My cross was well made, of graceful proportions, and braced with neatly beveled supports. I was proud of it. But also I was ashamed of whoever made it. Some skilled work-man had dedicated several hours of his God-given strength and dexterity to creating this instrument. And his hope was to change me from a being with human dignity into a weep-ing, cringing thing.

CHAPTER 10

No Hiding Place

EVEN AFTER MY CROSS WAS BURNED, BY REFUSING TO LOOK AT the Southern turmoil as a unit I was able for a year or two more to keep life in my old faith. Insults, threats, brutality, I laid at the door of the psychotic few. Other acts, each taken separately, I could explain on grounds of misunderstanding, special circumstances, and intentions or motives higher than appeared. By inches I retreated from belief that man's nature was loving and good.

As early as the summer of 1954, it began to be forced into my reluctant consciousness that people were not responding to the moral challenge of integration as they would if they were what I had always believed them to be—and that the contest would be both brutal and disappointing. But it wasn't until autumn 1955 that my altered image of Southerners broke through my defenses into words. Even then this ugly new image still wore soft garments of illusion.

Addressing the many Negro organizations that asked me to speak after the publication of my *Post* article, at first I blindly followed in my old groove, assuring them that the huge good will which existed in most white Southerners would shortly triumph. It was significant that whereas new data and points to support this thesis had flowed from me like a river until 1954, they then dwindled to a creek, later to a trickle. By summer 1955 my new speeches were composed almost entirely by rearranging parts of old ones. My brain had balked at what it unconfessedly knew was a fraud.

I thought I was just too overworked to be creative. But in September when the Martinsville, Virginia, branch of the NAACP sent a letter asking me to speak about the "personal difficulties which white Virginians encounter when they take a stand for integration," my noncreativity evaporated. The manuscript rolled from my typewriter as my early integration writings had done. More like an intense experience of reading than like the usual labor of forcing ideas into words, from one moment to the next I didn't know what was coming.

I wrote the speech at a sitting, and called it "No Hiding Place," after the well-known Negro spiritual. I said that we all know what courage it takes for a Negro to speak out against the existing order: He lays himself open to many embarrassments; he often risks antagonizing his employer; in some communities he is even threatened with bodily harm; in addition to these dangers he often suffers heartaches and disappointments as a result of the fact that unthinking, run-of-the-mill citizens are always dead weights for any leader who advocates change, no matter how much that change may benefit themselves.

But the minority member who makes an open stand for integration, I reminded them, has one comfort to sustain him on his difficult road. This is the knowledge that he is giving voice to the official position of his group. He knows that he can count on the approval and moral support of his press, and of all the outstanding leaders and intellects in the colored world.

He knows that if he is subjected to public embarrassment or reprisals, they will come from outsiders, from near strangers, who do not hold his heartstrings in their hands. Among his own, he will often be thought of as a champion. His clubs will commend him. His community on the whole will be kind, even though some individuals may not take much interest in his efforts. If he suffers greatly as a result of his brave stand, correspondingly great will be the sympathy and recognition of his friends. He will rightly be made to feel that he is a valued member of their society.

"But the white citizen who defends minority rights," I said, "does not have this comfort. He runs the same risks which his colored brothers run. His job is often endangered, his life is sometimes threatened. And discouragement hangs equally heavy on his heart. But unlike his colored brother, *he has no hiding place.* For his own people are the ones he has chosen to oppose . . ."

Suppose, I asked, a Negro believed that if he raised his voice to express his convictions he would grieve his parents, embarrass his sisters and brothers, and endanger his children's social acceptance? Suppose he expected his own people to receive him as a traitor and as a threat to their welfare? Suppose he anticipated that his clubs, instead of commending him, would feel obliged to apologize for him, and would consider his membership a blot on their good names? Suppose on Sunday he could look forward to curt nods and stiff smiles from such fellow churchmen as could summon sufficient Christianity, and the careful avoidance of those who could not summon it?

"If this were what you had to expect," I asked, "are you *sure* you would raise your voices then?

"Northern friends," I continued, "often say to me, 'Oh, but the love and appreciation of Negroes must compensate you for all you endure!' It certainly would, if it were forthcoming. For love is something which is precious to us all, and appreciation can put new heart in us in the face of almost any disaster. But I don't have to tell this audience that as a result of generations of betrayal, it's nearly impossible for Southern Negroes to trust a Southern white. No matter what he does or what he suffers, a white liberal is never established beyond suspicion in the hearts of the minority. He's never fully accepted. *He's always on trial.*

"You know and I know that a white Southerner can fully expend himself for years in a fight for human rights and then if he does or says one thing which is misunderstood, he will be classified as a phony overnight . . ."

Two factors made it possible for me to continue the fight, I told them. One was my faith in God. The other was my "vast and unshakable faith in man."

After having thus emptied my heart honestly in this speech, I then felt on solid ground in returning to my old affirmation that indeed there was more good will in the South than most of us suspected. We mustn't make the mistake, I warned, of thinking that the large majority who appeared to oppose us were really solid in their opposition; for many were moving quietly toward integration at every point where they saw the chance. Our real enemies were thunderously noisy, but fewer than either we—or they—thought.

In reality we had only one enormous common enemy whose name was Fear, I insisted; and if only we could destroy Fear in ourselves and in those who opposed us, we would find that all the disputes and conflicts in the South automatically would disappear.

I then explained that this entire recital was merely to show them the reason for the silence of good-willed whites— for, I said, "I want you to see how your white brothers really can be your brothers in their hearts and still not join their voices to yours."

In the next several months I delivered this speech repeatedly. It was well received by Negroes and was joyfully snatched up, published, reprinted, and distributed by liberal whites. For myself and fellow humanists I had cunningly salvaged our faith in man by giving a sympathetic twist to the very behavior which was smothering the Southern Dream. I had even implied that hearts remained steadfast, warm, and loving as their owners fled for cover.

The speech reflects my struggle to believe what both my senses and good sense told me could not be. By year's end 1956 I could not have written it. By then I had broken through the partition which shielded me from the realization that love and fear will not be mated, and that where there is love enough, there is also courage enough.

In the last months of 1955 and throughout the following year, violence struck like lightning in many Southern and border states. Mobs surged and roared, bombs boomed, guns cracked, knives flashed, fists bludgeoned, crosses flared. Yet more shameful and disheartening to me, even than these atrocities of a depraved few, was the inertia of the average well-respected white citizen, and the poor counsel shouted by our leaders and our opinion makers.

Prophecies of "blood running in the streets" by press and politicians gushed like geysers, with approval or condonation often plainly to be seen—an invitation to the underworld to act. In speeches from high places, brutality passed for boldness, threats of law defiance for courage. Cries for "Interposition!"* began in Virginia and spread, echoing and re-echoing, throughout the South. Governors sounded like hoodlums, clergymen like bad little boys, and liberals like goldfish.

On February 1st, 1956, Autherine Lucy, a qualified lone Negro girl was admitted by court order to the University of Alabama, then greeted by howls of hatred and student riots. The *Richmond Times-Dispatch* ran an editorial which deplored the violence but pointed out that it had been

* The official refusal of a state to obey a Federal law.

predicted and was simply to be expected when attempts at integration occurred.

My tortured feelings poured out in a letter protesting the editorial. The letter appeared February 15th beside two others also denouncing the editorial—for *its criticism of the violence.* One inquired, "What Else Could Opponents of Integration Do?" The other stated that the "Negro Student Was 'Asking for Trouble.'" Mine was appropriately titled "Reader Says She Is Ashamed to Be White." It was an anguished cry to the South I had thought was the real South—a plea to rise:

"Where are the ideals, the human warmth, the gallant courage and the love of God and man which we were taught were the warp and woof of Southern ways? Where are the clear voices to balance the bellows of poor souls caught in the quicksands of reaction and fear? If those who ache at the leadership we receive would shout that they are sick at heart, a different leadership would rise. No matter what we individually stand to lose, we've no right to be silently indignant now.

"This is no time for silence. Gasping, decency is going down for the third time. What will you believe about yourself tomorrow if you stand by now with dry feet?

"Are colored citizens the only ones left with courage?— such courage as Miss Lucy showed when she stood alone against the state of Alabama and was unshaken in her resolve before a hate-filled mob?—such courage as a 14-year-old child showed when he would not . . . grovel to save his life?* Haven't we even the grace to bow to courage any more? Neither the editorial nor Ross Valentine† made such a bow.

* Emmet Till, lynched in Mississippi in September 1955 for "making passes" at a white woman and then refusing to say he was not as good as any white man. (Reported by W. B. Huie, *Look,* Jan. 24, 1956.)

† Feature writer for the editorial page of the *Richmond Times-Dispatch.*

"The time has come when one is ashamed to go unscathed. It is now insufferable to be comfortable, unattacked and secure. I remember with what gay pride my grandparents bore their poverty following the Civil War. Are there no white Southerners left who will take punishment with pride? Isn't there, for any of us, solace enough in knowing that we stand for what we believe?

"Long ago I learned not to be proud I'm white, but I had never thought to be, as I am, ashamed . . ."

CHAPTER 11

The Power of Evil

In a referendum in January 1956, two thirds of Virginia's voters agreed to changes in the state constitution which were aimed at cheating the Negro out of his court victory.

I was incredulous. My estimate had been that two thirds would vote *against* it. The only explanation I could think of was that the people hadn't understood the implications.

Later, surveys indicated that they had.

"It's only leaders we need," I cried.

Quite likely it was. But the fact is that such leaders did not appear. Moreover, whatever good leadership the people might have *accepted*, their *preference* in leaders was sadly clear. Leaders who offered the least Christian, democratic, and honest approach to the issue were repeatedly by large —often by overwhelming—majorities endorsed at the polls.

Early in January 1956, two highly respected professors of education at a distinguished institution jointly issued a statement which pointed out the untenability, in principle and practice, of "massive resistance"* to integrated schools, and offered a carefully worked-out plan for proceeding toward integration "with all deliberate speed" yet with minimum dislocation.

* Our official state policy of refusing to allow integration even in districts where the officials and people desired it.

Liberals rejoiced. The tide had turned, we thought. Under this unimpeachable leadership, professors and other teachers at last could rise without fear of isolation and make themselves heard. Behind them, in turn, individuals could safely rally.

It was announced that *before* releasing their opinions both our leaders had secured positions quite a distance from the Southern scene.

Under the strong leadership of its president, the Ministers Association of a large Virginia city adopted and circulated widely a statement of conviction condemning efforts to preserve segregation and "social custom violating the dignity of the Negro." In heavy type the statement invited other groups and individuals to endorse it. At last! I thought. The clergy will give unified, all-out support to the second commandment in Jesus' summation of the Law, and all liberal church people can confidently rally to their standard.

Of the score or more ministers associations in Virginia, only two—of which ours in Albemarle county was one—came forward with endorsements. Public and private attack on the statement was enormous, and within five months the courageous clergyman who was president when the statement was framed resigned from his pastorate and moved to the Middle West.

But the little face-to-face incidents, more than the history- and headline-making acts of important people, were my undoing. Had I been personally less active, I might have evaded certain facts and their implications, and have come through the contest, like many others, with my main faiths intact. But I could not stand by idle.

I labored on. Through mass media there poured, unchallenged, the destructive lies of demagogues and racists. Once having gathered with ease fifteen signers of letters to the editor, I resolved to ask various authorities to answer misstatements in their fields. To a well-known historian-author

I presented an editorial claiming that "history shows" that a collapse of culture always follows integration. He exclaimed, "Asinine!" then documented his verdict.

"Uninformed people believe such things when they aren't denied," I reminded him. "Won't you state in the paper what you just said?"

"It would be undignified. That tripe doesn't deserve a reply."

When some speaker declared that disease epidemics always follow integration, newspapers joyfully headlined his words. I appealed to a respected physician: "Is there any truth in that?"

"It's nonsense."

"Then please write the editor and say so."

"I'm a doctor, not a writer."

"I'll ghostwrite it, if you'll sign it," I hastily offered.

"Facts don't need a medical degree. I'll tell you what to say; you sign it."

So it went with biologists, sociologists, psychologists. The rationalizations varied, but they all said, No. I made a point of introducing my request by first getting each one's opinion on whether it would improve the situation if influential people would take a public stand. Each person thought it would, but when he learned I was paging him, each had a *special* reason why he personally was ineligible:

His job was shaky. . . His wife was a segregationist. . . He thought it did more harm than good. . . His voice wouldn't carry much weight on this issue because he was not a Southerner, or he was known to be liberal, or he had been under attack for something else, or he was not influential enough. . . His daughter was in school and might be embarrassed. . . He had no children in school and therefore had no right to speak on a school issue. . . He had too much faith in the people of Virginia to fear such lies. . . He was an employee of the state and shouldn't speak against state policy. . . His boss was a segregationist. . . His department head was a segregationist. . . His mother-in-law was a segregationist. . . His father was in poor health and would be upset if there was a controversy. . .

At first I listened with understanding and credulity to these "reasons" for not witnessing to the truth. But if you interview twenty-five people and twenty-three of them have a special reason and the other two admit they haven't the nerve, you may still understand but now you understand too well. Something inside you shifts. It may happen when a respected friend is saying the familiar words with the same ring of sincerity, vibration of conviction, and quiver of regret which in recent years you have heard fourscore times —or is it four hundred? All at once your trustfulness is gone, replaced by a great weariness, nausea, aridness, despair.

In 1956 and '57, I traveled around the state for the Virginia Council on Human Relations, soliciting members, gathering funds, and attempting to stimulate liberals to organize locally. Everywhere I found reactions similar to those which bruised me when my article first raised a storm. Many, who at first had enthusiastically endorsed the organization, wanted no connection with it after the inevitable attacks on it began. Donations from whites were usually small, anonymous, and—to ensure the gifts not being traced to their donors—sometimes unbelievably roundabout. Since for economy in time I approached only old friends and known liberals, my illusions broke around me like a roomful of soap bubbles.

One reputedly courageous liberal, a stranger to me, when asked to donate, counted out twenty-five dollars in cash, then telephoned a friend to come get the money and have a certified check made to the Council. He was too businesslike to hand this much cash to an unknown solicitor, but he was taking no chances on even the bank clerk knowing that the money was coming from him.

When I solicited white members, instead of joining, it was common for them to hand me a cash contribution equivalent to yearly dues, plus praise for the Council's work. I minded most when the person added, "I'm with you all the way!"

Not even this untraceable connection with us was dared by some. Once I confidently approached a close friend who, with his wife and daughters, had so often privately boosted my confidence by energetic applause that I reserved my visit to them for a day when my courage sagged with failure. Having recently discussed with him his $50,000 remodeling plans for his already ample and charming home, I unhesitatingly asked him to take out a life membership at a hundred dollars for each person in his family.

Leaning forward on a thousand-dollar couch, he murmured: "We just can't afford it, darling. How I wish we could!"

Surprised but still trustful, I pointed to our twenty-five- and ten-dollar classifications, then added: "And we've a minimum membership at just five dollars for husband and wife jointly."

Nervously twisting her diamond-encrusted watch, his wife broke in hastily: "Not even that, honey. You see, with the new addition and all— But don't think we aren't *with* you. You *know* how we feel."

Several hours later I began to cry—in a way that I do only when I have had a stunning blow—with my face lifted up instead of bowed, and without covering it or wiping away the tears. The transparency of this can't-afford-it excuse was an affront to honest friendship, and now all the private applause I had ever got from the voiceless good-willed assaulted my self-respect.

I cried because these particular friends—dear to my heart as they had been—had deserted all that I was trying to stand for, but even more I cried for the many other much-loved and once-trusted friends who, though silent while I spoke and inert while I struggled, had made me feel their approval and had seemed to be passionately concerned. In my heart I had felt their quiet backing. But now I wasn't any more a front-rank soldier with an unseen regiment behind me. I was a lone sniper in a tree.

Although I tried to brush it off, mistrust of kind voices and noble assurances crept upon me like a huge, dank insect.

Some of my heart-dragging little surprises and moments of undoing resulted from incidents which might have happened in ordinary times. I think it significant that they did not. For nearly half a century of my life, such experiences were so rare that I easily buried them in constructive thinking. Now they mobbed in on me. Where there is mass tension, individuals and groups drop veils which hide their blemishes. Jealousy, malice, deceit looked at me from long-dear faces.

Miss A. and Mrs. B. were two elderly friends of mine and of each other. They filled me with multiple joy by successively rushing to me with congratulations when my *Post* piece came out. Arriving first, Miss A. said a lovely thing, which I gratefully quoted to Mrs. B. when she, too, offered generous words. Mrs. B. did not share my pleasure. "But *I* mean it," she said sharply, then—apparently not caring how much she hurt me—repeated in ruthless detail remarks of Miss A. which little resembled those Miss A. had made to me.

You might think it rare that a desire to be the *only* one who is loyal to a friend will outweigh a desire for his welfare. Among the few who were loyal to me, I found it common.

When my unpopularity was just beginning to become high fashion, I felt doglike gratitude to a friend, whom I will call Jenny, for the way her dark eyes snapped with indignation as I told her of little blows and jabs which made my days sad. Her empathy so bound my wounds that I rushed to her with a rare little triumph, eager to share that, too. I had been asked by a group of church women to set forth my Christian reasons for believing in integration, and as I talked to them I had seen many faces light with comprehension. "It made me see that I'm not as alone as I was beginning to feel," I told Jenny.

I waited for her rejoicing. Mouth set, eyes hardened, her gentle voice drawled: "I've felt awful for not being there to protect you."

"You're sweet but this once I got along fine. Everybody came up afterward and said—"

"*Everybody?*"

"Well, no, but even if you talk about gardens to a garden club, not everybody—"

"At least they were polite," Jenny said, "but the way they talked to me about it, I wanted to scratch their eyes out!"

Some people still invited me to parties and, although hecklers stifled my pleasure, I doggedly went—until a hostess followed her invitation with a rising note of self-admiration on this remark: "*I'll* never drop you, darling, if it costs me every other friend I have!"

I fought to feel grateful—and lost. Other experiences combined with this and suddenly the pattern leaped out. This was not love, but exploitation. Mrs. B., Jenny, others, now this woman, were creating noble self-images by means of my wounds. At last I understood why Negroes didn't appreciate our "love." It was more repellent than the conscious sadism of foes.

My prospective hostess waited, beady-eyed, for me to gratify her with a gush of gratitude. I tried but I could not. In a strained voice I thanked her and said I could not possibly make it this time.

A disconcerting feature of the incidents was that even though I saw through these egocentric efforts, and thus they boomeranged on the evildoer, nevertheless evil triumphed. Justice was accomplished in that a chill replaced my old warm glow when I thought of Mrs. B., Jenny, and my party-giving friend, but nevertheless their efforts to oust all others from my heart were successful. A chill also— though I fought it—replaced the old glow when I thought of these other persons who, I fully realized, may have been maligned. The power of evil struck me with new force.

CHAPTER 12

The Kiss of Death

THE CHIEF THING WHICH SUSTAINED ME NOW WAS HOPE THAT I contributed to bringing about a better South. This lifeline, too, rapidly frayed.

I knew that silent liberals often maintain that vocal ones do more harm than good. But members of the Virginia Council on Human Relations didn't propose to be silent, so when we organized a local chapter, I thought I would be just one of the gang. I couldn't have been more wrong.

It was my opinion then, as now, that my lifted voice made no dent in the opposition—and resulted only in attacks on me —mainly because none who believed I was right would say so. If, when I first made it, a few others had endorsed my claim that many whites would welcome integration, I was sure that "Massive resistance!" would not have become the battle cry of the demagogues. But, since the heart of my message was that others shared my views, when not one in my own community certified it, I was reduced from a spokesman to the South's prize fool, thus cutting the power of my voice, even as a lone one, to a minimum. In the summer of 1958, State Senator Edward O. McCue felt able to say in a widely distributed press release that I was the only white person in my area (where he himself lived) who wholeheartedly favored integration in public schools. And *no one denied it.*

However, when the local Council was organized, I discovered that most of its members thought I had brought attack on myself. "If done right," they as good as said, "one could openly combat the status quo without incurring anything worse than grudging respect."

This was precisely what in 1951 I had thought about those under heavy attack. The poetic justice of being myself the victim of such thinking made me smile in the midst of my shock.

Measure for measure, I was now rewarded for my earlier attitudes. Whenever I had heard of a shamefully vicious attack on some liberal, how smugly I had assumed that doubtless there was more justification for it than met the eye. Southerners being high-minded and kindly people, I reasoned, you could be quite sure that if someone was mistreated and none in his community rose to his defense, there was more against him than his stand for the brotherhood of man!

A favorite explanation of mine was that he had stupidly gone about his efforts in the wrong way. He was tactless, rude, or belligerent—in short, unnecessarily offensive. If only he had gone about his work courteously and intelligently, he wouldn't have had any trouble. *I* hadn't had any.

Having thus carefully analyzed attacks on others in my efforts to prove to myself that Southerners would follow gladly if led properly, I well knew that I could expect no quarter from those who had not yet become targets. They had a stake in believing that I foundered merely because of obvious blunders of my own. If they blamed me entirely, they could feel safer and more hopeful as they launched their own efforts into the Southern gale.

So instead of feeling strengthened and supported after the local Human Relations Council was formed, I felt more alone than ever—and more useless. Not even the lessons I had learned so dearly could be passed on to those who had more zeal than experience. In one board meeting after another, my suggestions were consistently ignored and overwhelmingly voted down. I could not escape the fact that rejection of my offerings was automatic.

Quickly, if not painlessly, adjusting to this new challenge, I gagged my ideas and resolved to contribute only my energy, experience, and skill in carrying out projects suggested by others. Again I crashed into a stone wall. It was better, I was told, if I did not represent the Council in any way; since I was identified in the public mind with "extremism," and the Council's influence depended on its establishing itself as "moderate."* They would not, of course—they said—ask me to stop expressing myself publicly, provided I made it clear that I wasn't speaking for the rest of them.

Licking these new wounds, I plunged into a round of tedious, spirit-draining, behind-the-scenes chores.

We need not concern ourselves with the degree of justification for the contentions of the local Council leaders, but only with their effect on me. They may have been right. They certainly did an outstanding job of what they attempted, and perhaps their most intelligent act was to put me down the drain. However, one of the things I had not questioned in 1951 was that I would have impact on others —that I would be listened to, even though I might pay heavily for speaking. Now I felt I was in a soundproof cell.

With the vocal opposition consistently misinterpreting me, and the liberals I worked with ignoring whatever I said, I felt that I could shout and beat on the wall and still not be heard. My ineffectuality clutched and strangled me like an Old Man of the Sea.

So heavy was this last straw of rejection that I staggered

* The word "moderate" soon lost its obvious original meaning when Southern liberals began applying it to themselves but in the beginning it was thought to be conciliatory.

under it and might have fallen but for one thing: Just at this moment, dark hands reached out and clasped mine. Negroes were listening! For them, attacks on me were not proof of failure, but diplomas, certificates of merit, postgraduate degrees. And the fact that I still stood four-square with them despite all at last convinced them of my sincerity.

Scattered individual Negroes had from the beginning treated me as a person of unquestionable integrity, but on the whole, even among those who made a point of being nice to me, I was conscious of being forever sized up, forever on trial. Now the barrier of general suspicion lowered. From individuals and organizations flowed a sweet acceptance and warm respect which so resembled my imagined "club" relationship of long ago, that it was like a bit of home in the midst of the strange land which for me the South had become.

The first Negro organization to offer me official recognition was the Virginia Voters League. In September 1956 they gave me their annual award. The citation said that I had earned it for "relentless, consistent, unselfish, untiring efforts on behalf of all citizens . . ." Two months later, the National Council of Negro Women gave me their annual human relations award, stating, "Your profound understanding and sensitivity to the times . . . are candles of light."

Framed and treasured, I read these citations many times in the months ahead. Belief had been growing in me that I contributed nothing whatever, but if those I had tried to serve really thought of me this way, I couldn't let them down by not at least continuing to try.

My feeling of hopelessness was shared by others, for as racial prejudice stretched upward to its full height, flexing its muscles and roaring its determination not to give an inch, across Virginia with few exceptions the handful who had rallied and raised their voices now moved in swift retreat to safer positions.

Probably they were unconscious of it, but the over-all implication of what they said was that they "certainly were not Negro lovers" and were making their stand entirely on "white man's grounds," such as to "save our schools," obey the law, and keep the tourist trade. I knew that they thought they were doing this to gain the ears of as many people as possible for their message. But I thought I could not bear it, both because I knew how it sounded to Negroes and because Virginia's avowed liberals were her last hope of decency.

Christmas day 1956, I published in many papers a letter which was a plea for retreating liberals to halt. I said that I had noted with distress the increased ugliness of the attacks on integration and on those who wished to achieve it, and I had waited hopefully, as I knew many colored Virginians had waited, for fitting replies from white Virginians who desired integration for warmhearted reasons.

Instead of these I had seen a steadily increasing tendency to defend integration only on grounds of obedience to the Supreme Court, of preserving our public education system and of other equally chilly reasons—reasons all remote from a natural reaching out toward others, and from an identification of human beings with each other in their sorrows and their problems.

This, I pointed out, was deeply wrong; wrong because it was a concession to hatred; wrong because "the simple, honest, uncalculating truth, spoken from the heart, has more power to sway than all the careful wording of a thousand tactical experts; and wrong because the expression of personal, individual feelings is important on any issue and especially on this. . .

"And so as a Christmas card to all colored Virginians and to the many white Virginians who feel as I do, I wish to say that I want integration partly because I love my colored friends, and find their company worthy and often inspiring, and I wish to see them freed from their many humiliations —for my heart is with them in their struggle for recognition.

"The fact that the accepted ideals of our democracy and of our faith support me in my feeling is something for which I am profoundly grateful. But even if I knew nothing of these, I hope and believe that from the deepest wells of my own being the truth that humanity is one would rise, and that I should somehow know that it is right to feel as I do. Into the very structure of the universe is built the truth that we are members one of another and Jesus came, not to invent, but to reveal this truth.

"There are many white Southerners besides myself who will feel personally freed when colored Southerners are free to move among us and the hearts of our children are free to recognize human worth. And though the crosses burn and the stars shiver on the bars, I think we should calmly, persistently and very audibly say so."

As far as I know, this is the only frank, clean-cut defense of, and call for, what some Southerners refer to as "nigger lovin'" that has appeared in Virginia newspapers during this crisis, and I still don't understand why this is so.

Letters appeared in the press and my mailbox attacking me for it, but also it drew a little public, as well as private, support, both white and colored. Briefly I felt listened to and useful again.

Though invitations to speak in more and more distant places indicated that some people thought me helpful, one's home-town folk have enormous power to warm or chill the heart, and as rejection tightened here, I felt increasingly impotent. The feeling mounted in me that I had never made a contribution of value, and I knew it would be generally appreciated by my co-workers if I would now just shut up.

Some local Negro leaders—though mercifully not all— appeared to agree with new white acquaintances in the Council. "You've worked yourself entirely out of a job," one told me, seemingly without malice and unaware of what such a comment would do to the interior of one who in doing that job had lost most of what she had once held dear. Another said, as though it were quite a foregone conclusion that I was retired: "I guess you're glad you have to step back now and let others do it all."

He was right at least that I was weary of combat. I felt as if I had run too hard to catch a bus, or as if it were four o'clock on a day when I forgot to eat lunch. But my weariness wasn't from overwork. It was from my severance from human fellowship, and his remark was another slash. It was as though all my life, without knowing it, I had been invisibly connected with other people, drawing from them nourishment, comfort, and strength, and now the unseen connections were cut. A puny thing I was when separated from the rest.

When my cross was burned, community reaction made me feel as if I had some unmentionable disease. In 1958 and '59, I felt that people regarded this disease as contagious, and that everyone probably unconfessedly wished I were dead. In all directions white liberals began to draw away from identification with me in their search for more neutral ground than that on which I stood.

In a distant Virginia town, a letter was published, hotly defending me against an equally hot attack which had said that its writer was "calling upon the Board of Visitors of the University of Virginia, to either muzzle her and her activities for the Negro organization (the NAACP) . . . or else take this family off the neck of the Virginia taxpayer."

My defender replied:

". . . Christian people know that Mrs. Boyle knows what she is talking about, and what's more she is not afraid to say it. There are people who know right from wrong concerning the race question and are afraid to let it be known for fear of their neighbors. But not Mrs. Sarah Patton Boyle.

"Also, there are people who fear the KKK. But, not so Mrs. Boyle. She stands for truth, justice, love and mercy for all people and if ever she loses her bread and butter for such a stand as that I shall supply it until she can do better. So there! ! !"

This vigorous bit of literature was signed "Another White Southerner."

Assuming it to be the voice of a stranger who had heretofore been silent, I was greatly encouraged to think that I had such a power-filled unknown friend. But a few days later I received a note from its author. Then I knew that one who was perhaps my last white supporter had thought it best to take cover. The most courageous and outspoken person in her quarter of the state, to my knowledge this was the first time she had ever failed to sign her name to a published letter concerning integration.

But it was a local liberal who neatly summed up my worst fears. I don't think he was being consciously cruel, but rather, was quite unconsciously trying to banish his own fears by scapegoating them on me—for next to myself he probably was the most conspicuous integrationist in town. We were discussing the sad paradox that in integration activities success is a handicap. Whereas in most work, the more you do and better known you become, the greater your power and influence, in a fight against the status quo the reverse appears to be so, and your usefulness declines as your reputation mounts. This is what he said:

"You've done such a good job that your usefulness is permanently over. Anything that has your name on it is automatically doomed to failure." Then he added a telling phrase. "You're the kiss of death."

I doubt if I could have borne it had not a letter appeared just then (September 5, 1958) in the *Richmond Times-Dispatch*. It was signed with a name I didn't recognize, William A. Smith, Newport News. It said:

"Negroes should never become antagonistic or vindictive because of the suffering inflicted and being inflicted upon us. Out of suffering come wisdom and strength. . . One human with courage constitutes a majority, and as long as Virginia can claim just one Sarah Patton Boyle, hope will spring eternal in this commonwealth's breast."

I cried for shame of my self-pity when I read that letter. Then I resolved to fight on.

CHAPTER 13

Whitewashed Tombs

MY HOPE THAT "THE PEOPLE" WOULD RISE AND RECOVER THE Southern Dream died a slow and groaning death. Each time I thought it lifeless, a little warmth would return and it would gasp again. Once, even, it briefly rose from its sickbed.

In the spring of 1957, the Virginia State Chamber of Commerce arranged a dinner honoring distinguished ex-patriates. Invitations were sent to six hundred Virginians who had become outstanding in other states. Then poetic justice struck: Unknown to the committee who issued the invitations, and despite scrupulous screening of the original list, six of these distinguished Virginians who received invitations were Negroes.

I laughed, then rejoiced. Here at last was vivid drama-tization of the idiocy and injustice of assumptions based on race. Here was both an appeal to man's admiration for the underdog who triumphs, and a challenge to common fair-ness—to say nothing of our long Virginia tradition of courtesy! Here, in a nutshell, was an exposure of our worst and a call to our best. Despite all that had happened, I did not doubt that in the name of good sportsmanship, justice, and love, Virginia as a whole would rise—humbly, peni-tently, gracefully—and welcome her distinguished colored sons and daughters who had so shamed her lack of faith in them.

The Chamber withdrew its invitations from all colored recipients.

"Now the people will rebel!" I insisted. "There'll be a flood of protests."

Only one of the white distinguished expatriates rebelled. Lambert Davis, Director of the University of North Carolina Press, responded as I had hoped great numbers would. He wrote a scathing open letter rejecting his invitation, implying, that, in such a context, it was more an insult than a compliment. Five hundred and fifty other white people attended that ignominious meal without a visible blush.

I felt myself drying up inside.

Much as I loved my own region, I would have been less in despair could I have made my disillusionment apply to it specifically. But I had learned my hard lesson about segregating certain groups of people and attributing to them special characteristics. I knew that what I was observing was not just white Southerners in action, but *man himself,* and that it would be the same with any group of people in similar circumstances. There was no refuge from my disillusionment, no hiding place.

A new concept of the nature of man obtruded upon me from three sources: First, from the people's own public behavior (stupid as well as graceless); second, from my personal experiences with friends and foes (self-deceiving, cowardly, cruel); and, third, from my mail, which with awful clarity substantiated what was acted out around me. The total picture thus revealed resembled my original image of man about as much as the character of Adolph Hitler resembled that of Albert Schweitzer.

In this new concept, the role of self-deception in man's nature loomed large. People's self-images, I saw, bore little resemblance to their real characters, and the greater part of their thinking was rationalization. They acted with utter selfishness, simultaneously attributing to themselves the most laudable motives they could pluck from the air.

Worst of all, merciless cruelty resulted from their efforts to make these noble motives convincing. For example, I had noted an effective technique for destruction of those who disturbed the status quo. This technique when unconscious had a ghastly machinelike ruthlessness to which many of its perpetrators probably would not have given conscious consent.

In a Virginia town, the director of the public library had in seven years received few critical suggestions from the library board. But at the meeting immediately following his "exposure" as having hired a Negro assistant, the board asked the director to resign. Their reason? Incompetency!

Indignation rose among liberals and semi-liberals, and a ground swell of strong protest began. It halted when the board published passionate assurance that the request for resignation had no relationship whatever to the librarian's having a Negro assistant. Persons delegated to interview members reported that their sincerity was unquestionable.

The result was threefold. First, the librarian was separated from the help of supporters. For who would feel justified in pressing for the retention of an unsatisfactory worker, merely because he happened to be liberal? Second, he lost much sympathy and esteem even among his friends. After a burst of indignation at an injustice, one cannot but feel disgusted upon discovery that the person only got his just deserts. Third, he inevitably suffered much loss of faith in himself. When those to whom you are responsible exert themselves to prove that you're not, and never were, worth your salary, even if your rational mind hotly repudiates the charge, your heart half believes.

Indeed, what puts the sharpest teeth in this method is that there always is some truth in such accusations. The most gifted and competent people are ineffectual in some ways. Probably not one successful man in five hundred is so flawless in performance that no justification for firing him could be found by those who desired to see him in a bad light. Therefore an employer not only honestly, but also easily, convinces himself that a newly discovered integrationist has long deserved the ax.

In each individual case, if separated from all others, a fair-minded person usually will find it possible to give the employer the benefit of the doubt. But after one has studied the records and has seen repeated scores of times the pattern of firing newly discovered integrationists, then all doubt disappears. One fully grasps the significance of such facts as that the library board had never before, in seven years, thought the librarian's faults necessitated action— never until he hired a Negro assistant!

One of the things which baffles the inexperienced investigator in such cases is that the person (or persons) responsible for dismissing a liberal often seems fully sincere and entirely unconscious of wrongdoing on his own part. He obviously really believes his story that the views of the fired man had nothing to do with his dismissal. Of course he believes it! He has a large stake in building up a case which will convince himself. A normal man can't fire another for his convictions and loyalties, and then sleep without sedatives.

But his greatest cruelty often lies in his very effort to clear himself of guilt feelings. If you know you have treated an employee unjustly, you will try to make amends by helping him find a better job. But if you convince yourself that he thoroughly deserved the treatment you gave him, how can you ethically recommend him to another?*

---

* It should be noted that this pattern of firing revealed integrationists is followed by those who substantially agree with their views as well as by those who sharply disagree. The employer has his eye on others (everybody else is prejudiced) rather than on what he himself may feel

I began to see why Jesus kept hammering home the fact that self-righteousness is worse than crimes punishable by law. It is distressing that we who consider ourselves Christians probably lead the modern world in the commission of this unpunishable crime. Indeed, Christian lay leaders commit it against courageous Southern clergymen with monotonous frequency:

Reluctant to admit that they would penalize their pastor for his Christian convictions alone, churchmen have sought, found, and written into their own minds and into the records an array of ministerial faults which, though real perhaps, would have been readily overlooked had the clergyman refrained from witnessing to his belief in the brotherhood of man. The rejected minister's wounds are thus doubled, while the people who inflicted them go conscience-free.

Toward the end of the decade, though I was in no position to be fired—not being employed—this same devious pattern of rejection wove itself into nearly all my relationships.

I think it began early in 1958, when I testified for the National Association for the Advancement of Colored People against the state of Virginia. Special laws had been passed aimed specifically at the destruction of this, the one organization which was really effective in combating segregation. The NAACP went to court in an effort to prove the laws unconstitutional.

I was able to give pertinent evidence and they asked me to be a witness. Other whites were called as witnesses, too, but by now I was thoroughly identified in the segregationist's mind as public enemy number one, and news stories featured my testimony, especially in our local paper.

Later the same year, our local NAACP branch held a

---

about the matter. The fact that he may personally agree with the man he fired, or at least not care at all what the private views of his employees are "just so they do their job"—this fact he uses to bolster his rationalization that the firing was not related to the exposure of the man's views.

workshop (much advertised in advance as integrated) to prepare parents and children of both races for the schools, which were under court order to integrate in the fall.*

Local white liberals agreed that identification with the NAACP would end their usefulness in the community, so it developed that I and my school-age son were the only white people who registered†—a fact also much publicized, though my son was referred to only as a "white child," his name mercifully omitted.

The result was a writing me out of the white race with a finality which surprised even me. One white "moderate" voiced an opinion which I sensed was widespread but which, until then, I had heard only from the opposition: "You don't belong with us; you belong with the Negroes."

I was grateful that the coveted annual Russwurm Award, of the National Newspaper Publishers Association—all Negro—had just given me welcome assurance that informed Negro leaders thought the same.

I do not know at what point genuine rejection faded into imagined rejection. Common sense assures me that this happened sometimes. But only through believing in a chain of farfetched coincidences could I doubt that most of what I saw was real. That it was not imagined is evidenced by the fact that discovery of this new pattern of rejection was unexpected. I even valiantly denied it at first. Also, later, its abrupt suspension underscored its existence, especially as this, too, took me by surprise. Here is how it worked:

I willingly admit to my share of faults. However, these faults were not of such nature or virulence that for fifty

* Our school board appealed the case and actual integration did not take place until the fall of 1959.
† One white mother, whose children were below school age, sat in on a couple of sessions; three white ministers, of whom my own was one, successively opened sessions with prayer; and on the closing night, four or five of the Council's eighty-some white members came to hear the guest speaker.

years associates were not able to take them in stride. I kept the same friends for decades, and found making new ones easy. But in 1958, slowly at first, then with relentless acceleration, my faults were pulled forward, my virtues pushed back in almost all my relationships within the white community. There was a mounting tendency to interpret whatever I said or did in terms of its lowest, rather than its highest, implications, especially in matters *not* related to the integration issue.

I fought hard against seeing it as a pattern, hard against letting it slip in among the many other patterns of self-deception which the skyrocketing tensions brought into bold relief. It was no use. The psychology behind the shift in emphasis was too elementary, the elements too obvious:

Friendship with me had become very costly in the white community; yet could any friend or liberal retain his self-respect if he pulled away from me for this reason alone? Acceptable justification must be found. How? Well, if he quarreled with me on other grounds than my integration activities, or if he saw in my character reprehensibility which he had been too charitable to see heretofore, why then, naturally, he could withdraw from the association without damaging his self-image.

With some, efforts to pick quarrels with me were only gentle, steady pressures, and I resolutely found other explanations for them—keeping each separate—until the blatantly ludicrous efforts of others forced me to recognize the unconscious design. Attempts to twist my most patently innocent words and actions into something offensive often were so irrational and ridiculous that I felt shaken, helpless, at bay. Though not everyone moved in even the milder manifestation of this paradigm, I found forms of it in so many whom once I had most trusted that my sense of security in any human relationship utterly dissolved.

The enormous dark pull of many unconsciously seeking

excuses to retire to a safer distance from me was like a strong undertow. It carried me down several times before, comprehending its current, I was able to brace myself against it. Even then, it dragged off my belief in my own worthiness. With desperate, heavy-footed weariness, I fled from a new and loathsome image of myself.

For people to accomplish this switch in themselves and in me was easy. Every virtue has its counterpart in a vice. If you wish to like Jack, you can applaud his will power; if not, you can lament his stubbornness. Ted's devotion to his mother is either beautiful, or an Oedipus complex, precisely as you choose, and Susie is innocent or a prude.

Such psychological bows and blows are standard daily dozens in personal relationships. Though there is some limit to the reversability of character traits, we usually can go straight down the line of the virtues and faults of ordinary people and, by an act of simple choice, turn the shield and reveal the trait's counterpart in reverse.

Having tended to be charitable in my own interpretations, through the years I perhaps had more than my share of shield-turning in my favor. An unbelievable loneliness crept through me as the contrary process began. Despite my frantic efforts to keep it down, a wall grew slowly or rose abruptly between me and each of the few I still thought of as friends. One after another, small areas of my heart went numb, while a central, over-all pain mounted.

A depressing awareness possessed me that the Negroes who long ago had shocked me with their cynical assessment of what was to be expected from Southern whites had been proven right. Indeed, their worst predictions had fallen short. Those who had gladdened my heart by listening with shining eyes to my assurances of the reality and depth of silent good will had had their sweet hopes falsely raised. A man's real and deep feelings are surely those which he acts upon when challenged, not those which, mellow-eyed and soft-voiced, he spouts in easy times.

Seeing the faith we had shared crushed from Negroes who also had believed in a hidden beauty in the South, seeing glowing faces replaced by haggard faces, as they saw, heard, endured as I did, weighted down my days. "You can't trust anyone," I heard them say in low, still half-disbelieving voices. Once I would have cried out, "Oh, you can, you can!" Now I could only answer in a voice as low and shaky as theirs, "It does seem that we can't."

Some told me about white friends of whose loyalty they had been sure, and how, as the fever of white supremacy rose, these friends had stiffened and drawn away. "I can't believe it even yet," one said. "It just seems as if it *couldn't* be. Was it a phony friendship all along?"

I could only put my hand on hers and say, "I know, I know."

I knew. And I knew also that those guilty of such betrayal never confronted themselves with it. They burrowed under it, leaped over it, by-passed it on the left. Thus they avoided making conscious moral choices. But conscious or not, choices were made. Drawn faces, wounded eyes, inner emptiness among the innocent betrayed attested to the reality of those unadmitted choices.

Early in 1959, Federal Court decisions having rendered the official "massive resistance" program of Virginia unworkable, it was quickly abandoned for a policy of "containment." This meant that a few Negroes would be accepted in white schools, but—by various devious means—the number would be kept to a minimum. In February, seventeen Negroes were sprinkled into six white schools in Norfolk, and small numbers into various schools in Northern Virginia—with whites boycotting in some cases, in others, not. The Charlottesville school board agreed to admit eleven the following September.

Whispered cheers went up from sideline liberals, and loud

ones from Northern supporters. "How happy you must be!" one wrote me.

But all that I had fought for was lost.

I had not battled for the fact of integration. This was in the hands of judges and Constitutional lawyers, and was assured. I had expended my heart and strength, mind and soul for an integration accomplished with love and grace, courtesy and thanksgiving, in a land where justice was done when injustice was seen, where graciousness and courage were standard equipment like sun and rain, and where principles were more important than one's self.

CHAPTER 14

Discredited Currency

As September 1959 moved closer, I tried to tell myself that there was yet time to make of integration something more than grim necessity. I hoped until the day our local schools opened that a statement from a small group of parents and teachers, or a delegation of them, would publicly welcome the Negro children who would soon be so lonely in our midst. As the first day of school came and went, this last sick little hope quietly died.

For me personally in the final two weeks before integrated classes began in Charlottesville, and the first two weeks afterward, sharp experiences and dull pain were at their worst. In a great flood tide, fears had risen that violence would break out, disease run rampant, delinquency spread, and scholastic standards hurtle downward, when the handful of dark little ones crept timidly into the big white schools. And I was closely identified in the public mind with "Negro aggression"—the cause of all this horror.

Eyes which in the months just past had looked at me merely with a stony chill now stared with snapping anger. A few, even, were glazed with a still more engrossing rage. The unforgettable note of grinding harshness, grown familiar to me on the telephone, was often heard in voices of people as they greeted me, or replied to some casual, impersonal remark of mine. No hour of the day lacked reminders that I was hated, despised by many, while avoidance of me by friends and fellow liberals was so frequent, conspicuous, and visibly shamefaced that my efforts to believe it imaginary miserably failed. I was sure everybody wished I were dead. I did.

The first week came and went without disaster—or even difficulties—then the second. About the middle of the third week, a sigh of relief went up from the community which you could almost hear. As tangibly as the dark cloud had settled down in the summer of 1954, I felt it lift. The heavy air became mountain-fresh. The sun sparkled on still waters. Then something happened which I had not even dimly anticipated:

Quietly but quickly, white society opened its gates to me again. Of course I don't mean that everyone consciously altered his opinion. Doubtless many, even most, traveled in the same thought grooves concerning me, some in the same emotional grooves. But whatever their secret opinions and feelings, something within them changed enough to make their spontaneous expression toward me quite different; different enough for daily woundings to cease and daily pleasantries to command the field again; different enough for me to feel that in many directions the next move in re-establishing myself was up to me.

With some perhaps the change resulted from a release of good feeling toward me which various fears had suppressed, with others maybe it was impersonal—simply an exuberance of relief which found expression with everyone they met. With still others it may have been a feeling of "now let's let bygones be bygones." But for me it was as though an eclipse of the sun had ended. Day was day again.

Eyes softened, voices warmed, former friends and foes paused to add a few extra words to a passing greeting. "Why don't you come and see me?" was a question I heard again. Among segregationists I was no longer made to feel like a rattlesnake. Now I was treated as a fellow Virginian with "a different opinion." Among the neutral, I no longer felt I was merely a curiosity; subtly, somehow I was once more an old friend. Among liberals, I didn't feel I was the kiss of death, but a hard-working, hard-fighting veteran within their ranks.

The change happened with such rocket speed that at first I thought it an hallucination. It just *couldn't* be that within the space of less than a fortnight I had ceased to be a sheep in wolf's clothing, forced to keep lonely vigil on a distant hill, and had become again a potential member of the flock! But day by day the inviting looks, voices, words persisted. There seemed no longer a doubt: I was free to re-enter the fold when I chose.*

Then came the last and worst shock in this decade of destruction. *I did not choose to re-enter!* I didn't warm to the warm looks, voices, words! They filled me with repressed fury. Gestures of friendliness, which once I would have gone out to meet like an ocean wave, left me unmoved, or moved to recoil.

An old friend took my hand on the church steps, and said with low-voiced tenderness, "I've thought of you and prayed about you so often in these months. Can't we get together? I've so much to tell and ask you."

I wanted neither to listen nor answer. What was the

* I continued to doubt my senses at times until I saw the results of a painstaking survey of Charlottesville people published six months later by sociologist Dr. Johan Galtung. Selecting 200 names at random from the city directory, Dr. Galtung and his assistants had interviewed all these persons in the spring of 1959 and again in the spring of 1960. In the latter interview, about 30% had switched to a more favorable attitude toward integration. This was conscious opinion, and probably a subconscious shift occurred in a still greater number, finding expression only in social overtones such as those I had sensed. At any rate, Dr. Galtung's findings supported my conviction that the change in attitudes toward me was no illusion.

good of trying to communicate? Even if one could succeed, what difference would it make? Tiredly, I tossed out the expected cordial words:

"What a good idea. I'll phone you about it when I can."

A sweet-faced woman caught my arm in a store and said, with melting eyes, "You'll never know what you meant to me through all this. You saved my faith in the South."

I only wanted to slap her smooth cheek and hiss, "Why didn't *you* save *mine?*" I managed a wan smile and said faintly, "Thank you."

A brawny, six-foot man of thirty-some smiled ten inches down at me and rumbled in a nice bass, "You spoke for us all. I didn't ever feel I had to say anything, because you said everything that needed to be said—*so* beautifully."

I looked down—he probably thought modestly—to keep him from seeing the rage and contempt in my eyes. I wondered whether I would feel better or worse if with all my might I kicked his shin.

I examined myself in horror. Had I descended to hatred? —or lower? My desire wasn't to hurt these people but only to strike out, as you kick a chair you stumble over. That was worse than hating: Reacting to a person as though he were a chair is further from love.

The self-image with which my own unworthy feelings now confronted me was uglier than any that others had ever been able to make me see. Was I really so unforgiving, small-natured, frozen-hearted? These people were sincere. It was written plainly in their faces. Whatever they had done or not done a few months ago, they *meant* what they were saying now. They wanted me to feel good about what I had been through—or wanted to forgive me, as the case might be.

It made no difference to me whether or not they were sincere. I didn't care at all.

Why? *Why* didn't I care? Suddenly I knew.

Warm looks and kind words once had meaning for me because I thought they represented something beyond, and more important than, themselves; something dependable and enduring in the hearts from which they came. Like paper currency, smiles, praise, words of welcome, shared laughter, and shining eyes draw their value from what stands behind them. If there is no gold in the vault, other currency is worthless.

You have seen photographs of proud homes leveled by tornadoes: All is rubble and rubbish—nothing remains. It was so with the house of my faiths. In 1950 I had many inner mansions—built of the loftiness of man, the mellow loveliness of Dixie, the steadfastness of friends, my own capacity to give and take. Nothing remained of all this now.

For a while I would not admit that my heart was void. I tried to blame each individual for the way I reacted to him or her with nothing, with aversion, anger or contempt. By segregating each case, I was able for a little to attribute my reactions to faults in a particular personality.

But after a while, I knew I had to stand still and face the truth: I had nothing to give others any more, and there was nothing I wanted from them. So I had no reason for living.

"I'm spiritually bankrupt," I admitted very slowly. "Inside me, I'm a pauper."

This time I had struck rock bottom. I was all the way down. I didn't see any hope anywhere—unless there was a little in what Jesus said about the poor in spirit.

Part 3

THOU SHALT LOVE

CHAPTER 1

Decision

I LOOKED THROUGH MY WINDOW AT THE FOOTHILLS OF MY once beloved Blue Ridge Mountains without a breath of response to their enchanted, haze-veiled beauty. They had no *meaning*. Once this beauty of Virginia's countryside had seemed the symbol of a deeper, total beauty. "Sacrament" is defined by the Book of Common Prayer as "an outward and visible sign of an inward and spiritual grace." Virginia's beauty had been to me a kind of sacrament.

Now I viewed it with distaste. We chill to the loveliness of an angelic face when we learn that its owner's conduct is in another category. I chilled to Virginia's fraudulent physical glories.

The bitterest aspect of my condition was that nothing seemed to have been *accomplished* by my inner destruction. No ranks of the enemy had been broken, no bridge, pass, or gate had been held against the foe to give meaning to the sacrifice of all my joy.

In the middle 1950's I had thought of myself as a finger-in-the-dike until help came. I had to keep back the withering brine of hatred and fear only until Virginia's brave thousands came quickly forward with sandbags, determined that there should be no inundation of our green land. But down the miles of dikes where I had thought to see hordes at work, I saw only scattered individuals who like myself were thrusting numbing fingers and arms into holes in the crumbling dike. The good people of Virginia rushed, not for sandbags, but for safety, while chill, brackish waters flooded in.

The futility of my expenditure was like a great weight. I was tired in my stomach, bones, brain. I wanted neither to think nor act:

What profit hath a man of all his labor which he taketh under the sun? . . . The wind goeth toward the south, and it turneth about unto the north; it whirleth about continually . . . In wisdom is much grief. Eccles. 1:3; 6, 18.

Yet deep in me something said that it would not be well to have less wisdom. I didn't quite wish I had not begun this bleak journey. I was in the desert because I had believed in something better than my experience demonstrated. The goodness I had imagined was worthier than the facts which had confronted me. My lot was cast with the best. I could not regret it.

Moreover, my discovery of the realities of human character was somehow related to goodness, even though what I had discovered was not good. My disillusionment itself was not a part of evil, of futility. It was in the category of progress. Perhaps the desert I was crossing symbolized progress from dream goodness toward real goodness.

Real goodness? Was there such a thing? All around me there was only desolation. To die would comfort me. It was past midnight in my spirit and death was a turned-down bed.

I didn't believe in anything. It wasn't so much that I actively doubted the tenets of my religion as that I lacked faith in them. All my beliefs that I had been in a position to test had been proven untrue. The Negroes I now knew bore little resemblance to the Negro I had envisaged since childhood. The white South with which I was contending was an utterly foreign land. The friends and relatives who had peopled my heart, since 1954 had not demonstrated the qualities which once I had taken for granted. And now I, too, stood revealed as a puny thing, soon spent, empty-hearted, defeated by less than a decade of adversity.

No confidence was possible even in those few relationships which so far were undestroyed. Having witnessed easy disintegration of many loving bonds I had trusted, I could not doubt that only accident preserved any of them. When a nearby blast shatters most of the crystal and porcelain in a china shop, the small number of objects left unbroken are not necessarily sturdier than those smashed: Mere chance intervened. I knew people to be other than I had believed. This encompassed *all*.

Aware of the gap between what we claim to think, feel, intend, and our actual performance in friendship or combat, I found conversation with even my nearest and dearest ones devoid of meaning. No matter what its nature or who the participants, a discussion represented merely a string of unconscious falsifications. Thus, no exceptions to my mistrust of people existed, or could exist.

I felt homeless in a vast sense. The South I had believed in was no more. Golden-hearted mankind was dead within me. The whole magic world of nobility, kindness, and fellowship I had once viewed with joy was just a painted backdrop. If I had been projected far into space, with no hope of returning to my home-world, I couldn't have been more alone, purposeless, or without hope.

Nothing anywhere seemed firm or dependable. All I had thought solid and durable was quicksand. Once I had had many convictions, certainties—now, none. I couldn't even think, for there was no way to begin, or any incentive for beginning—no premise from which to start.

"If only I had one thing I really believed in," I told myself helplessly, "I could try to rebuild. Or maybe I could
use it like a tuning fork."

Without volition something stirred in me. Without conviction I said, "I believe in God." Then I made a flat statement which surprised me: "I *choose* to."

A tiny thread of returning life ran through me: I had
chosen a premise, a place to stand. My mind took hold of
the truth that believing in God *is* a choice, an act of will, a
decision. I had thought of it as a conclusion reached after
weighing internal evidence. But the existence of God is an
hypothesis which I could neither prove nor disprove. Reason, therefore, could play no real part in my belief or unbelief. Either was a free-will choice.

After choosing, reason could come into play, ordering
my thoughts so as to make sense of my chosen hypothesis.
But at this crossroads I must choose belief or unbelief, then
follow the road of reason which took me in the direction I
had chosen. Perhaps it was better to say that I must choose a
premise, then build upon it, as elaborately as I wished, a
house of reasoned thought.

I examined the bit of ground I had chosen, welcoming
its firmness. God being universal, eternal, indestructible is
not subject to disintegration as my world of idyllic backdrops
and much-adorned images had been. To myself I said, "If
I build here, my house will stand."

This was strange, for I had thought my old house had
stood there. In my family, God was an "inherited" assumption (almost like an inherited talent) the taken-for-granted
foundation of everything. Yet something significant was
added when I *chose* to believe, something solid and important which had not been present before.

It was rather like a person's life being flavored and influenced by a talent for art from childhood up. He sketches
when he should be studying, he pores over photographs

of great paintings. But it isn't until the day he says to
himself, "I'm going to be an artist," that the course of his
life is changed. In the same way, the assumption that there
is a God who can be approached and called upon had
colored much of my life and guided my choices for many
years, but a new type of involvement had now come into
being. Indeed my position was new in at least three ways:

First, never before had I believed *only* in God. I had been
so wealthy in beliefs that an implied "and" stood in front
of my Christian creed: "*And* I believe in God, the Father . . ."
Shuffled in with a host of other beliefs—in myself, in man,
in many institutions and optimistic formulas—belief in God
may have been near the edge of the pile.

Second, I hadn't before ever taken a real "leap of faith."
When I believed in so much, it would have been silly not
to believe in God, too. Why leave out just that one thing?
Now, no longer believing in the worth of anything, it was
logical to discard a God who would create such a world.
Yet from the rubble-heap of convictions proven untenable,
I had searched out and chosen this one belief as sound.
Therefore it was mine.

Third, my religious faith had never before had *finality*.
I used to pride myself on remaining "open-minded" to the
possibility that atheists or agnostics might be right. I
weighed their philosophies with interest, lifting from them
whatever seemed of practical value. Resultant snarls of
conflicting doctrines didn't bother me because I never tried
to straighten them out.

But now I wanted no more of such dabbling. It belonged
to the old quicksand. I needed a definite, firm, permanent
faith, never to be questioned or doubted again—one that
could be both my premise and compass in outside confusion.

Never to be questioned again. That was vital. It made of
the decision a foundation rather than just another experiment in thinking.

Often I had heard the claim that "the leap of faith has power to alter any life." Obviously it would have. With it one's whole interior life changes focus. I felt more detached, relaxed. I still felt defeated but *how* I felt mattered less. "The will of God" ceased to be a cliché phrase and became a guide line, leading I knew not where, but having definite direction. The importance of what had happened to me diminished as the importance of following the will of God loomed large.

All I had heretofore taken for granted would now have to be re-examined. I must also re-examine much that I had tossed aside as not worth consideration. I had a new starting point for all my thinking, and this meant that everything must start fresh. In short, with the leap of faith, my old way of thought stopped, another started, and I had to bet my life that the new way, with unknown rational and spiritual consequences, was better than the old. Few will take such a leap until their old life is pauperized of meaning.

For me there was no inner resistance when the leap confronted me. My old way had proven to be quicksand, and here was rock: I believed in God. Upon this faith I would build my life. I felt eased and comforted. I felt as if I were standing up straight instead of thrashing about in desolate sands. But I knew I couldn't just stand there. I had to make sense of my choice, line up my thinking in such a way that it would be parallel to, and co-ordinated with, my new feelings. Otherwise, I would be a house divided against itself.

I must decide what kind of God I believed in, must take another leap of faith, and choose to believe that God is good. Without this, life could have no lure or purpose. I made it: "I believe *in* God, not just that He exists."

This excluded all the terrible possibilities which some people fear in religion—that it will make of this life a dungeon in which guilt, remorse, fear, and repression replace normal pleasures and satisfactions of earthly living. To believe *in* somebody is to give him your confidence. A cruel, far-off, an unjust, indifferent, or helpless God can't be believed *in*.

With this foundation established by faith, I felt I could go on to build by reason. The next step loomed. Since God is the Highest, He must represent the highest good I knew. Then if I thought of everything in the world as somehow related to this highest good—either stemming from it or promoting it—I would have a faith I could live by and act on because it would have built-in consistency. With this clear-cut criterion of a single, over-all good, I would know what decisions to make, how to live and act.

But what was the highest thing I knew? Astonished, I realized I had never thought it through.

A feature of my old thinking had been a point of reference which I called "the highest that we know." But this, I now saw, was a *group* of qualities, principles, ideals of first magnitude, as compared to secondary ones. For instance, I knew that those qualities which call for service and involvement are higher than those which permit one to be an island. Sideline liberals who enthroned tolerance and reason above justice and mercy were manifestly not choosing the highest, for tolerance and reason, while good, don't necessarily lead us beyond our separate existences.

To use an extreme illustration, with full tolerance and reason a person could stand calmly by while a man tortured another to death. He would not himself resort to torture, for a tolerant, rational man would be without motive for such action. But to prevent the torture would mean thwarting another human being who had decided what he wanted to do. Our man would ask himself if he had the right to interfere. He must be either just or merciful before he would be prompted to set the screams of the tortured above the rights of the torturer. Of themselves, neither tolerance nor reason would demand that he even point out to the torturer that his acts were intolerant and ultimately irrational.

In short, it was clear to me that the highest things are those which so intertwine us with another that we cannot stand apart from our brother in heart, mind, or body. They guide us into making his joys, sorrows, and problems our own. But among these highest, which is highest of all?

I must find out before going on. Here would be the key to my God's character. Otherwise, He would not satisfy my soul; and if God is supreme in the world, supreme satisfaction must follow right belief in Him. So my question should be phrased: "What is the best possible thing that God could be?"

Perhaps my greatest disappointments would point to my highest hope. What had I expected in people and not found? Courage? The awful timidity of nearly everybody had been one of my greatest shocks. But no, courage wasn't even among the highest things. It supplemented evil as readily as good. Beauty, then? The stark, unexpected ugliness— But beauty could be empty. My God was more than a God of beauty.

I went on down the list. Integrity? (Oh, that duplicity!) Concern? (The indifference, the callousness!) Loyalty? Kindness? Strength?

I halted. All these seemed to rest on some other, more primordial attribute from which they drew their importance or meaning. Just being strong, for instance, has no value in itself. A purpose behind the strength is implied. You are strong for the accomplishment, or the protection of something else. Kindness seemed closer to what I sought than the others but wasn't it more a result of something than a first cause?

Dependability? Oh, that was enormously important. The value of everything is immediately reduced if you can't depend on it. We even feel that we would rather have an inferior thing we can depend on than a better one which we can't. My discovery that I couldn't depend on the constancy even of a person's most characteristic attitude was one of the things which had made quicksand of my world. First, last, always, my God was dependable. But—what was the matter with me?—dependability isn't even among the highest things. You can be dependably evil!

I tried a different approach. What did I myself originally have—now lost—which had made every little thing seem significant? I reviewed my list from this angle. Again, dead end. "Concern" rang a tiny bell, but I was looking for a great clanging bell.

I tried once more. What experiences in my life had been *satisfying in themselves* quite apart from what resulted from them? Ah, now the great bell clanged! How could I have missed the one thing upon which all real happiness and all meaning finally depend! Like polished gems scattered among common pebbles, certain moments in my life shone. They were the times when my heart went out to someone or something so that in that moment I seemed to myself less than this other person or thing and for this other I would be well spent—and spent in joy.

"I believe that God is love."

It has been said that the affirmation "God is love" is heard *ad nauseam.* If our only acquaintance with it is hearing others rattle it off, doubtless this is so. It is *not* so if we have discovered it in our own experience.

Heard only from others, as I had heard it until now, it is one of the world's tritest statements—quite on a par with another overfamiliar affirmation: "I love you." But the words "I love you," spoken or heard when you yourself are experiencing them to the full are extravagantly exciting, incredibly, creatively new. In them the world is reborn for you. And in the words "God is love," experienced by you in the only way they can be fully experienced, in poverty of spirit, you are reborn.

I wish I could say that my rebirth took place just then with suddenness and drama, as happens with some. But it was more like the slow recovery from a near-fatal illness than like bursting new into the world with a cry. At this point I felt merely as if I had just passed the final crisis of a disease and, though still sick in mind and heart, was safe. Disintegration had been halted, healing begun.

The only thing quickly and tangibly restored was hope. The blank wall which had confronted me, close to my face, was shoved a long way back. Before me was a future for the making. I was still too weary and weak to do more than think about it a little, but knowing the space was there was important. When I was able to step upon it, a path awaited my tread.

Of course I had long believed the words "God is love"—or, rather, had not disbelieved them, for true belief is more a part of one's inner structure than my admission that God is love had ever been. My belief in man had been my vitals and bones. Not so with any beliefs about God.

But today there was newness in the quality of my responses. The old rote words stirred with life. As I pondered them, a fresh world picture dimly formed before me. What would it be like to live in such a world?—a world in which I looked to God for all the wondrous, warm responses I had once sought in man? What if I believed in God with the vitality of conviction which once characterized my belief in man? What would happen to my inner being if I loved God with the same outpouring of faith, admiration, fellowship, identification, and tenderness which once I felt for certain people?

It was as though in the midst of winter I had smelled new grass and early blossoms. I had glimpsed a green land on the other side of my desert. Like a mirage, the picture faded. But the bleakness of the desert no longer penetrated me so deeply. I had seen my destination. I knew I should survive to reach it. Some day I should be able to love again, and this time my love would be stored "where moth and rust doth not corrupt." In all of me that was weary flesh, and in all that was above weariness and flesh, I knew that by starting from the premise *God is love,* no life I remade for myself, no inner world I reconstructed, and no outer world I strove to realize could be without purpose, meaning, and worth.

CHAPTER 2

Love

"I BELIEVE IN GOD AND I BELIEVE THAT GOD IS LOVE." WITH this as my foundation (never to be questioned again) my alien, barren world began to hold a faint interest. A pulling forward and pushing back of values began; a clarifying, a rearranging, a shifting of emphasis.

What did I mean when I said "God is love"? First, that love is the standard, the measuring stick whereby I could judge the value of all things. Second, that by examining what I knew of love—how it makes us act, the goals and motives it seems to engender—I could make as sensible a guess as I was capable of concerning the character and intentions of God. And, third, that love is God Himself in the sense that my hand and what it does is myself in being and in action. Thus when I experienced love in its purest forms, I was experiencing God to the fullest degree that a limited creature like myself can experience Him.

Evidence that God is love spilled around me like spring sunshine. I saw that the broad trend of history, despite its specific horrors, points to God-is-love as man struggles upward, seeking to be increasingly humane. Accumulating knowledge converges on the truth that God is love as it uncovers the unifying principles which bring each element into creative relationship with others. And every individual discovers, either through his richest moments of fulfillment or his great gaping lacks, that love is what matters most.

It was clear that if I really operated on the assumption that God is love, not only would love take precedence over all else, but also I could measure the value of all else in terms of it—that is, in terms of whether it springs from, leads to, or promotes love. If it does none of these, I should question its value. Looking around me, I suddenly saw that in our age we evade love in an overwhelmingly inclusive way. By systems and analyses on every side we avoid love, wherever it appears. Emphasis on analysis and organization rivets our attention on mechanism rather than on essence, and love is essence.

Even charity has become organized charity, and we tend to feel guilty if we give aid spontaneously, rather than through "proper channels." Machinery of mercy so far removes us from personal participation in the lives of those we wish to serve that the word *mercy* loses all meaning. In the operation of caring for the "needy" and the "underprivileged" there is little place for the pouring out of hearts in identification, sympathy, empathy, affection.

Yet I saw that if our lives are controlled by physical, institutional, and psychological robots—machines, organizations, social customs, rules, methods, indoctrination, personal habits, fixed patterns of all kinds—then we must have robots assigned to do works of mercy, or they might not get done.

A mechanism of some kind stands between us and almost every act of our lives. Few of the young mothers I had known in bygone years raised their children from their hearts in natural creative and spontaneous joy. Instead, they studied rules, growing tense and rigid in a struggle to make the machinery of a particular theory work in raising their particular child. The child himself was often seen as a kind of machine that would do certain things if certain things were done to him, instead of as a center of creativity with a free and flowing—not a mechanical—inner being. Is this perhaps one reason why, as these children have become teenagers, delinquency has risen alarmingly?

We are like mechanics, so intent on listening to and analyzing the knocks and gratings of an imperfectly running motor in our car, that we have no eyes, ears, or thoughts for where the car is taking us. Anyone who has ridden through a lovely countryside with a man who is concentrating on the behavior of his motor, knows how blind, deaf, and absorbed he is. It would be the same to him if he were driving round and round within a prison wall. There is for him nothing outside the mechanism on which he focuses.

Many of us today live like this in all areas of our lives. We think about knocks and rumbles of our own, and of the various psychological patterns and systems around us. We seldom lift our thoughts to our rich surroundings as we travel through creation, or think of the purpose for which all mechanisms are set in motion. And if our thinking moves from psychological patterns to pulsing human need, right away we rivet it again on mechanisms of organization—organized aid and how to make it function more efficiently.

Humanity is like a busy mother who knows no tenderness because she is spent with the concentrated effort to keep her children clean, well fed, on schedule, and trained in a variety of proper habits. In short, we are more like an orphanage run on routines and formulas than like true parents to the children of men.

This avoidance of love, this escape from the claims of love by means of many mechanistic avenues, may be the great sickness which I had sensed among Virginia liberals when integration tensions rose. It may have been this that made thoughtful people inactive, active people devious. For always a mechanism stood between each person and his real resources, the power and creativity of love. Always there

was a mechanism—habit, custom, law, formula, theory—
between him and man's rightful goal, spontaneous self-
giving. When we lose love, we lose also our identification
with the universe and with eternal values—an identification
which alone makes it possible for us to lay our lives on the
altar for what we believe.

In all directions I saw discouragements to every kind of
love. Hardly anybody "believes in love" in the sense meant
when the phrase was coined. Even when we are *in* love we
seldom believe in the kind of deathless love which was a
generally accepted fact at the time *Evangeline* was written.
Such a man as the hero of this poem would be thought
neurotic today, pigeonholed with an analysis of his psychological mechanism, the essence which sustained him dismissed without a glance.

An unconquerable loyalty, springing from love and love
alone, is neither cultivated nor searched for today. Passionate love of country in an ordinary citizen is called fanatical
or sentimental. Only in a great leader is it viewed with respect. "Oh, say, can you see," though still sung, never could
have been written today. Sweeping mother love is categor-
ized as silver-cordism. No educated adolescent dares to be
consumed with a really deep love for either parent, knowing
the name it will be called. And what chance would Damon
and Pythias have today?

I pulled my thoughts up sharply. Was I heading toward
the vague, the spineless, the gooey? I thought not. If God
is love (not to be questioned!) the danger lies in the direction of too little, rather than too much, emphasis on
love, and the devil must be chuckling contentedly over
our modern fear of too much. There's nothing vague about
an emotion so impelling as love. Spineless? Indeed not! We
can confidently set the courage of love against the courage
of wrath. And sentimentality isn't inherent in love but, rather,
in the way certain persons approach anything precious.

True, sentimentality is at its most repellent when applied to love, but that is because the great musical masterpiece of the human heart is heard in love. Any false note, therefore, is at its most offensive.

I doubt if anyone who has experienced love denies its intrinsic value. He may say that it isn't worth having because one can't keep it, but in itself this is a confession of a longing to keep it if only one could. Every endeavor, every relationship glows, lives, is magically new when love is added. The dullest type of work if you love it sings through you like a masterpiece. The drabbest-seeming people when you learn to love them are revealed as full of rich harmonies. A long illness can be an area of peace in your life if you are nursed and tended in constant love. Even pain endured for the sake of love mellows and makes radiant the one who endures.

In my past, my surrounding world, my imagination, no situation or effort could be seen which I thought love would not aid, except those which are aggressively evil—war, crime, climbing to success upon another's failure. I recalled no one so repellent that he could not be made shining if only he loved his labors, surroundings, and others. Like salt, love sharpens all the flavors of life and merits of personality. It is significant that the re-enthronement of love is taking place in the social sciences, that psychiatry discovered that love is essential to mental health. If God is love—never to be doubted—then love is the power, key, and goal we seek. Yet we persistently fix our attention on our countless mechanisms, not turning to follow this living glory.

If God is love, so much follows: The most valuable attainment and possession must be love, and the way to be greatest is to love most. When we love, it truly is more joyful to give than to receive; and the Ten Commandments can be obeyed without conscious effort, like breathing, when we love enough.

Frank Lauback, who has taught illiterates to read their native tongues in more than two hundred languages and dialects, says he has proved in his experience that love is the common language of all peoples, and that you are safe among the most savage tribes if you only make it clear that you love them. A naïve hope? He has sojourned at length among cannibals.

As I pored over these thoughts, I felt as if, aching wearily, I had stretched out on a perfect bed. Here I could find renewed strength for the morning. I rested, then returned to my problem.

The tree of life was in sight, but how could I reach it? My capacity both to love and feel loved was lost. I still felt a clinging sort of affection for those nearest me, and terror that it might not be returned. But this bore little resemblance to a state of mind and heart which I could call real love. In some ways it was almost opposite: It bound me round with ropes of tension, compulsion, fear, whereas real love is freeing, ennobling, strengthening. These mere affections made me cowardly before possible loss, greedy for return. But with real love courage envelopes one like a cloak, and there is no asking—only answering without ceasing.

I didn't cherish the prison love I had now, having known something better. But how could I recapture my old freedom of heart in which giving and receiving love were equally easy? Even the first step eluded me.

But wait! I did see a first step. Couldn't I simplify my problem by reducing my two lacks to one? Was feeling loved essential, if without it I could still love? Here was the confrontation of an important truth which I had often brushed in passing. In 1950 I felt great emptiness in discovering that Negroes didn't love me, but was refilled when I reclaimed some of my love for them. Stronger and more creative than before, I had then returned to the struggle. And at the Public Education Hearing, it was no feeling of being loved which

dissolved my block and untied my fear. Rather, it was finding a way to love the people regardless of how they felt
about me. Here, too, I rose stronger and freer. When you
can love without being loved, you have not half success but
double success!

Now I saw that it isn't being loved which primarily
makes us feel happy and safe in a relationship. How do we
feel about being loved by someone to whom we are completely indifferent? Far from bringing us joy, it usually is a
burden and a bore. But if we care for someone who doesn't
care for us, a sense of triumph often mingles with our pain.
The most achingly rejected parent or lover seldom wishes to
love less in the sense in which I use and shall define the
word. To desire less, yes: but seldom to love less.

What is love? Searching all the fruitful and barren moments in my memory, I was satisfied only with the conclusion that it is a state of mind and heart in which we are
centered, momentarily or lastingly, in something or someone
so that the main fountains of our being flow to this other
center. It is the movement outward of that which is most
vitally ourselves. Moving with it flows appreciation, fellowship, sympathy, empathy, respect, affection, gratitude,
adoration—any or all. But love itself is neither any nor
a compound of all of these. I think it is the primordial, creative power behind all flows.

Love has been much analyzed and classified, thereby making it easier to think about. Yet in the larger sense I suspect
that more is lost this way than gained. Just as focusing on
the differences between ethnic groups leads away from consciousness of the overwhelming humanity of all, so the
categorizing of loves turns us from a realization that real
loves of all kinds are more like each other than like anything
else.

What I would call real love, whether for our home, work,
pet, friend, lover, parent, child, idol, or God, is characterized

by at least two tremendous qualities—the shift of our center of consciousness from ourselves to our beloved, thus enlarging us to include it or him; and the flow of ourselves toward the beloved, thus making self-sacrifice both natural and easy. There is no grim duty in service to a beloved. All giving is cheerful giving and bestows upon the giver pleasure, strength, satisfaction, peace.

The intrinsic, rather than the practical, worth of the object seems to have the largest bearing on how much of our being flows. We can love an inanimate thing—our home, our work—with our mind and strength, but only a living being can call forth our heart in tenderness and sympathy, and only a person can be loved with the full force of our spirit in gratitude and adoration.

Real love, I felt sure, no matter what its category, is not an in-pulling emotion. It moves only one way—out. The ultimate purpose of our need to be loved is surely not that we may know the joy of having this need filled, for this is a smaller joy than loving. The purpose of our need, by its very nature, can be no less than to draw forth love from another, so that he, too, may share in an outgoing heart. When our love goes to another, our consciousness extends to include him. This in itself is reward enough, yet there is another. Since God is love, when we love, we are united with the great, creative life stream of the universe. As St. John put it, "He that dwelleth in love, dwelleth in God and God in him." In the midst of such an experience, the reward of being loved in return is a pittance.

Everything of value in our lives stems from our moving *outward*. Perhaps it is the life force in us exploding as the universe is said to have exploded. We come alive when we feel love. Without it, we have no real access to others, no means of true contact, no awareness of anything except ourselves—perhaps not even of ourselves. No other cold prison walls are so grim as those of lovelessness. I knew that had I held to my love for those who had made a desert of my heart, only enrichment would have come from my bitter moments.

My thread of returning life had grown slightly stouter. My problem seemed less immense, less like poisonous mist. Almost it had gathered itself into one question: How could I love despite what I knew? Was there an answer?

I saw none. Yet Jesus had said, "Love your enemies," and your enemies always are pretty obnoxious characters—to you, anyway. Also, for nearly two thousand years all great Christian leaders had asserted both that man is a mess and that we should love him. There *must* be a way.

I didn't see it. The conception of man as "fallen sinner" and the Judaeo-Christian commandment, "Love thy neighbor," always had seemed to me an impossible paradox.

"Love moves spontaneously or not at all," I insisted. "And it won't move toward ugliness and evil. It is drawn from us by something lovely. To love our neighbor, we must believe him worthy and lovable."

I believed him neither. I had once seen in man something so richly warm and beautiful that my heart was liquid for him and easily flowed. Not so with this chilly version of him I now saw. And *this* was the truth about man, for it was what he acted out.

I could not love this true man. Yet we must love or stagnate, love or fear, love or hate—love or die. This ghastly inner death of not loving must surely be the hell the scriptures speak of with such foreboding. Here was true banishment from God. For how can you approach God, Who is Love, unless you have at least a little love within? I must have been very close to God in 1950, I thought. How easily and sweetly I had loved that lovely image of man.

Image! A realization struck me: Never had I loved *real* people. Just as the white Southerner never loved the real Negro but only the adorable image of him created in his own mind, so I, too, had loved only a man which I myself had made!

Moreover, this image I had both loved and worshiped. As with the ancient Israelites at Mt. Sinai, the Spirit of God was too abstract for me. Man was visible, tangible; hence, he had seemed more comforting. So I had made a golden man—a golden calf!

CHAPTER 3

Service

REALIZATION THAT MY OLD LIFE HAD BEEN FOUNDED ON A violation of the first of the Ten Commandments—"Thou shalt have no other gods before me"*—was a relief as well as a shock. A demoralizing aspect of my inner collapse was that it didn't make spiritual sense to me. The discovery therefore that I had been operating off base when I failed internally gave me hope for a future in which failure might be overcome.

Had I been far afield in other respects too? Among my faiths, belief in the value of service to others probably had been second in importance, for I willingly acted it out at dear cost. Was this a sound belief?

In these dark hours I doubted it. There were those who assured me that my efforts had achieved much, but to me it seemed I had accomplished nothing—at best, little—in service after years of Herculean exertion. The time, energy, and zeal expended would have paid heavy dividends if directed toward a personal goal. Was the columnist who had attacked me so viciously in *The Daily Progress* right when she charged that such efforts are essentially neurotic?

---

* Exodus 20:3, King James version.

Was it better to mind one's own business and pursue the "more realistic goal" of one's own happiness?

My answer was the realization that I wasn't sorry I had followed this course. Not sorry? Having achieved nothing that I intended, I was wrecked, empty, defeated in heart— yet I didn't regret it. Did that make sense?

Perhaps. For wasn't this always true of choices leading us beyond ourselves? At least, that is the testimony of many—of all, as far as I knew—who have made such choices in the history of man. Choose a selfish goal and suffer for it, gaining nothing, and we regret, bemoan our choice. Even when efforts are crowned with success, often little lasting satisfaction results. Not so, if our choice is an unselfish goal. Then failure to gain matters little—even pain matters little. We take griefs and distresses in stride.

Obviously we tacitly acknowledge something more important than our own much-vaunted happiness, more important, too, than our much-pursued success. True, we often hear that the way to be happy is to help others, so perhaps in this, also, we are only seeking our own happiness. But I thought not. In service I sensed a higher good. Happiness, indeed, appears to be, by its very nature, a by-product, not a goal. It never results from a direct search for it. And in the case of service, even when we are quite sure it won't bring us happiness, many times we choose to serve. Is this neurotic, or does service really offer a higher good?

Pondering, I thought I glimpsed an answer. Was this higher good enlargement of ourselves? When we love as well as serve, our consciousness includes that which we love-and-serve.

Suddenly my interest sat up. I knew I was on the track of an important insight. I began to pursue it with precision.

Service, I saw, is love in action, love "made flesh"; service is the body, the incarnation of love. Love is the impetus, service the act, and creativity the result with many by-products.

An important by-product is always *growth*. When we serve only ourselves, we are the size of just one person. When another is included our being is, in a sense, doubled, isn't it? This is the chief satisfaction in loving service. If we have this relationship with our community, we stretch to include it. If we love-and-serve our country, in a sense we *are* our country. If we love-and-serve an ideal we reach backward in time to its inception and forward to its consummation. To grow is sometimes to hurt; but who would return to smallness?

Another by-product is *freedom*. In loving service we escape the natural restrictions of self-centeredness which pull our horizons inward until they are like prison walls. The more we serve only our own interests, the less we are aware of anything beyond our own sensations and problems. We are like shut-ins. Indeed, occasionally one sees a shut-in like John Whetzel, the slowly dying man I visited in 1951, who led from his bed a larger, more adventurous life than is ever possible for the egotist, regardless of how far he travels. For the egotist never gets outside himself. It is not stone walls but our own egos which make of us real prisoners. In 1950, when I felt called to serve, I broke loose from my self-center and had a feeling of being magically free. And who will not suffer and sacrifice for freedom?

Peace is still another by-product. There's a mechanical monotony in self-centeredness which builds up tension. We escape this in dedicated service. When we pursue our own ends, we go round and round on our private treadmill, grinding out food for our desires which grow with feeding and demand more food. We go round and round, getting rich and never feeling rich, famous and never feeling famous, powerful and never feeling powerful. For the tumor of desire always grows faster than the body of achievement.

We joke about the multi-millionaires who cant, "I'm not a rich man," but in their hearts they are not, and never can be, rich. We don't see on the faces of those who pursue self-centered goals that look of relaxed radiance so often seen on the faces of those who serve in love, at no matter what great sacrifice.

Self-centered existence, once we're partly free of it (for we are never wholly free), appears as a kind of cancer life which, in attempts to increase only itself, results in self-destruction. It's better to be a member in the body of humanity, even if one suffers and dies in service to the whole.

A sense of belonging is a by-product of service—a feeling of being a member in the body of all creation rather than merely a thing unto one's self. For me this had been swallowed up in the pain of being excluded from the flock, but it isn't always so. If we serve along lines which are acceptable to the flock, our sense of membership in both the whole and flock greatly increases. Those who render such service make up the local and national rosters of loved and honored favorite citizens, and life offers perhaps no sweeter, more satisfying reward than such love and honor from those one has served.

There was still another by-product that I couldn't quite grasp. Was it safety? Not safety, surely! We always invite many dangers and losses in true service. Security? That was closer. Perhaps, in the larger sense, the only real security lies in loving service. When our conscious being reaches beyond our own borders, we are relatively secure, regardless of the degree of personal danger. None is so vulnerable as the self-centered man. All his eggs are in one fragile basket.

True, if you put some of your treasures into another, equally fragile basket, you gain little, if any, security. But when your consciousness includes many individuals, a whole group, or a large field of endeavor, your vulnerability is much reduced, and you feel fear slip away. When your consciousness includes service to ideals, your only devastating danger is disillusionment. Is this why frail-bodied idealists often show surprising moral and physical courage in defense of their ideals? Being centered in these, to lose them is worse than to lose their lives.

My area of solid ground seemed larger now. I could even comprehend some of my behavior and experiences of the past decade. In 1950 I had loved both white and colored Southerners, had acted on this love, trying to bring them all together in understanding and brotherhood. My consciousness, therefore, reached out and included them. That was why possible loss and damage to my little treadmill-self held slight threat.

Perhaps, too, this was why I had sensed that "bravery" was not the word for my lack of fear concerning my personal welfare—if, that is, bravery is the doing of one's duty despite a recognition of danger. I didn't feel in danger when my person or my material welfare was threatened because my life center was elsewhere.

Something important was still unexplained: Since I had served eternal principles, as well as many people, why wasn't I invulnerable? The early Christians were made invulnerable by their identification beyond themselves. I sensed that I was near the heart of my problem now. I knew I needed what the early Christians had, but what this was specifically—as compared with the Christians of my acquaintance—remained a mystery. I returned to lesser inquiry. What was my present state of mind?

Well, I wasn't self-centered any more. I cared hardly at all what happened to me. This was not in itself bad—perhaps even good, depending on what use I made of it. If I let it be the end, the final step in hopelessness, then it became just that. But maybe it could be used as a first step into a new life!

I didn't want to return to the sweatbox of self-centered

caring. Surely that in itself was a kind of proof that I was headed toward something better. Indeed, I had already tasted the something better. Since 1950, in my best moments I had been less self-centered than humanity-centered. The trouble now was that I wasn't humanity-centered either.

Suddenly I knew what ailed me. I had no center! I hung in midair, and so felt nothing, cared for nothing. You are centered in what you love, and I didn't love anything or anybody. Without love you are a homeless wraith, a ghost. Indeed, yes! that was how I felt—like a ghost. My human life was over, because there was nothing to draw me into the current of human living. Not only did nothing remain of my once lusty faith in the South, in people, and in myself, but also I had lost hope for a better world and for my making a worthy contribution toward it. In my emptiness, I knew St. Paul right in naming those three essentials to inner life, of which love was the greatest. Without them I had no incentive for action, no joy in reception, no peace in stillness.

Faith in people is necessary for a relationship. If you don't believe in their sincerity, dependability, goodness, or love, you really have nothing you want to say to, or hear from, them. And if you have no hope of making anything any better, effort becomes increasingly difficult until at last it is quite impossible. But if you have love, then hope and faith seem to follow: "Love believeth all things . . . hopeth all things." Without it, I neither wanted to speak nor to listen.

How impotent lovelessness rendered me. Having known the gushing spring of loving service, I recoiled from service without love. To others I hoped I as yet appeared little changed. My old habit patterns of friendliness and service were well grooved, and mechanically I went through most of the motions of normal human exchange. But soon the diminishing force of this momentum would be spent. Cour-

tesy, kindness, service are rigid, robotlike, without love.
⬛ penalty, not a gift, alike to server
⬛ the latter, imprisonment to both,
⬛ ive. Love is not genuine unless it
⬛ her is service genuine unless it

⬛ was worth attempting. All was
⬛ goeth down, and hasteth to his
⬛ e wind . . . whirleth about con-
⬛ unchallenged. I was ready to be
⬛ ad in other ways already. Hur-
⬛ ing premise:

"I believe in God, and I believe that God is love. Upon
this belief I will bet my life, for if it isn't true, life isn't worth
living. I believe in a God who is love. Starting from this, I
will remake my inner life."

A thought struck. If I really did that, wouldn't *God be my
center*? I felt on the brink of a great discovery, breathlessly
close to something I couldn't quite reach. How did you go
about becoming God-centered?

CHAPTER 4

Man

My old belief in golden man appeared to promote love, I pointed out to myself, and if God is love (not to be questioned), then the rightness or wrongness of a belief can be gauged by whether or not it promotes or sustains love. So wouldn't I have to consider this belief in golden man a good belief?

No, I decided, because my image of golden man could never be sustained except in superficial situations. My fragile idol could not endure the impact of reality, and when it broke, my love—lacking reason for living longer—inevitably died. Therefore, while this belief seemed to promote love briefly, it ultimately destroyed it, leaving me with a despair deeper than any personal wound.

Personal betrayals and rejections, though they smarted and ached, had not directly been my undoing. Rather, they had pointed always to something beyond the personal. As they heaped one upon another, something was being proved about people in general that I didn't want proved.

I had little feeling of being personally ill used—or, rather, little that it was important whether or not I was personally ill used. But the fact of being ill used had jarred me into clarified perception of how universal is the ill use which human beings make of one another.

At times I almost wanted to believe that I was being discarded because I merited it. But I could not escape the conclusion that my unhappy experiences were mere *examples* of an ignobility which people characteristically reveal under certain adverse conditions. We can depend on real friends to give us sympathy, moral support, time, even material aid, during brief periods of such standard trouble as illness, grief, or loss of employment. They expect no reward but our gratitude, a boost to their own self-respect, the pleasant feeling of serving a loved one, and possibly, though not necessarily, applause from approving onlookers.

I mean no belittling of such friends when I point out that actually these rewards are considerable. They are, indeed, enough to make the average normal person quite happy. Service which brings such rewards is far different from really costly service. Only when the latter is called for do we discover we are quite alone.

I had often read, without giving it modern application, the story of how Peter glibly denied Jesus so soon after passionate affirmations that he would die for his friend and Lord. Neither at home nor at school, not even at church, had I been given preparation for the shocking discovery that such behavior is simply to be *expected of friends*.

But the significant thing is that this lack of preparation was not peculiar to me. Agreed that, as T. J. Sellers said, I was "a naïve idealist," and that my image of man was loftier than most. Even so, I represented only an extreme example of a basic, general misconception. Although we have our quota of skeptics and cynics whose chief faith is in evil, you have only to read popular magazines and view the more popular motion pictures and television shows to realize that by and large the American people (and doubtless many other peoples) subscribe to a group of beliefs which under testing prove untenable. The empty, defeated hearts of our young men returning from our victorious wars should have convinced us that the foundations of our faiths will endure no tempest of reality.

Aside from social scientists and clergymen (whose business it is to understand the human heart), the minority of intellectual sophisticates, and the substratum of nonillusioned underdogs, there probably are few people who don't expect more of human nature than in fact it is able to deliver. Out of both my past and present life there loom faces of many who believe in others desperately, who set their whole faith in human friendship, integrity, steadfastness, and who look to human fellowship for personal fulfillment.

Yet the simple facts of the universe do not justify any such faith. The crushing discoveries I had made probably would be made by others if they were thrown into situations which revealed the truth. Since their activities do not challenge their illusions, naturally those illusions remain. But we cannot be assured of lives which will not challenge illusions, and it is not well to hold faiths which will surely betray us in times of greatest stress when we most need firm support. These flimsy faiths are like cardboard crutches made to resemble stout wood. Standing in the corner, they convince the eyes but when we throw our weight upon them, they crumble and we fall.

Except for the relatively few who have either natural skepticism or special education, almost everyone harbors certain hollow golden images of man which he worships, and in his own fashion suffers from the fact that his images little resemble the unyielding facts.

For instance, in any relationship which resists being fictionalized, such as marriage or parenthood, the result usually is the slow corroding of bright hopes, and the opening of great caverns between what we want to believe these relationships hold and what we secretly find they do hold. Our gleaming images of husbands and wives result in demands which cannot be met and thus too often, through disappointments and resentments, lead to retaliations.

Speaking of their broken marriages, people monotonously use certain phrases: "Before we were married *I thought* . . . *I believed* . . . *I imagined* . . ." Always the contrast is large between what he or she expected and what really happened.

Our idol images are cruel as well as costly. Many teenagers carry loads of guilt from the visionary perfection a parent projects upon them. Then they, in turn, thrust similar loads on relatives and friends. We expect others to be grateful for our high opinion of them, but upon them is laid the burden of justifying our impossible beliefs.

Romances dissolve in varying degrees of bitterness; friendships founder; parents view their children with pain; adolescents look resentfully upon their parents; husbands and wives try not to recall wistfully dreams of one another unfulfilled—all because we ask of others what no human being can give, the fulfillment of our hopes and the satisfaction of our hearts.

In ordinary comfortable circumstances, by shutting our eyes occasionally, we can hang on to rainbow illusions fairly well, because then we have slight opportunity to see man functioning without his pretenses. Disenchantments which force themselves upon us we isolate by blaming the particular individual "who let us down." Some of us spend our lives going from one broken relationship to another, making each disaster specific, and never once challenging our own false expectations.

Doubtless we would be less stupid did we not have full co-operation from others. In seeing a friend as golden, you will get his help. Indeed, you probably will simply be subscribing to his own self-image as he projects it. To most of us "a true friend, who understands" us is one who fully accepts our self-image.

We get aid, too, from a subconscious "gentleman's agreement." Partly as a mechanism of social grace, and often, too, in a genuine effort at kindness ("Do unto others . . . !"), practically all of us engage in efforts to help each other keep our illusions. We offer friends enlarged and expurgated editions of our own and other people's opinions of all their dear ones. The haste with which we change the tenor of our remarks in discussing someone once we know a friend or relative of his is present, should (but usually doesn't) lead us to pause and ask ourselves, "How close to fact are the images which support my own relationships?"

Finally, biographers and fiction writers help us make idols of men. With their eyes pardonably turned toward their royalty checks, they are encouraged to present man appealingly. Though there are notable exceptions, by and large golden man sells better than flesh man.

It is amusing to note that our very language exposes our enormous self-deception. Take the word "disillusioned" in its original meaning—that one simply has been disabused of an untruth. Then note that we usually use the word to describe a person who has lost something of value which he can't be expected to be happy without!

Searching for the original source of the gold with which I made my man image, I blushingly realized that I pilfered most of it from the Judaeo-Christian treasure house. There it rests as an ideal toward which we are expected to strive, a vision of God's will for us. In this form it has inspiration and no evils. It is only when we claim it as an accomplished fact that it becomes an idol and a lie.

And I had stolen the principles on which I tried to operate, ironically rejecting most of the theology which midwifed them, and which would have allowed me to function on such principles without being torn asunder. I realized that probably most Americans who range from semi-religious to non-religious belong to my gang of robbers, being sustained in some way by ideals and moral values originally spelled out and demonstrated by deeply religious people. To put it bluntly, we feed on the fruits of someone else's authentic relationship to God.

Apart from the sophisticated few, people often think of others as possessing virtues in much the way they possess physical characteristics, like the color of their eyes. We think of certain persons as being quite without cruelty, cupidity, duplicity, vindictiveness, and when the traits crop up in defiance of our flattering images of these persons, we quickly explain the incident in a way to cover up the trait. "John is a little thoughtless sometimes." "Alice sometimes exaggerates without realizing it." "There must be some mistake: Jimmy would be incapable of such an act! I know him well." Criminologists inform us that under certain conditions and pressures, internal and external, any one of us is capable of anything.

Amiable ordinary people often think of human virtues as deep, and human faults (unless they dislike the person) as more superficial. Orthodox Christianity has always stoutly maintained that man's sinfulness, not his virtue, is the thing on which you can depend. In different language, science agrees. Characteristics last acquired, it says, are quickest shed, and those of civilized man are very recent. Man can be expected to become less and less admirable and "human" when his pressures and problems mount.

That he sometimes flowers, not wilts, under the scorching sun of pain is a significant, mysterious truth which is missed if we expect him to flower. This flowering, says science, is evolution's occasional breakthrough of characteristics which one day will be common. Theology states it more simply: "It is the grace of God." In any case, my unrealistic expectations had robbed me of many joyful surprises. The cult of man, I could now see, distorts our whole outlook, giving false hopes doomed to be dashed, and withholding many of life's highest and most wondrous pleasures.

Where had I got my golden concepts of the content of nobility, my golden vision of what man ought to be? I said I got them from our Judaeo-Christian heritage. But wasn't I just pushing the question back a few centuries to the first people who had them? Where did *they* get them? Certainly not from their own depths, for our depths, we have seen, disclose worse, not better, more animal—not more godlike —qualities and yearnings.

Moreover, a vision is not something a man can make or even choose. It comes upon him, out of the stuff of the universe. When a vision of a nobler way of life does come, then he can choose to believe or disbelieve in it, but he cannot choose its coming. I think there is no simpler, more direct way to say it than that such visions are *sent*.

Indeed in almost every way the religious approach to life now struck me as simpler and more direct than those used by the more modern frames of thought. All the great facts, truths of existence, are set forth by religion in clear and powerful lines, the deep needs of the heart defined in free, strong strokes. Much that is "newly discovered" and laboriously traced in psychology was given concise and adequate treatment centuries ago in Christian doctrine. And doubtless much remains in religion which psychology would do well to discover.

I found that I had no need which some established doctrine did not completely fill. I had never taken orthodox belief seriously because I had not heretofore experienced enough despair of myself and my world to realize that here is a blueprint for making any life meaningful. Here is a road map on which are marked highways for every need and temperament, all leading from confusion and inner desolation toward an ordered and meaningful inner existence.

Reviewing the established doctrines of Christianity, I began to see the whole of life in a new and simpler way. How complicated, hazardous, and fraught with built-in defeat had been my attempts to practice Judaeo-Christian ethics with my eyes fixed on man instead of God.

Such attempts can succeed, I now saw, only when man's pretenses of nobility are unchallenged by threats to his personal well-being. One of the most obvious reasons why sound ethics can't be based on faith in man is that if man is our standard, our conscience is at the mercy of the kind of people we happen to know. Among gangsters we will be ashamed to neglect a chance to commit a profitable crime; among atheists, ashamed to go to church or pray; among segregationists, ashamed to treat a Negro as we would a white.

Centered in man, we feel guilty under man's disapproval, even if our behavior represents a higher level of morality than that of our critics. Flooded with such feelings in the midst of combat, even when we most surely know we are right, our strength is much reduced.

Man will not suffice as our frame and center. When our belief is in man, what alternative have we to dependence on his approval and trust in his judgment of our conduct? Only trust in our own, and this would call for insufferable conceit. Without a higher frame of reference, how can we believe we are right when many voices proclaim us wrong? Moreover, we must have a frame which both represents the highest that we know and is "the same yesterday, today, and forever." How well I knew the fatality of being at the mercy of man's shifting judgments!

Also, man will not do as a frame because his skill at self-deception is such that each person creates a maze of rationalization about himself which, if we take it seriously, will eventually create hopeless, exhausting confusion in our own thoughts. I could think of no one who was aware of playing the traitor to his own principles and to white and colored friends who defended them. Each saw himself as standing firmly with banners unfurled. When our eyes are fixed on shifting man, our standards shift easily without our knowing it.

We are like people seated on a railway train halted in a station, not certain whether our train or the one next to it is moving—unless we look out the opposite window at some fixed object. In times of tension and confusion we must have something fixed to look at, something which is the same yesterday, today, and forever. Because their eyes are fixed on shifting man, tolerance of the views of others becomes for so many Southern liberals—quite logically—a greater virtue than loyalty to principles. For principles, too, if you believe in man rather than in God, become only some people's views.

In short, the various humanitarian philosophies, once they pull completely away from religion, tend to defeat themselves. I suspect that it is nearly impossible to serve man in times of severe crisis when he most needs serving, unless we keep our eyes on something higher and more reliable than man—if not on God Himself, at least on some eternal principle which reflects some aspect of His Nature. For man always opposes an unfamiliar good. Man fights the inauguration of good in every form, calling each advancement evil, until the new form of good becomes commonplace. Attempts to serve man with our eyes fixed on man are like trying to steer a ship by fixing our eyes on its prow. God-is-love is our North Star. By it, even with rough seas, we can bring our vessel into port.

I had always felt superior to orthodox Christian theology, not seeing the simple realism of its view. But now that the mask of brave, kind, honest, loyal, and just man had fallen away, I found myself face to face with Adam, Cain, and the betrayers and crucifiers of all that saves. Stripped by strife of his bejeweled garments of pretense, the Biblical man of original sin emerged.

CHAPTER 5

God

THE REASONING AND INSIGHT OUTLINED IN THE LAST FOUR chapters did not occur to me in a short time. Long before autumn 1959 bits of them were coming, almost as irrelevant musings. Momentarily I would feel that I had got hold of something important, but when I tried to place it in my old house of faiths, it wouldn't fit, and I would lay it aside.

If you've ever seen an old frame house in the process of falling down, you know how long it takes. It sags in the roof, leans to the left, collapses on one side, and you wouldn't dare go inside for months, even years, before it finally groans and splinters to the ground. It was so with my house of faiths. In 1956, it became untenable. In 1959, it fell.

I collected materials for a new house and pored over mental and spiritual architectural blueprints long before I chose the site. By then nearly all the building materials were gathered. I had only to salvage them from the rubble and arrange them in a logical way, then start to build.

After I laid my new foundation, it was clear that I couldn't go on without love. Yet I saw no way to get it again. You can't make yourself love. Love rules and will not be ruled. It smilingly ignores all orders. It must be drawn, not pushed. It flows of itself or not at all. Command

it, and you find yourself shouting to an empty room. Before
I could love, I knew I must find the lovable. But where?
The worthy, darling people I had once envisioned were
products of my own thoughts, while man in his reality was
not such as to draw forth my heart.

"If only there were one person I could believe in as once
I believed in all," I cried. "Someone whose goodness is so
dependable that it is never for any reason set aside, maybe
my heart would thaw in one spot, and I could use this little
warm place as my pathway to life.

"*Just one person* who is utterly good and lovely?" I
repeated haltingly. "Why, God is like that. Maybe I could
love Him."

Could I? All my life I had heard about loving Him. It had
seemed a figure of speech. By it you merely meant that you
took Him seriously. It was a new thought that I might be
able to feel for God that sweet outrush of the heart I used
to experience when I loved a friend.

I had learned by rote Jesus' summation of the Law: "Thou
shalt love the Lord thy God with all thy heart, and with all
thy soul, and with all thy mind. This is the *first and great
commandment*. And the second is like unto it; Thou shalt
love thy neighbor as thyself. On these two commandments
hang all the Law and the Prophets."

Halfheartedly, I had even made attempts to understand
what it might mean to love God with one's whole content,
one's *all*. Now and then I tried to love Him; but my failure
hadn't troubled me much, since loving mankind seemed
really the same thing. Didn't Jesus say, "Inasmuch as ye
have done it unto the least of these, ye have done it unto
me?"

But I wondered now if Jesus hadn't meant specifically
acts of kindness—the filling of man's desperate needs. After
all, the only way you can be kind to God is to be kind to
man for God's sake. But attitudes and emotions are in a

different category. We are told to worship *only* God, and to love man second, not first. I hadn't even loved God second. I just hadn't loved Him.

But maybe I would be able to love Him now, for I had incentive. Like the leap of faith, to love Him was no longer just a difficult chore, but a life-saving measure! I must, therefore I could—and would.

But how? If love will not be compelled, aren't we commanded to do the impossible in Jesus' summation? Or is it possible *by indirection*?

Something below the conscious level stirred. I felt truth back there, hidden. An adage, rooted in farm life, pushed itself forward, almost making me laugh at its incongruity: "You can lead a horse to water, but you can't make him drink."

Yes, hearts and horses were alike in this. As a child I would take my horse to water, then just stand there until she was good and ready to drink. Sometimes she would thrust her nose in eagerly, and I had joy with her in the visible slaking of her thirst. Other times, if I took her to the wrong drinking place, she would sniff the water, back off, paw the earth, snort and debate before she would take even a tentative sip. Once, even, I had to ride her many miles home to her own stream because she wouldn't drink the trough water in a strange stable. She was sick with thirst after two or three days of refusing to drink.

The human heart, too, must have the right water before it will drink. It would have none of ugliness and evil, of the unloving and the unlovable. You had to take it to the right water, and then just—

I sat upright in bed where I lay musing. If I took my heart where there was something lovely and lovable, surely it would love! Almost like St. Paul, I seemed to see a blinding light, and wanted to fall on my face before it. Thoughts which I had touched only lightly now seared into my consciousness.

Again I asked, "Where would the human animal—who becomes less human, more animal, the deeper into him you go—get a vision of such loveliness as I and others had had? Obviously, *obviously*, not from his own depths. Where then? There must exist an objective Reality from which the vision of nobility and lovability comes like a radiation. Since man is not like the vision, God must be. Not only is He Love, but also He is lovable—and being infinite, is infinitely lovable. To His lovableness there can be no end. I could love Him with *all*."

I saw that my wildest vision of lovableness would inevitably fall short of what God is. I must take my heart to Him, and then stand and wait. Surely it would drink.

But if all this was so, why hadn't I loved Him all along? It could only be because *I didn't know Him.*

No one could love the God I had called mine for most of my life. I had the supposedly enlightened concept of Him as a great beneficent power, essence of goodness. The concept of God as a Person had seemed anthropomorphic to me. But unless we are prepared to concede that pure energy or abstract substance is higher than the totality of man, my old conception of God was hardly logical.

What colossal ego it fosters! If you conceive of Him simply as a great power, no matter how perfect and good, you quite unconsciously assume Him to be either merely an inaccessible First Cause or else there to call upon, to *use*—a sort of Aladdin's Lamp rubbed by your prayers. In the one case, He is little more than a word to you. In the other, you, not God, are the center of your universe—though you hastily point out that He answers other people's prayers, too.

One almost inescapable result of the latter position is that faith in His goodness becomes contingent on His services. The fact that you may call this It a "Him," only thinly disguises the necessity of thinking of yourself as the one who really gives the orders ("asks") and God as the one who obeys ("gives"). If He disobeys you often, you just fire Him ("stop believing"). No wonder I had never quite understood why humility was considered such a virtue!

My first spontaneous smile in many weeks came as I saw how, down the ages, man has steadfastly inflated his own ego by conceiving of God as something lower than himself. This effort probably has reached its most triumphant success in our mechanical age with a conception of Him as the kind of thing which runs our man-made machines! Even the ancient conception of Him as a bird-headed lion, or other composite animal, at least allows Him a low form of consciousness and will.

This tapestry of errors would be impossible if we didn't evade Jesus' First and Great Commandment. Any serious effort to love God immediately reveals our "enlightened view" as the lowest rung on the ladder. A composite animal possibly can be loved at least as a pet. But what heart could go out to vague, pervading power? It would be like loving a tankful of gas—or, rather, like loving the electric current which helps us in countless ways.

You can't even be grateful to such a thing. You can be glad it's there, dependent on it, and frightened at the idea of its sometimes failing you, but that's a long step from its stimulating your highest feelings of fellowship, gratitude, or love. Since these are the feelings we must have for inner health, if our God does not inspire us to pour them out, of necessity we turn to man and place him on our highest throne.

Of course we must realize that God is far more than any human person, but certainly He is not less. All power and all good essences His Person must assuredly include, but also it must tower above all this, as the personality of man towers above the sum of his feeble merits. If love is the highest thing we know, then the *most lovable being we know* must be the the concept closest to the truth of God

which our finite minds can grasp. Well knowing, and pro-
claiming, that He was vastly more, the Hebrew prophets
visualized their God as very human indeed. The result was
a profound and majestic faith.

I pulled my thoughts back from this reconnaissance to the
problem at hand. How could I get to know the Person of
God, so that I could find life through loving Him?

Well, I thought, what do you do when you want to know
a human person? You think about him, go where he is, talk
to him—about himself, not you—and learn about him from
others.

That seemed clear enough, so I pitched into the program.
I got a shock. When I tried to think about God, or talk to
Him about Himself, in a few seconds I ran out of things
to think and say. From having thought that I was rather
close to God, I had to face the stark fact that He was more
a stranger to me than any human stranger.

How glibly I had spoken to other "dedicated Christians"
of my sense of His Presence with me. I now realized that
I felt this Presence in much the way you feel that of a tenant
who rents your spare room but who keeps such odd hours
that you never see him. You know you're not alone in the
house, and you're thankful for the check he leaves on the
hall table. But that's all you know about him—and you're
probably glad of it. God had been my tenant.

The worst of it was that until now (along with most of
the other people I knew) I had considered such a relationship the utmost in faith. In trying to think of God as at
least no less than a human person, I had learned how far
below the human level my relations with Him really were.
Even if I were an orthodox Southern Segregationist with
a Confederate flag in my lapel, I certainly wouldn't have a
single friend if I treated people the way I treated God.

Suppose I talked to human friends as seldom, as reluctantly, as I did to Him! Suppose when I did condescend to

speak, I rattled on entirely about myself—worse!—often only about my troubles, problems, lacks. Suppose I showed friends that there were literally hundreds of things I would rather do than be with them! In my hasty talks with God I seldom even listened to see if He wanted to reply!

Of one thing I was sure: Along with any sincere effort to obey the First and Great Commandment would go a new way of life, a whole new World. I had a strange, exciting feeling that I was about to step through the Looking Glass, not into the reflected world in which everything is backwards, but into the real world, from this crazy backwards world in which nothing was as my heart told me it ought to be.

I paused and drew a long breath, then plunged again into the struggle for the survival of my will to live.

I had been proud of the "high quality" of my prayers because I sometimes gave thanks for the beauties and wonders of the world, and I had often smugly noted in past years that I reaped the benefit (got my reward) in a sense of well-being which much exceeded that of most persons in better circumstances. We can't be fully aware that we have a thing until we're thankful for it, and the thanks I sent skyward kept me conscious of everyday blessings which most people take for granted.

My pride now took a nose dive as I realized that even in this manifestly right mode of prayer, my thought hadn't really focused on God. It was thankfulness, not gratitude I felt. In thankfulness, you're glad *you* have the thing; in gratitude, your consciousness opens out and includes the one to whom you are grateful. How my heart would have poured out to a human person who had given me the things for which I thanked God with dispatch!

Suddenly I had an overpowering feeling that I didn't want to think any more—an almost panicky desire to close all the doors of my mind. I knew what it meant and steeled myself: I was about to have insight I didn't want!

An innocent-looking thought approached: I recalled having been well pleased with the frequency with which I asked God's forgiveness—especially considering how little I needed it compared with everybody else I knew . . . In a flash the innocent thought snatched off its mask, and I shrank back in pure horror.

All my requests for forgiveness had been a string of paste-pearl words. The only prayers I had ever prayed with deep feeling were the unverbalized ones I silently offered in hearty thanksgiving. In spirit they were modeled after the prayer of the Pharisee: "God, I thank thee that I am not as other men"!

In the first honest, humble slump of my life, I sank to my knees and prayed the familiar prayer of the General Confession from the Book of Common Prayer. I had repeated it a thousand times, usually by pure rote. Today every word of it was mine: "I have offended against Thy holy laws. I have left undone those things which I ought to have done; and I have done those things which I ought not to have done; and there is no health in me."

Having put little into this prayer before, I had got little back. This time there stole through me a sense of having been cleansed and refreshed. Moreover, I felt the heretofore steadily thickening wall between me and others crack and crumble at least in one place. When my fellowship with golden man disintegrated, no fellowship of any kind remained. Now there awakened in me a less lovely but more relaxed sense of the great fellowship of human failures, of sinners, among whom I could be humbly at home.

In one corner of my heart I had retained a vision of myself as golden even while, as I gazed, other persons became mere flesh. I had experienced, and fled from, terrible brief glimpses of a version of myself which others forced upon me.

But in my heart of hearts I didn't believe I was unworthy like the rest! I was separate, different. As my other idols broke, I cast them down but I had remained on a tiny throne. Now I, too, was fallen—and with the others again.

Although through accidents of personality, it had been easier for me to speak out, easier to take an unpopular stand, than it was for most, on many occasions when I should have done so, I had not—for fear. Like all the others, I had hastily explained these lapses, lied to myself, refused to face my real motive for silence. Intent on their own way of doing the job, others had not backed me up in my efforts to make the Southern Dream come true. But I, absorbed in my own method, had many times ignored the struggles of those with whose methods I did not agree—and had passed by on the other side when they lay defeated by these methods which I thought wrong.

With a wry smile I realized that I couldn't have recognized duplicity in others had I not contained it. We have no access to the workings of other minds except through our own. Were we not all set in the same mold there would be no human nature and each heart would be a mystery to every other. Even language would be impossible!

Jenny, Miss A., Mrs. B., and my party-giving friend had exploited me no more than I had them. I had not loved them for themselves but because they made me feel good. And when I decided that they were less than I had thought, hadn't I politely frozen them out of my life, just as my top-of-the-pyramid friends had frozen me out when I became an object of unpleasant publicity?

Had not disillusionment, with all warmth gone, looked from my eyes at my middle-of-the-pyramid friends, just as it had looked from theirs at me? They had nothing to say to me when they found that I harbored thoughts they repudiated. Had I not done exactly the same to them?

At some time in some form I, too, had been guilty of all

the heartless, vainglorious, deceitful, and cowardly acts I had seen done. Sins of commission and omission alike had been mine. No more than the worst of them had I been true either to my brother or to my God. We have all fallen short of the Vision of what we ought to be. There is none who has not failed. And I now saw that those who feel contempt for the failures of others are the worst of all.

This was my judgment: That I had let my heart freeze with censure. Having seen the Vision of Loveliness, I had not sought its Source, but stayed with the graven images I had made in the Vision's likeness. I had looked upon the Living but had remained behind with the dead, of which I had become one.

CHAPTER 6

Christ

SINCE I KNEW TOO LITTLE ABOUT GOD EVEN TO CONTACT HIM, I tried to get information from others by asking about their personal experiences with God and what steps they had found effective in learning to love Him. Quickly I discovered that if there's one thing most Christians regard as more crackpot than taking seriously the Second Commandment in Jesus' summation of the Law, it is taking seriously the First! So I resolved to do most of my seeking through reading or at occasional religious retreats.

With doggedness I pursued the search, being sure of at least two facts—that my life depended on my learning to love God, and that to do this I must think of Him not as nonhuman, but as human-and-more. Inescapably I was confronted with the Christian conception of Jesus Christ as truly Man and truly God.

I suspect that no intelligent person, with or without religious faith, will deny that there's something seriously wrong with modern Christians. Is it simply that not one in a hundred—perhaps in a thousand—even among clergymen does what he is told and makes it his first concern to learn to love God?

One can't but smile at the almost continuous efforts of

serious Christians to evade this unequivocal requirement. A favorite means of evasion is simply to ignore it, as I did, by sending my mind quickly off to other quarters whenever I was presented with it. Another is to define love in tenuous terms, some of which are so watered down as to amount to no more than nonhate.

For instance, unless some kind of horrible knot is tied in your emotions, you wish everyone well to the extent that you vaguely hope he will have a pleasant, successful life—health, a happy family life, enough of this world's goods, and his share of personal triumphs—provided he thereby does no real harm. Such a hope is merely healthy neutrality, and if you don't have it you may be sure you have a serious emotional problem. Your good will doesn't rise above neutrality until it presses on you at least a little and urges you toward some effort or sacrifice aimed at realizing the pleasant hope. Yet one often hears this normal neutrality described as love.

Granted, the achievement of such an attitude toward persons who seek your destruction often represents a gigantic spiritual triumph. But it is not love. For neutrality is stillness. Love is the wind-and-wave outsweep of your heart. If we wish to know God, we must face the disturbing fact that neutrality is not enough. We must pour forth service, seeking, yearning, joyous tenderness, before we can claim to love with our strength,* mind, soul, and heart.

I'm quite sure of this because even at my greatest depths of emptiness, I still felt this neutrality. I wished nobody harm, and had I been offered a push-button device for good and ill fortune, halfheartedly I would have pushed good fortune for everybody, feeling while pushing it neither pleasure for friends nor reluctance for enemies. This only meant that I hated no one and was still sane. As I noted at the time, I probably was further from love than if I had

* Mark 12:30, and Luke 10:27 add "strength" to the list of faculties which must be fully employed in loving God mentioned in Matthew 22:37.

hated. For hatred is at least a living, moving force, filled with creative power, and with it goes full awareness of the hated one.

Neutrality easily becomes indifference, in an extreme of which we wouldn't even choose a good-will button, but would push at random. Such an inner void is the truest death. Love more easily switches to hate than to indifference. When we are angry with one we love, we will momentarily hate him enough to want to hurt him, but we will never altogether blank out interest in what happens to him.

I was proud of having outgrown anthropomorphism, and so, reluctantly at first—clinging to my pride—but soon with increasing peace and pleasure, I found that the answer to all my questions concerning how to love God were contained in the Christian conception of Jesus Christ as fully Human yet also fully God. I think that this pride and its accompanying shame in appearing foolish were chiefly responsible for my plodding progress along a path which many travel with speed. But as my great need compelled me to thrust pride and shame aside, with sharpened focus I pursued knowledge of Jesus.

Light soon flashed on a passage of scripture which for me had been dim: "Except ye . . . become as little children, ye shall not enter into the kingdom . . ."

Again reluctantly (for out must go my pride in special insight, knowledge and "good taste") I learned that the tritest, most naïve conceptions of Jesus often were the ones which helped me most to understand and love Him as man and more-than-man. Simple, piercing, stirring visions of Him are found, for instance, in old Gospel hymns—badly written, often ungrammatical—which no sophisticated choir leader would allow sung even by his children's choir:

"There is love with the pain in the Savior's eye, As each day He dies for you and I." I heard an old farmer sing those words softly to a haunting tune as he waited for a bus, and suddenly I saw Jesus as present and as caring for me and what I did here and now. Though the glimpse was lightning brief, something of its wonder remained.

I do not mean to imply that such qualities as good taste and intellectual dignity are necessarily incompatible with the Companionship of Jesus, for these are good things and all good things are of God. But what is good in one place often is bad in another. Moreover, pride in all its forms is generally recognized as an insurmountable barrier to a relationship with God, and I had been proud of having good taste and intellectual dignity in regard to religion.

It is worth noting here that there are at least two other vitally important human activities in which these two qualities almost always are irrelevant and can be real barriers. These are play and love-making. Here again a childlike unselfconsciousness is required.

One utterly childish practice I rediscovered proved to be a magic key to a relationship with God. As a country youngster, though our house in summer was filled with numerous young visiting cousins, in winter I was often lonely. I resorted to imaginary companions, as lonely children often do to quench a thirst for fellowship. The thought came to me now in my mature need, "Why not take the Lord for an imaginary companion?"

I knew this was a good idea because it kept recurring, but I didn't see quite how it could be implemented. My childhood imaginary companions were like me and therefore easy to talk to, but I didn't know what to say to Jesus. After reiterating several dozen times that I wanted to know and serve Him better, I was terribly bored with the "conversation" and thought He must be too. Yet what else was there to say to one's Lord?

At a CFO (Christ For Others) religious retreat I met a man named Blair. He was the first person I had known who openly practiced companionship with Jesus, and I listened eagerly to his advice:

"Never say anything to yourself. Say it to Him, no matter how ordinary it is. 'Lord, why doesn't that fly leave me alone?' 'I think I'll take a drink of water now. Come with me while I get it. . . Oh, thank you, Jesus; that was so cool —like your hand on my temper.'

"You'll feel like a fool talking that way at first," Blair said, "but soon you'll find He's right there with you, *interested* in your simple needs and remarks. He never gets bored with you or anything you say or do, because to Him it all has infinite *meaning*. Nothing is trivial or unimportant to Him. You'll find that those who know Him best think everything is interesting and important, just as He does. They don't know what it is to be bored." Then he added: "Remember, He wants to be with you, too. He's on your side. He'll seize every opportunity if you'll just give Him a few."

I have since found truth in all that Blair said. It is, of course, a basic Christian doctrine that nothing is too minute to take to the Lord—"every hair of your head is numbered" —and it was Blair who brought this important doctrine into reality for me. It wasn't until I fully realized that my smallest problems have an infinite dimension in the Concern of God that I could begin to be free by "laying my burdens on the Lord."

Following Blair's instructions, my sense of distance between myself and God began to lessen. I saw that I could confidently take things to Him which would only pester an earthly friend. Hence *all* my tensions began to ease.

But of the many truths he pointed to, the first I experienced was that I certainly did feel like a fool when I tried to practice the rest, and he failed to warn me of how long "soon" sometimes seems. After months of constant struggle, I would have abandoned his method but for his own conviction that by this means one could not fail. My chief block probably was that I felt such a fool as I practiced. When finally I succeeded in putting this feeling away, I immediately got results. And with the first came a shock:

My childhood imaginary companions were poor substitutes for real ones, and were instantly shelved upon arrival of my young cousins each summer. But after a taste of Jesus Christ as Companion, I knew I had never known real satisfaction in friendship before, and that thereafter He must be a third in every relationship if I wished to experience it fully.

He is the archetype, the original of which all other friends are poor imitations. He was what I had been seeking when I projected humanly impossible images upon others. To me it seems probable also that it is the humble, ever-forgiving, ever-loving Lord who endures rejection and still remains to serve and to comfort, whom the white Southerner seeks and subconsciously thinks he has found in "his Nigras." Perhaps it is for this reason that he feels so bitterly betrayed when he is faced with the aggressive "New Negro" who wishes to be free of whites and to seek his own ends and material welfare. It also may be why he often feels so sure that this type of fulfillment for the Negro is anti-Christian.

But to return to my main point, not only did I find Christ more satisfying than any human companion; also I found Him more *real*.

Let me here insist, for it is very important, that it makes no difference whatever to *the point I'm here making* whether or not the historical Jesus greatly resembled the Christian Christ. There's much evidence that He did, and no proof that He didn't, but this is immaterial to my point. It would not matter even if it were proven both that the Christian Christ was entirely invented by the Apostles, and that God is only a figment of the human imagination.

For Christ still would represent an image which could

have come only from that which is higher than any individual man, and therefore—for convenience and for want of a briefer name—we might call "God." Christ still would have "come down from heaven" (from an ideal beyond man's current capacity to achieve), not up from man's animal depths; and to my point it matters not whether this Son of God came to our earthiness in the form of the one man Jesus or in that of the combined ideas of many men who were struggling toward light. The concept exists, is *real*, in either case, and rises eternally from all crucifixions and all tombs.

By whatever means it came, the concept of Christ, the Person who is man and more-than-man, did come into the world and is real. This Concept (this Word) is more real to those who seek Him than any merely human person could be, for all-that-is-best in all persons is caught in an archetype. Therefore, to "know Him" is to be redeemed from our woes in a very tangible way.

Having a religious background, I prefer to use religious concepts and language in dealing with this theme, but, in common with most modern people, I'm not entirely happy if a religious experience fails to make sense on the purely psychological level as well. This one does. Even if there were no great objective Reality which we may justly call God, and even if my Companion were indeed entirely imaginary, "creation" of Him provided a solution, both practical and poetic, to a problem which seemed to have no solution.

Once satisfied that my religious experience made sense psychologically, I discovered a serious emotional block from which I had long suffered—a secret fear that acceptance of Jesus as living and present might be more destructive than helpful to persons who wish in a modern world to dedicate themselves to the common good. Deep within me lurked a fear which for many people may be an unconscious barrier to belief.

The fact that when you have God for a Companion you need no other had somehow got confused in my mind with an idea that to accept God meant to reject man. Instinctively I felt that to reject man is wrong, and therefore I feared to accept Christ. Once I realized that a childlike acceptance of the Person of Christ did not endanger human relationships but, rather, preserved and heightened them, then the wall of my fear crumbled, and His Reality became apparent.

To put it bluntly, I had to be sure that the existence of Christ, even if it were only an hypothesis, is the best working hypothesis for an effective, satisfying, and useful life. Once this was done, all my doubts fell away and I was able to see that in point of fact His existence is no mere hypothesis but a self-evident reality.

Of course by 1957 I had nothing to lose by believing in anything I could believe in. Whatever I could have hung my life on would have been better than the slowly growing vacuum. I would have been better off if I had believed in any of the non-Christian great religions—even Communism, which is, of course, a kind of religion. But being based on faith in man, for me Communism was automatically eliminated. As for the others, even apart from the obvious fact that in a Christian country one would need considerable perversity deliberately to choose a non-Christian faith, I was confronted with the Christian God when I discovered in experiences both rich and barrenly bitter that love is the highest thing we know. Although I have always recognized enormous merit in every great religion, I think that Christianity makes the best three-point landing on the claim that God is love.

My turning to God admittedly was a fox-hole type action, and for those who think that fox-hole religion isn't genuine, I'll counter that I strongly feel the opposite. My impression is that this is the only kind of genuine religion which any of us ever has—though in saying this I am, of course, broadening the concept of fox hole to symbolize all situations in which one discovers that there's nothing to turn to but God.

True, once out of his fox hole, a man often ignores or rejects his discovery that ultimately God is all we ever have, but this doesn't mean that the insight wasn't authentic. Actually, unless his over-all dream bubble has burst, as mine had, everyone—even after he has fully accepted religion—follows this pattern of turning to, and away from God as his woes wax and wane, until at last he sees that a fox hole is simply where we live every day, all the time.

Besides satisfying myself that Christianity is the best "working hypothesis" for me, I had to satisfy myself that others also would be better off believing in it. Why was this necessary? Because individuality, while real, is superficial. Fundamentally human beings are all one, physically, psychologically, spiritually. Every human institution—science, art, and religion—is based on this assumption. Even language is based on it, for we could not make ourselves understood to a being basically unlike ourselves. Since religion deals with the deepest fundamentals of our lives, there could be no such thing as a workable individual religion.

To the casual observer modern Christianity presents a confusion of denominational ornamentation. But a more searching look reveals a fundamental structure simple and lovely to the heart in its proportion, grace, creativity, freedom, and strength.

If anyone doubts this, let him take the three essentials of Christianity—God, love, service—and study them in terms of each other and of his own life. If he does this seriously for several months, and then selects any other three motifs and does the same, I think his experience will be similar to that of one who studies the work of some great, immortal painter, musician, or writer (whom he may even dislike—

it doesn't matter) and then returns to the work of some minor artist in the same field who had delighted him. The shock is painful, but enlightening. Greatness has a way of revealing itself to us whether we like its specific form or not.

All great religions contain these three motifs in some form, and this in itself is proof of the basic truth of these motifs, but I think that no other religion presents all three in such bold relief, and links them together in such obvious interdependence. Studying Christianity after having learned that its basic motifs are God, love, and service, and that the rainwashed skeleton of its design simply affirms that each is inseparable from the others and that a beginning in understanding one involves some grasp of the other two as well, I began to foresee that at last I would find the total fulfillment I had sought and not heretofore found.

It is my hope that even nonreligious people will be able to make some kind of sense out of what I discovered. For obviously it is a solution which anyone could apply on any of the many occasions when his images are broken and the solid-looking world he thought he stood on softens and dissolves under his feet. It has often been noted by Christian theologians, twisting Voltaire's point a bit toward their own ends, that if Jesus Christ did not exist, it would be necessary to invent Him. I hope that in its small way my experience supports this truth.

But I hope, too, that some readers will be struck by what seems to me a quite simple and obvious fact: That the illusion lies not in our religious faith, but in our everyday lives; that not Jesus, the true Archetype, but everyone else we know is an imaginary companion. We have seen that the lovable people I adored existed only in my thoughts— and perhaps in their own! Also, that to a lesser degree this projection of images which we can love is a universal practice among all people.

Moreover, as I have hinted, it really is our dim glimpses

("through a glass darkly") of the Archetype which we project onto all whom we love. Therefore He is the reality —The Reality—in the images of our human loved ones, and genuine companionship, free of self-deception, is possible only with Him. The truth of His Reality easily can be proven if we spend as much time with Him and take Him as seriously as we do a close human friend. Ask anyone who knows Him and he will assure you that he found it so—found it so especially in times of great weariness, pain, grief, and disaster; found it so in times of need, and of opportunity; above all, found it so in times of love.

I was slow to know my Divine Companion, but no other labor has rewarded me so well. Despite the near impossibility of such a task, therefore, I shall try to give you glimpses of what I found.

I must begin by saying that all the most trite, silly, and sentimental remarks made about Friendship with Him by the most unschooled and simple folk, to my amazement, turned out to be factual statements. For instance, when they say, "If you jus' got Jesus, you don't need nobody else," it is a piece of exact information, like saying, "If you have an electric blanket, you don't need other blankets."

Because, as Archetype, He is the composite of all the highest things that we, and others down the ages, have been able to visualize as right and good and lovely, He supplies us with every possible value which we could get, or thought we could get, from others. If we don't believe that one electric blanket is all we need over us in cold weather, it's because we never tried sleeping under one. And if we don't believe that Jesus' Companionship (His imaginary companionship, if you will) is more than sufficient for all our needs, it's only because we have never had it.

Testimony to this effect has been proclaimed and reiterated for twenty centuries, and I was long among the majority who pay not the slightest attention to it. I can think of at least three reasons why we don't.

For one, bringing such a companionship to fruition is a laborious task, like learning to play a difficult instrument, and one who attempts it halfheartedly will succeed only in convincing himself that it is impossible.

For another, man has long exerted his considerable intelligence in finding substitute satisfactions for this hard-to-achieve friendship with God, and has accumulated a large stock pile, ranging from alcohol and tranquilizers through hundreds of distractions and amusements to hundreds of arts and cultures of the mind. He will usually go through quite a lot of this stock pile, trying each item, before he is prepared to concede that nothing has brought him the fulfillment he hoped for, and that his deep longings have been satisfied only briefly, if at all.

A healthy, averagely fortunate person may in easy times go to his grave with his substitute satisfactions (like his illusions) functioning so well that only a few skillful dodges are needed for him to maintain belief that all is well with him. For almost half a century, I certainly made this claim. But having recently had the experience of all actually being well, I look back in wonderment that I could have thought so before.

A third reason why we ignore testimony that Jesus Christ is all we need is that as long as human fellowship is intact, as long as we have dear ones whom we believe in and who believe in us, there usually is much drag against acquiring our Divine Companion. For it appears, though it isn't really so, that we must lose people in order to acquire Christ. Therefore, it usually isn't until we have already lost at least the people we most value, that we will seek Him.

We appear to lose others when we seek Him because we must stop believing that they truly are the lovely images which in fact are dim reflections of Him. Otherwise, we find it hard to isolate Him in the maze of gods and goddesses around us.

For many months one great truth has pursued me at every turn: My relationship with Him is more real, actual, than any other I have known. His presence is more completely *with* me than any human person ever has been. From this mysterious overpowering fact alone I would suspect that here is the Source, that now at last I deal with the basic Substance from which all relationships are made. Moreover, unlike the rest, this One when made transcendant does not diminish, deaden, or crowd the others out. Rather, It revives, heightens, and includes them all. Love of God is never, I think, a rival to any other love. It is the means by which all loves are made constant, dependable, and strong.

I can't here review the lengthy adventurous drama of my search. Briefly, I sought Him by reading the Gospel stories over and over, studying interpretations of His life and thought, listening to simple hymns, questioning the few who seem to know Him, talking to Him, thinking of Him, doing my housework for Him as though I were His housekeeper, and by many other means.

At first nothing seemed accomplished, but slowly His Personality took definite shape in my mind, and His Presence began to move with me as I moved. Then, quite without warning, one day my fragmentary thoughts about Him drew together and fell into their proper places. For an indescribable moment He was real, present, and living in my midst. My frozenness melted. I had looked upon the Lovable. As I had hoped, the result was love.

CHAPTER 7

Children—of God

IN THE FALL OF 1957, I GAVE SOME TALKS IN LOS ANGELES, and while there I often visited Pershing Square, notorious as a gathering place for bums and hobos and for those who wish to harangue them into seeing some kind of light.

Among the many people I saw exhorting each other to various philosophies and religions was a half-witted boy who sang and preached continually to gatherings of idlers who neither looked at him nor listened. A glance told you he was mentally deficient, and he sang abominably written hymns in that terrible, off-key voice the deficient sometimes have. But his homely face wore a look of unearthly beauty as he sang and preached his sermon consisting of two non-original sentences reiterated without variation:

"I'm a fool for Christ. What are you a fool for?"

If you smile, I hope it is because the message went home. I had heard it before, and had thought it a shallow play on words, but coming from this boy, I felt the impact of its wisdom, outreaching even Lincoln's point that we all must die but not all can die *for* something.

Of these three things we can be sure: We must die; we have betrayed the Vision; we are fools. If a man thinks he can escape any of these fates, the more fool he. Never is the question, "Will I, or will I not, be a fool?" It is, "What will I be a fool over?" On the numerous occasions when each of us has found himself foolish, how often had we a purpose which gave meaning to humiliation?

When the lawyer asked how he could inherit eternal life, Jesus said to love God and man, then added, "This do, and thou shalt live." If we will not be fools for love, we choose death, not merely for the dim future, but for the eternal now.

If I live, it is partly because as I struggled through my self-made mazes toward love of God (so freely offered), I remembered the half-wit's sermon and knew that I had been running from the fear that if I became "as a little child" I would appear a fool to those few who still thought well of me. Had I not stopped running, I think I wouldn't have found the key to loving again. Then I would have been a fool for fear.

Many results and discoveries have already followed my recognition that Jesus' First and Great Commandment was meant to be obeyed. Many others are still to come, for much that is living truth to some people remains only unmeaningful doctrine to me. But by and large, from a religion which was a mixture of Humanism, New Thought, and hodgepodge, I have found myself moved firmly down the path toward orthodox Christian theology.

I find it fascinating that this happened through no knowledge of, or desire to follow orthodoxy, but through trial and error. I still know virtually nothing of either theology or Church history, but informed persons tell me that I have relived and relearned some of the hard lessons of the Church which resulted in the orthodox position. Conventional theology had always seemed to me dogmatic in the worst sense, and without practical basis or value. But when burdens too great for personal strength rested upon me, *only orthodoxy worked.*

That it has worked when no other hope was in sight, my whole internal life attests. Moreover, it has worked creatively. Had my recovery resulted from the lifting of community rejection plus pardonable pride that I weathered the storm, I would have felt the change most at first, satisfaction would have tapered with familiarity, bitterness remained, and fear of a recurrence of rejection would have been inevitable. But the mark of Life is upon my renewal in that it grows, flowers, bears. It bears in energy, joy, meaning, purpose, wholeness and, above all, in a sense of corporateness with all mankind.

A new world, greener and sweeter than the one I lost, stretches before me while within is a growing will and strength to serve all people and judge none. Decreasingly I think in terms of the "worthy" and "unworthy." A belated but growing sense of my own unworthiness moves me haltingly away from self-righteousness toward true worship of Righteousness Himself. Through the humility bestowed by glimpses of true Goodness, a deeper sense of fellowship with all that lives has begun to rise. I'm more at ease and at home in all situations and among all people than ever I was when I believed in golden man.

Never before was life so persistently alluring. I begrudge even the few hours' sleep which my body demands. Each morning that I wake in love with God, I feel like a child on Christmas. So many, many gifts await my opening.

Indeed, to whatever extent I am enabled to love Him, each moment is like a gift, and every future moment lies waiting wrapped in ribbons with bows. I may have discovered a little of what the early Christians had, for it does not matter that some of my packages hold woe. Wrapped in the love of God they are still gifts, and I shall have wisdom of them, I shall have strength, and in acceptance of them I shall have peace.

I know that the worst of my troubles may lie ahead.

Scattered attacks still warn that expense and effort are deemed well spent to bring me grief. My future status hangs on Virginia's political strategies, on the choices of Negro leaders, the conduct of integrated Negroes, and the general behavior of the Negro group as a whole—besides on whether this book is read in the language in which I wrote it, or is translated into a more familiar stereotype tongue. In man's world I have no reason to feel secure. Having learned how easily man's kindness is turned aside by little things, I should be both fearful of the future and too weary to face what it probably holds. I should be saying, "I'm not as young as I was and I've served my term. I want peace now." I would lose no face. Few would blame me. Many would applaud my good sense. Were it not for my Companion, I think I should find it necessary to say it.

In acquiring a sense of His Friendship, isn't there danger of delusions of infallibility, of feeling that we have an inside track to Divinity? Less, I think, than when we are self-centered. Our status as a grain of sand is never so clear as when we turn our faces toward God. And Jesus' Second Commandment keeps our feet on the ground while we practice the First. Without this Second Commandment, we might indeed get so elated by the practice of the Presence of God that we would identify ourselves with Him. This danger looms if we forget that Jesus gives not just one Command, but two.

And He does not say to identify ourself with God, to love God as ourself. He says to love God with our whole heart, soul, mind, and strength. This pouring out of our total being for God is quite other, and much more, than identification. But we are not to rise off the dusty earth with our outpourings. On the contrary, with a heart made paradoxically full by pouring forth, we are to identify ourself with every man, to love every man as ourself. Filled with our love for God, we are to empty it out upon all.

Moreover, we are to love man not merely in high and kindly thoughts, but in very physical, earthy acts. Not for an instant will He allow our feet off the ground in the lifting of our hearts to God. He leaves us no avenue of escape from His meaning in the parable of the judgment: Whatever we do or fail to do for any man, even the worst, "the least," in God's eyes we do or fail to do for Himself. Our status and our responsibility couldn't be plainer than they are made by Jesus' two Commandments plus this parable.

So there we have it: We are not little gods, but big children of God. We are not better than the most wicked or wiser than the worst fool—except once in a while, by grace, via love. We are man in all his helplessness, emptiness, propensity for wrong. Each fool, each villain, holds a mirror to our face.

Yet as we glimpse, love, and serve Him, God Himself becomes our own, and in these moments of truth we are freed. That they are so few and so feeble should of itself keep us more lowly minded than we were wont to be before we sought Him. Those who attempt great things discover their limitations. If we never try to make Him monarch of our life, we may possibly think we can. Boldly to reach for the highest is humbly to learn what we are.

The story of Jesus' last days is the basic plot of a story repeated with variations over and over in any era of tension and change. As each of us learns it in our own tender viscera and brittle bone, we are faced with the truth that we are alone under distant, unknowing stars. This knowledge is the Terror which pursues us from crib to coffin, and much of our unworthy conduct may stem from our panicked flight.

From this hell of horror there is no escape but one. A single steep path connects us with anything at all. We know and can be known by that which we love. We possess and are possessed by that which we love. If we love nothing, we are quite alone.

But if we love God we are never alone. Rather, if we know it is God we love, we know we are never alone. For only He is lovable, and always it is only His spirit and His expression that we love. We glimpse His shining in man, and thinking that it is man who shines, how can we feel other than betrayed when man acts like a man, not a god?

But when we learn to love God for Himself, we recognize Him everywhere, and we know that never have we been betrayed, never deserted. Pursuing us as the Hound of Heaven, love, loyalty, courage, honor, and honesty have dogged our footsteps dependably, appearing now here, now there. For so silly a reason as that they didn't show themselves monotonously in the same places, I thought them unreliable.

Once we know that God is love and that we can love Him—can be *in love* with Him—we have our catalyst which brings meaning and adventure to all we must learn and do. We have a new and equable conception of the pulsing radiance in man. Breath comes and goes, to come again. This is the rhythm of living.

I have moved far since, two years ago, man's paper currency was to me counterfeit, its offering to me insult. Today each paper dollar represents the whole golden treasury. Even in pretenses of kindness, I see recognition of its value, and can accept such currency with a warm heart, which is itself a draft on the Treasury.

Within and without, I see new dimensions: Nothing is senseless, separate, fearful. All is new-born and ready for new challenge. "One man and God are a majority," it is said. Yes! For God is Personification of all that you value in every man, and standing with Him, you stand in a sense with all people. There is no greater majority.

Only by fits, starts, and fleeting moments can I live the

new life. Habits of a lifetime drag at me, and I still treat my Companion less well than I do earthly friends. Yet my poor efforts move me consistently toward restoration of all the inner values I lost, plus new treasures. God must indeed be meeker than any man, since He responds to such poor performance of love and loyalty and grants me glimpses which I never could have earned.

I know well that my foot is only a step along a path up which many have gone far. Already I have found more than I am able to tell. Still I shall try: I have found that there is glory and holiness in us through which we can live and be free. We have touches of it in the best moments we have known, and the best we have seen in others, the best in our own thoughts and in sky and land and sea.

These divers glories belong together. They have affinity. They are members, one of another, parts of one whole. If we gather them all in one place in us; if we steadily seek to feel that they are moments with a Person who is all these and more, whose stature rises above them as the stature of a man rises above the sum of his thoughts; and if we try to keep this concept with us until we are weary of even wanting to try, then rest, and grow weary again, and rest; after a while our weariness and resting becomes a rhythm, which after a while becomes both a soft, low tune and the breathing of the great, primordial Life which is in us and beyond us, and which Itself lives. It is the Person of Love, the Meaning for which we have been spent. But He is not ours until we love Him, and we are not loving Him until we respond to Him by loving man—not man the golden image, but man the common clay.

Here is the last of the discoveries which have renewed me: When you obey the First Commandment in Jesus' summary, the Second is not only your balance, but also your reward. As soon as you love God, you love man. Once you love God, you cannot help loving man. It follows as quenched thirst follows drinking. Surely this is the meaning of St. John's much misused warning that we only delude ourselves if we think we love God yet do not love man.

"... The truth shall make you free." I think it really shall. For even with the little truth I have so far garnered, I have found it so. I have become free to face my own iniquity, and hence to enter truly into the sweet and humble brotherhood of man; free to touch the hem of His garment, and thus to glimpse the restoration and shining hope of the Fatherhood of God; free to be grateful and glad that I lost my life, and therefore found it; above all, free to love a little, thus gaining strength to seek, learn, and love a little more.

CPSIA information can be obtained
at www.ICGtesting.com
Printed in the USA
LVHW051416030621
689226LV00010B/103